THE COMPLETE

ALL-IRELAND
SENIOR FOOTBALL
CHAMPIONSHIP

1887-2019

First published in 2019 by
Litter Press
Ballygarran
Wexford

Author: John Ó Néill
© John Ó Néill 2019

ISBN 978 1 9993008 2 1

Typesetting in Bahnschrift and Garamond by Litter Press.
Cover design by Emma Byrne
Front cover image licensed by Sportsfile.

CONTENTS

INTRODUCTION

This book contains the records of the All-Ireland senior football championship from it was first staged in 1887 through to the most recent championship season in 2019. The results of the 4,400 games played to date are organised by year and laid out according to the format of the draw in each year.

Obviously, this format has changed over time. In 1887 there was an open draw and the individual games given here by round and then by date within each round. Where a game had to be replayed, it is listed directly below the previous game between the sides. From 1888 to 2000 counties played off within their provinces with the winners progressing to knockout 'All-Ireland' rounds. These results are listed by round and date as for 1887, but with the provincial championships given first, then the All-Ireland series of games. From 2001, as teams were eliminated, they joined a knock-out competition and these rounds are listed in a 'Qualifiers' section following the records for the provincial championships that year.

Records for the early years of the All-Ireland Senior Football Championship are by no means complete. A list of provincial titles awarded to each county in this book is based on newspaper reports both of the championships as won on the field of play and by determinations of the Central Council or Provincial Council in years where, for various reasons, a championship was awarded when no games or final were played (see below for more on this).

Championship Formats

In 1887, as mentioned earlier, there was an open draw and no provincial championships took place. In the early years of the championship, counties were represented by the club who had either won the county's own club championship or were nominated by the County Board. In these years (where counties were represented by a single club) the clubs involved are named underneath the county they represented. In those early years, there could be long delays in holding provincial championships as they could only start once the club championship, and the frequent

3

appeals against the result of games, had been brought to a conclusion. To be eligible to participate both the county and the club also had to be properly affiliated to the GAA. As not every county had an eligible club some years this prevented a county being able to participate in the championship.

The more familiar format of provincial championships began in 1888 although, due to a tour of the USA, only the provincial championships took place that year. Official records of the early years of the championship are incomplete and information is sometimes confined to newspaper reports. A good example is the 1888 Connacht Championship. Mayo and Sligo drew in the final and while there are no reports of a replay, later newspaper reports state that Sligo were the 1888 Connaught champions (e.g. see *Sligo Champion, 24/8/1895*).

In some years provincial championships were awarded by default. The rationale given for this was that counties that had not completed club championships forfeited "their claim to the championship" (e.g. see report from G.A.A. Central Council in *Drogheda Independent*, 28/9/1889). Another issue could be that only one county had a club that had paid the appropriate affiliation fees. Thus, in 1889, Antrim (Belfast Gaelics) and Galway (Dunmore) were due to play in the All-Ireland semi-final. A full draw had been made for the provincial championships that year (see *Freemans Journal*, 6/5/1889) but clearly most matches were never played. Galway had a walkover in Connacht as correspondence published in the *Western People* (2/11/1889) states they had been awarded the provincial championship as Mayo were ineligible and Leitrim refused to take part. Antrim must similarly have been able to claim the Ulster title.

From 1892 counties were now formally represented by a 'selection' of players rather than a single club. In practice, after 1892, counties were still often represented by a single club but that club now could (legally) select players from other clubs to play in 'inter-county' games.

As it had done in 1889, Galway again won Connacht uncontested in 1890, while Roscommon did the same in 1892. Both are also clearly described as 'Champions of Connaught' in press accounts. In 1897, though, teams were reported as 'nominated' by Connacht and Ulster rather than selected as 'champions'. The distinction is minor but, in terms of titles awarded, it forms part of the basis for the records included for each county at the end of this book. In 1895 the Central Council made a draw for just two provincial championships, one for Munster and one clearly labelled 'Leinster and Ulster' (eg see *Irish Examiner*, 7/8/1895). This is the only occasion on which an amalgamated provincial draw was made.

Galway and Antrim were also deemed as winners of Connacht and Ulster in 1900 as the only eligible entrants (see *Freemans Journal*, 22/9/1902). Antrim are credited with the 1900 Championship by the Ulster Council in its GAA Centenary Ulster Final programme from 1984 (the listing in this programme is consistent with the other Ulster Championship records used here, apart from 1889). In 1901 the game organised and clearly named by the Ulster Council as the 'Ulster Championship Final' was actually between two Antrim clubs (see *Irish News*, 26/3/1903) and so is given here in that format (see records for 1901 on page 114). Galway had another walkover in Connacht in 1902.

Throughout the 1900s there were long delays in progressing provincial championships. Coupled with appeals and objections, this meant that, on a number of occasions, championships were awarded for successive years by default or not at all. The delay in completing the 1904 Ulster Championship meant that it was instead awarded as both the 1904 and 1905 Championships. When this occurred again, in 1907/1908, no Ulster Championship was awarded for 1907 and only the 1908 Championship was awarded (to Antrim).

Further delays in completing the 1910 Connacht and Ulster Championships meant that (in line with a ruling at Congress in April 1911), they were also to be deemed as the 1911 Championships. Subsequent provincial championships were only awarded if won on the field of play. More recently, the overall format of the championship was significantly re-organised in 2001 with the introduction of the qualifier series in which defeated teams were admitted to a series of knockout games for a place in the All-

Ireland quarter-finals. The All-Ireland quarter-finals have been replaced by a group stage since 2018. As far as possible the rounds of the competitions, either provincial or All-Ireland, are given using the nomenclature used at the time (e.g. first round, semi-final etc). Note that provincial championships formats could be unusual with teams receiving a bye in multiple rounds or direct to the final. For ease of reading current county names are given for Laois (for whom Queen's County, Leix and Laoighis were used previously) and Offaly (previously King's County).

When comparing the scores and scoring rates between different eras, a number of rule changes should be borne in mind. Scores for individual teams are given in the conventional Gaelic games format of goals and points (for instance, '1-10' is one goal and ten points). In 1887, 'forfeit' points were included at the end of the score which was written as 1-10-3. A 'forfeit' point was awarded to a team when a team played the ball over their own end line (now given as a '45'). Five 'forfeit' points were equal to one point. This rule was then changed and, instead of a 'forfeit' point, the opposing team was awarded a free kick out (today this is taken from the 45m line). From 1887 to 1891 games were decided on goals scored and points were only counted towards the score if both sides had scored an equal number of goals. From 1892 a goal was given the value of five points and the winner was then determined by the combined value of the goals and points. The value of a goal was reduced to the current value, three points, in 1896.

For games that had been arranged but where one side either failed (or refused) to field or otherwise had to concede is denoted by a score of 'w/o' (for win outright) appearing beside the team which was deemed the winner.

Where teams had to replay a game the result is included here directly below the result of previous meeting of the two teams. Often, particularly in the early years of the championship, games were re-played following an objection or appeal. Such games can be recognised by the fact that the scores were not tied at the end of the previous game. Where objections and appeals led to a replay, it was generally the reason for such long delays between rounds of the championship as decision on the outcome of a game often had to wait on the next council meeting.

It is also worth noting that the standard duration of football matches first was sixty minutes and continued that way until 1970 when provincial finals and All-Ireland semi-finals and finals were extended to eighty minutes. From 1975 the rule changed again and all games were to be seventy minutes in length.

Sometimes, newspaper reports on the same game contain slight variations on the final scores (although obviously agreeing on the most fundamental detail of who won or lost). In this book, no newspaper is given precedence where different results are available. Where a variation in the reported score does occur, a local newspaper is assumed (rightly or wrongly) to be more likely to be accurate. And rather than listing a source for each individual game, the date for each match is included so a report can be easily found in the contemporary press. In two instances – Clare v Limerick in 1910 and Antrim v Armagh in 1916 – the score doesn't appear to have been reported in the press, only the name of the winning team (Clare and Antrim).

As the Gaelic Athletic Association adapted its playing rules over time, players and teams had to adjust their tactics. In the first few years after the playing rules were agreed, the team who scored most goals won and points were only taken into account if teams were tied on the number of goals scored. So, in those early years of the GAA goals literally won games. This began to change as the value of a goal was first set as equivalent to 5 points, and then, in 1896, reduced to the equivalent of 3 points. This had the effect of making scoring points (as opposed to goals) a more worthwhile tactic in its own right.

In the years prior to the rule change, the winning team in games tended to have 3-4 more points (as well as their goals) than the losing team. As 3-4 points was less than the value of a goal (5 points), intercounty team tactics appear to have prioritised scoring goals since the reward was much greater. After the value of a goal was reduced down to 3 points, the winning teams over the next few years then started scoring, on average, 6-7 more points than the losing team (as well as scoring more goals). So clearly teams adapted and began to evolve tactics that got them into positions to score points and keep their overall score up. This can be seen in the chart below which shows how the change in the value of a goal in 1896 saw teams try to score more points in subsequent years. The light grey bars show the average before 1896, the black bars the average after 1896.

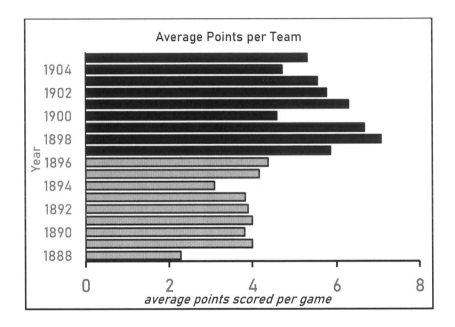

The impact of individual rule changes can be seen throughout the history of the All-Ireland Senior Football Championship. This can be neatly illustrated by looking at the average number of goals and points a team scored in a game for each year from 1888 to 2019 (see next page). In the graph on the next page the top line shows the average number of points and the bottom line shows the average number of goals scored. It is clear, looking at the date of key changes, that despite the impact of a new playing rule, teams eventually adjust to the new format and with time improve their scoring return per game.

8

Five key events can be seen to have immediately impacted on scoring and are visible as abrupt changes to the direction of the graph. These are marked by arrows and numbered 1-5 as below:

1. The value of a goal reduced from 5 to 3 points.
2. Goalposts changed.
3. Rules/refereeing of hand-pass.
4. Hand-passed scores banned.
5. Hand-passed points permitted.

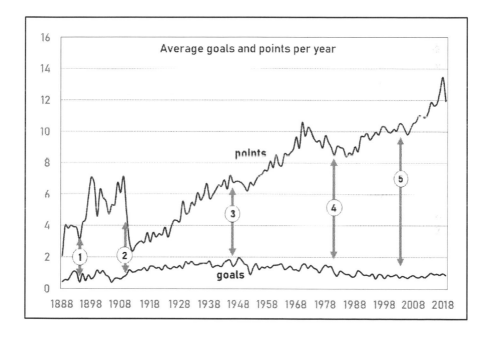

After 1975 all games were seventy minutes in duration. So, to make the long-standing comparison in the graph meaningful, the average team scores for games after 1975 are reduced by one seventh (i.e. to make them the equivalent of sixty minutes).

Most people now barely remember that until 1975 the standard duration for games was sixty minutes (apart from the experiment with eighty-minute long finals in the early 1970s). Obviously longer games might favour some teams, such as those with better fitness. The impact of the shift from sixty to seventy minutes on the overall number of scores in a game is shown below. The graph includes the average number of points scored per ten minutes of a game from 1950 to 1995. The average score per ten minutes was increasing through the 1950s and 1960s and at the start of the 1970s. Then the number of points scored in an average ten minutes begins to drop and continued dropping until the end of the 1980s then returned to the level it had been in the mid-1960s. So, while there were longer games after 1975 the scoring was still at the same rate.

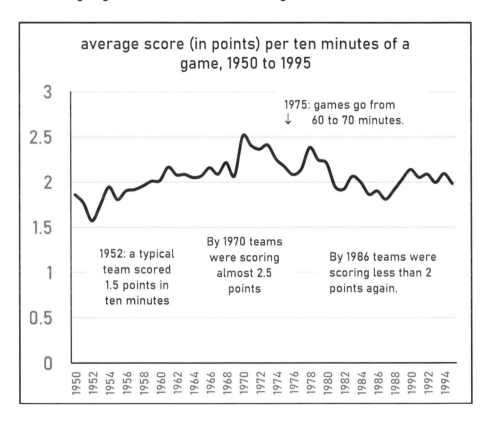

Physical Changes to the Game

While early Gaelic football games looked considerably different to todays matches, there are very few high-quality images of early football games. The limitations of early cameras meant that there are few action shots of Gaelic football games and good quality photographs of early matches are very rare. These two images below are part of an early set of good quality images published in the *Illustrated Sporting and Dramatic News* (on 12/12/1908). The photographs were taken at the 1908 Munster final between Kerry and Waterford, played in Cork. The photograph on the left shows the earlier style goals, while the photograph on the right shows the Waterford goalkeeper (Clashmore's Eddie Duggan). The Waterford team was mostly made up of Clashmore players and wore the club's red jerseys in the final (which Kerry won 0-7 to 0-2).

An alternative to photographs for recording events was sketches, which were sometimes used as a substitute for photographs by the newspapers. The example on the next page is from the second replay of the 1903 All-Ireland Final between Kerry and Kildare, which was considered to have been instrumental in popularising Gaelic football at the time.

This sketch also illustrates details of the earlier style of goal posts used for Gaelic football which were soccer posts with no nets and extra uprights either side (the modern form of goalposts was only introduced in 1910). You can also see the goal umpire, flag in hand, directly behind the goal. Fencing to keep spectators out of the playing area had been brought in to stop crowds encroaching on the pitch during matches.

AN EXCITING POINT IN THE KERRY v. KILDARE MATCH.

That nimble player, T. J. Fitzgerald, securing first score—a point—for Kerry, despite the desperate resistance of the Kildare keepers. Fitzgerald was seen to equal advantage later on. The picture is typical of many incidents in the big match.

(*Irish Independent*, 17/10/1905)

While the shape of footballs has remained the same, the weight of the football and the air pressure within the ball have changed over time. The type of boots needed to kick the lighter modern ball (and the needs of fitness) can also be seen in the prevalent style of boots used by the typical intercounty footballer during the championship. The style of football boots has actually changed quite slowly since the 1880s. The early boots, which partly covered the ankle, were eventually displaced by 'continental-style' boots from the mid-1950s. These are shown on the next page.

[The images are from: top left - *Munster Express* 28/10/1922; top right - *Connacht Tribune*, 31/10/1936; middle left - *Kilkenny People*, 8/9/1951; middle right - *Sunday Independent*, 28/2/1954; bottom left - *Irish Independent*, 23/9/1963; bottom right - *Ulster Herald*, 8/10/1988.]

County Records

The main section of the book with results for each year of the senior football championship is preceded by a section providing a summary of each county's championship record (the counties are included in alphabetical order). This includes it's overall performance (in terms of games played, won, drawn and lost), a win ratio, All-Ireland and provincial championships won and a county-by-county record of the biggest winning and losing margins over the years.

The book also includes a section (beginning on the next page) with an overview of performances, rankings, scoring feats and other analysis. The performance of counties over the decades is broken down to show the top six ranked teams in each decade (see page 26). This changes considerably over time, with Tipperary top in the 1880s, Dublin in the 1890s and 1900s, Wexford in the 1910s, Kerry in the 1920s and 1930s, Cavan in the 1940s and 1950s, Down in the 1960s, Dublin in the 1970s and 1980s, Meath in the 1990s, Kerry in the 2000s and Dublin in the 2010s. Unsurprisingly, after the 1890s, with the exception of the 1990s, in the decades where Kerry was not the top ranked side, it was ranked second.

CHAMPIONSHIP TITLES UP TO 1905

(Leinster records include 1895 'Leinster and Ulster Championship')

Titles

Connacht
Galway (4)
Roscommon (3)
Mayo (2)
Sligo (1)

Leinster
Dublin (9)
Kildare (2)
Kilkenny (2)
Wexford (2)
Laois (1)
Meath (1)

Munster
Cork (7)
Tipperary (5)
Kerry (4)
Limerick (1)
Waterford (1)

Ulster
Cavan (4)
Antrim (3)
Armagh (2)
Monaghan (1)

All-Ireland
Dublin (8)
Tipperary (3)
Kerry (2)
Limerick (2)
Cork (1)
Kildare (1)
Wexford (1)

BIGGEST WINS UP TO 1910

All-Ireland: Cork 4-16 Mayo 0-1 (1903)

Connacht: Mayo 2-16 Galway 0-1 (1907)

Leinster: Dublin 7-17 Laois 0-3 (1900)

Munster: Limerick 5-6 Kerry 1-1 (1895)*

Ulster: Armagh 3-17 Antrim 0-0 (1890)*

[*goals = 5 points]

BIGGEST COMBINED SCORE UP TO 1910

Meath 0-5 Louth 6-19 (1901)

MOST GOALS SCORED BY ONE TEAM UP TO 1910

Dublin 7-17 Laois 0-3 (1900)

MOST POINTS SCORED BY ONE TEAM UP TO 1910

Wexford 2-24 Carlow 0-5 (1898)

CHAMPIONSHIP TITLES UP TO 1921

(Leinster records include 1895 'Leinster and Ulster Championship')

Titles

Connacht
- Mayo (11)
- Galway (9)
- Roscommon (5)
- Sligo (1)

Leinster
- Dublin (14)
- Wexford (8)
- Kildare (3)
- Kilkenny (3)
- Louth (3)
- Laois (1)
- Meath (1)

Munster
- Kerry (13)
- Cork (11)
- Tipperary (7)
- Clare (1)
- Limerick (1)
- Waterford (1)

Ulster
- Antrim (9)
- Cavan (8)
- Monaghan (6)
- Armagh (2)

All-Ireland
- Dublin (12)
- Kerry (5)
- Wexford (5)
- Tipperary (4)
- Cork (2)
- Kildare (2)
- Limerick (2)
- Louth (2)

BIGGEST WINS 1910-1939

All-Ireland   Cork 6-6 Antrim 1-2 (1912)

Connacht: Mayo 9-2 Leitrim 3-3 (1935)

Leinster: Kildare 9-8 Carlow 1-1 (1921)

Munster: Kerry 6-11 Clare 2-0 (1919)

Ulster: Cavan 6-13 Tyrone 1-2 (1933)

BIGGEST COMBINED SCORE 1910-1939

Wexford 7-10 Longford 6-2 (1927)

MOST GOALS SCORED BY ONE TEAM 1910-1939

Kildare 9-8 Carlow 1-1 (1921)
Mayo 9-2 Leitrim 3-3 (1935)

MOST POINTS SCORED BY ONE TEAM 1910-1939

Cavan 0-18 Donegal 0-2 (1925)

CHAMPIONSHIP TITLES UP TO 1939

(Leinster records include 1895 'Leinster and Ulster Championship')

Titles

Connacht
- Mayo (22)
- Galway (14)
- Roscommon (5)
- Sligo (2)
- Leitrim (1)

Leinster
- Dublin (21)
- Kildare (10)
- Wexford (9)
- Laois (4)
- Kilkenny (3)
- Louth (3)
- Meath (1)

Munster
- Kerry (27)
- Cork (12)
- Tipperary (9)
- Clare (1)
- Limerick (1)
- Waterford (1)

Ulster
- Cavan (12)
- Monaghan (11)
- Antrim (9)
- Armagh (2)

All-Ireland
- Kerry (13)
- Dublin (12)
- Wexford (5)
- Kildare (4)
- Tipperary (4)
- Galway (3)
- Cavan (2)
- Cork (2)
- Limerick (2)
- Louth (2)
- Mayo (1)

CHAMPIONSHIP TITLES UP TO 1959

(Leinster records include 1895 'Leinster and Ulster Championship')

Titles

Connacht
Mayo (27)	Sligo (2)
Galway (24)	Leitrim (1)
Roscommon (11)	

Leinster
Dublin (26)	Meath (8)
Kildare (11)	Laois (5)
Wexford (10)	Kilkenny (3)
Louth (8)	Carlow (1)

Munster
Kerry (41)	Clare (1)
Cork (18)	Limerick (1)
Tipperary (9)	Waterford (1)

Ulster
Cavan (32)	Tyrone (2)
Antrim (11)	Derry (1)
Monaghan (11)	Down (1)
Armagh (4)	

All-Ireland
Kerry (19)	Cork (3)
Dublin (16)	Louth (3)
Cavan (5)	Mayo (3)
Wexford (5)	Limerick (2)
Tipperary (4)	Meath (2)
Kildare (4)	Roscommon (2)
Galway (4)	

BIGGEST WINS 1940 TO 1974

All-Ireland: Roscommon 5-8 Cavan 1-3 (1944)

Connacht: Mayo 7-10 Sligo 0-2 (1949)

Leinster: Dublin 10-13 Longford 3-8 (1960)

Munster: Kerry 9-10 Clare 0-4 (1947)

Ulster: Cavan 8-13 Tyrone 2-3 (1946)*

[result was equalled in later years]

BIGGEST COMBINED SCORE 1940 TO 1974

Dublin 10-13 Longford 3-8 (1960)

MOST GOALS SCORED BY ONE TEAM 1940 TO 1974

Dublin 10-13 Longford 3-8 (1960)

MOST POINTS SCORED BY ONE TEAM 1940 TO 1974

Cork 0-25 Kerry 0-14 (1971)

CHAMPIONSHIP TITLES UP TO 1999

(Leinster records include 1895 'Leinster and Ulster Championship')

Titles

Connacht
Galway (42)	Sligo (3)
Mayo (38)	Leitrim (2)
Roscommon (20)	

Leinster
Dublin (43)	Louth (8)
Meath (18)	Laois (5)
Kildare (12)	Kilkenny (3)
Offaly (10)	Carlow (1)
Wexford (10)	Longford (1)

Munster
Kerry (66)	Clare (2)
Cork (32)	Limerick (1)
Tipperary (9)	Waterford (1)

Ulster
Cavan (37)	Armagh (8)
Monaghan (14)	Tyrone (8)
Down (12)	Derry (7)
Antrim (11)	Donegal (5)

All-Ireland
Kerry (31)	Tipperary (4)
Dublin (22)	Louth (3)
Galway (8)	Mayo (3)
Meath (7)	Offaly (3)
Cork (6)	Limerick (2)
Cavan (5)	Roscommon (2)
Down (5)	Derry (1)
Wexford (5)	Donegal (1)
Kildare (4)	

BIGGEST WINS 1975 TO 2019

All-Ireland:	Kerry 7-16 Kildare 0-10 (2015)
Connacht:	Roscommon 9-19 London 1-10 (1980)
Leinster:	Meath 6-19 Kilkenny 0-3 (1979)
Munster:	Kerry 9-21 Clare 1-9 (1979)
Ulster:	Tyrone 3-19 Cavan 0-7 (2005)

BIGGEST COMBINED SCORE 1975 TO 2019

Cork 2-20 Mayo 0-27 (2017)

MOST GOALS SCORED BY ONE TEAM 1975 TO 2019

Kerry 9-21 Clare 1-9 (1979)
Roscommon 9-19 London 1-10 (1980)

MOST POINTS SCORED BY ONE TEAM 1975 TO 2019

Kerry 0-32 Clare 0-10 (2018)

CHAMPIONSHIP TITLES 1979 TO 2019

(Leinster records include 1895 'Leinster and Ulster Championship')

Titles

Connacht
Mayo (17)   Sligo (1)
Galway (14)   Leitrim (1)
Roscommon (8)

Leinster
Dublin (24)   Laois (1)
Meath (9)   Westmeath (1)
Offaly (4)
Kildare (2)

Munster
Kerry (26)
Cork (14)
Clare (1)

Ulster
Tyrone (12)   Derry (3)
Armagh (9)   Down (3)
Donegal (8)   Cavan (1)
Monaghan (5)

All-Ireland
Kerry (13)   Armagh (1)
Dublin (9)   Derry (1)
Meath (4)   Offaly (1)
Cork (3)
Tyrone (3)
Donegal (2)
Galway (2)
Down (2)

24

TOP RANKED COUNTIES BY DECADE

Here's a breakdown of the top performing teams by decade and all-time. Teams were scored based on 3 points for a win and a point for a draw and then ranked.

The top six counties are listed in order of rank with the highest ranked county on the left and lowest on the right.

1887-2019	Kerry	Dublin	Cavan	Cork	Galway	Mayo
2010s	Dublin	Kerry	Tyrone	Donegal	Mayo	Kildare
2000s	Kerry	Tyrone	Dublin	Armagh	Galway	Cork
1990s	Meath	Dublin	Mayo	Derry	Kerry	Cork
1980s	Dublin	Kerry	Offaly	Meath	Cork	Mayo
1970s	Dublin	Kerry	Derry	Offaly	Galway	Roscommon
1960s	Down	Kerry	Galway	Cavan	Offaly	Dublin
1950s	Cavan	Kerry	Louth	Meath	Cork	Dublin
1940s	Cavan	Kerry	Meath	Roscommon	Dublin	Carlow
1930s	Kerry	Cavan	Kildare	Mayo	Galway	Armagh
1920s	Kerry	Cavan	Kildare	Dublin	Monaghan	Mayo
1910s	Wexford	Kerry	Louth	Dublin	Cavan	Antrim
1900s	Dublin	Kerry	Cork	Kildare	Louth	Kilkenny
1890s	Dublin	Cork	Wexford	Kildare	Limerick	Meath
1880s	Tipperary	Kilkenny	Limerick	Louth	Laois	Wexford

MOST COMPETITIVE PROVINCE

So, which was the most competitive province over the years? One way of trying to answer the question is to look at how big (or small) was the typical winning margin in games within the provincial championships.

The graph below shows the average number of points that was the winning margin in games in each province over the decades. The figure on the left is the average winning margin in points and the individual lines each represents a province. The most competitive province can be identified by which line is lowest (and the name of the province with the lowest average is indicated below the relevant part of the graph).

Since the 1960s Ulster has had the lowest winning margin since the 1960s. Before that it was Connacht and then, for several decades, it was Leinster. Munster has tended to be the least competitive since the 1940s although the introduction of New York and London to Connacht often saw both counties lose by large margins increasing the overall average winning margin in the Connacht provincial championship. The growing gap between Dublin and the rest of Leinster in recent years has seen a similar increase in the average winning margins in the Leinster championship.

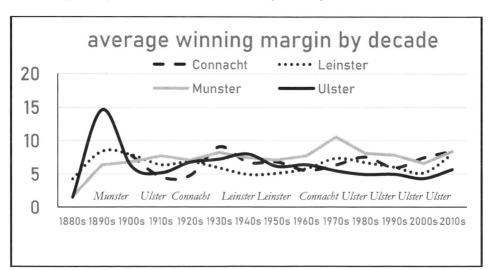

CHAMPIONSHIP TITLES 1887 TO 2019

(Leinster records include 1895 'Leinster and Ulster Championship')

Titles

Connacht
Galway (49)	Sligo (4)
Mayo (46)	Leitrim (2)
Roscommon (24)	

Leinster
Dublin (58)	Laois (6)
Meath (21)	Kilkenny (3)
Kildare (13)	Carlow (1)
Wexford (10)	Longford (1)
Offaly (10)	Westmeath (1)
Louth (8)	

Munster
Kerry (81)	Clare (2)
Cork (37)	Limerick (1)
Tipperary (9)	Waterford (1)

Ulster
Cavan (37)	Down (12)
Monaghan (16)	Antrim (11)
Tyrone (15)	Donegal (10)
Armagh (14)	Derry (7)

All-Ireland
Kerry (37)	Louth (3)
Dublin (29)	Mayo (3)
Galway (9)	Offaly (3)
Cork (7)	Tyrone (3)
Meath (7)	Donegal (2)
Cavan (5)	Limerick (2)
Down (5)	Roscommon (2)
Wexford (5)	Armagh (1)
Kildare (4)	Derry (1)
Tipperary (4)	

RECORDS BY COUNTY

Includes records for every county in Ireland as well as London and New York. Scotland and Glasgow were included in the draw on a number of occasions but as no Scottish team played a game, they are not included here. Counties are listed by alphabetical order based on the English spelling of their name.

The county record includes the number of games played, won, drawn and lost with a percentage for games won; a list of the individual provincial and All-Ireland honours; and then a list of the biggest win and defeat against each other county (including the year in which the result took place). Where counties have never met, that part of the table has been left blank.

ANTRIM/AONTROIM

Overall Record		
Played	228
Won	77 (33.8%)
Drawn	11
Lost	140

TITLES

Ulster 1889, 1900, 1901, 1908, 1909, 1910, 1911, 1912, 1913, 1946, 1951 (11)

All-Ireland none

HEAD TO HEAD
(biggest win/loss; blank if counties have never met in championship)

Armagh	*Win*	Antrim 1-12	Armagh 0-6	1946
	Loss	Armagh 3-17	Antrim 0-0	1890
Carlow	*Win*	Antrim 1-13	Carlow 2-9	2011
	Loss			
Cavan	*Win*	Antrim 3-4	Cavan 0-1	1911
	Loss	Antrim 0-4	Cavan 6-13	1940
Clare	*Win*			
	Loss	Antrim 2-9	Clare 1-13	2006
Cork	*Win*			
	Loss	Cork 6-6	Antrim 1-2	1912
Derry	*Win*	Antrim 5-10	Derry 0-5	1950
	Loss	Derry 4-14	Antrim 0-8	1957
Donegal	*Win*	Antrim 2-8	Donegal 0-3	1947
	Loss	Donegal 3-19	Antrim 1-9	2017
Down	*Win*	Antrim 4-10	Down 0-1	1932
	Loss	Down 5-4	Antrim 0-4	1941
Dublin	*Win*			
	Loss	Dublin 2-12	Antrim 0-2	1903
Fermanagh	*Win*	Antrim 1-6	Fermanagh 1-3	1913
	Loss	Fermanagh 1-21	Antrim 0-11	2015
Galway	*Win*	Antrim 0-11	Galway 0-10	2012
	Loss			
Kerry	*Win*	Antrim 3-5	Kerry 0-2	1912
	Loss	Antrim 1-10	Kerry 2-12	2009

Kildare	*Win*			
	Loss	Antrim 0-14	Kildare 1-25	2019
Kilkenny	*Win*	Antrim 3-1	Kilkenny 1-1	1911
	Loss			
Laois	*Win*	Laois 1-16	Antrim 2-15	2015
	Loss			
Leitrim	*Win*	Antrim 0-13	Leitrim 1-8	2001
	Loss			
Limerick	*Win*			
	Loss	Limerick 3-11	Antrim 0-15	2014
London	*Win*	Antrim 2-11	London 2-9	2012
	Loss			
Longford	*Win*			
	Loss			
Louth	*Win*	Louth 1-11	Antrim 2-16	2019
	Loss	Louth 1-17	Antrim 1-11	2013
Mayo	*Win*			
	Loss			
Meath	*Win*			
	Loss	Antrim 0-13	Meath 5-12	2005
Monaghan	*Win*	Antrim 2-7	Monaghan 0-2	1962
	Loss	Monaghan 2-18	Antrim 0-4	1983
New York	*Win*			
	Loss			
Offaly	*Win*			
	Loss	Offaly 2-30	Antrim 1-15	2018
Roscommon	*Win*			
	Loss			
Sligo	*Win*			
	Loss	Sligo 0-22	Antrim 3-7	2017
Tipperary	*Win*			
	Loss	Tipperary 0-10	Antrim 0-8	2012
Tyrone	*Win*	Antrim 2-9	Tyrone 0-3	1963
	Loss	Antrim 2-9	Tyrone 2-23	2019
Waterford	*Win*			
	Loss			
Westmeath	*Win*	Antrim 0-16	Westmeath 1-7	2011
	Loss	Antrim 1-10	Westmeath 0-14	2002
Wexford	*Win*			
	Loss	Wexford 4-4	Antrim 0-1	1913
Wicklow	*Win*			
	Loss			

ARMAGH/ARD MHACHA

Overall	Played	314
Record	Won	148 (47.1%)
	Drawn	29
	Lost	138

TITLES

Ulster	1890, 1902, 1950, 1953, 1977, 1980, 1982, 1999, 2000, 2002, 2004, 2005, 2006, 2008 (14)

All-Ireland	2002 (1)

HEAD TO HEAD

(biggest win/loss; blank if counties have never met in championship)

Antrim	Win	Armagh 3-17	Antrim 0-0	1890
	Loss	Antrim 1-12	Armagh 0-6	1946
Carlow	Win			
	Loss			
Cavan	Win	Cavan 1-4	Armagh 2-7	1938
	Loss	Cavan 4-10	Armagh 0-2	1929
Clare	Win	Armagh 2-16	Clare 1-15	2018
	Loss			
Cork	Win			
	Loss	Cork 1-15	Armagh 0-0	1890
Derry	Win	Armagh 4-11	Derry 1-5	1953
	Loss	Derry 1-19	Armagh 2-1	1976
Donegal	Win	Armagh 3-15	Donegal 0-11	2004
	Loss	Donegal 2-16	Armagh 1-7	1993
Down	Win	Armagh 0-15	Down 0-1	1905
	Loss	Down 5-7	Armagh 2-3	1948
Dublin	Win	Dublin 0-11	Armagh 0-15	2003
	Loss	Dublin 4-16	Armagh 1-6	1904
Fermanagh	Win	Armagh 2-13	Fermanagh 0-5	1985
	Loss	Fermanagh 3-8	Armagh 0-8	1966
Galway	Win			
	Loss	Galway 1-11	Armagh 0-9	2013
Kerry	Win	Armagh 1-12	Kerry 0-14	2002
	Loss	Armagh 1-11	Kerry 3-15	1982

Kildare	Win	Kildare 0-17	Armagh 1-17	2017
	Loss			
Kilkenny	Win			
	Loss			
Laois	Win	Armagh 2-17	Laois 1-11	2005
	Loss	Laois 1-10	Armagh 0-10	2016
Leitrim	Win	Leitrim 0-10	Armagh 8-13	2013
	Loss			
Limerick	Win	Armagh 4-10	Limerick 0-11	2003
	Loss			
London	Win			
	Loss			
Longford	Win			
	Loss			
Louth	Win			
	Loss			
Mayo	Win			
	Loss	Mayo 3-9	Armagh 0-6	1950
Meath	Win	Meath 0-13	Armagh 0-18	2014
	Loss	Meath 0-15	Armagh 2-5	1999
Monaghan	Win	Armagh 5-9	Monaghan 0-5	1961
	Loss	Monaghan 2-9	Armagh 0-2	1922
New York	Win			
	Loss			
Offaly	Win			
	Loss			
Roscommon	Win	Roscommon 1-12	Armagh 1-17	2014
	Loss	Roscommon 2-20	Armagh 3-11	1980
Sligo	Win	Sligo 1-13	Armagh 1-19	2018
	Loss			
Tipperary	Win	Tipperary 1-15	Armagh 1-17	2017
	Loss			
Tyrone	Win	Armagh 7-13	Tyrone 2-3	1951
	Loss	Armagh 0-1	Tyrone 3-13	1941
Waterford	Win	Waterford 0-8	Armagh 2-21	2003
	Loss			
Westmeath	Win	Westmeath 1-11	Armagh 3-16	2018
	Loss			
Wexford	Win			
	Loss	Armagh 0-12	Wexford 1-14	2008
Wicklow	Win	Armagh 2-21	Wicklow 0-2	2013
	Loss			

33

CARLOW/CEATHARLACH

Overall Record	Played	190
	Won	52 (27.4%)
	Drawn	19
	Lost	119

TITLES

Leinster 1944 (1)

All-Ireland none

HEAD TO HEAD
(biggest win/loss; blank if counties have never met in championship)

Antrim	Win			
	Loss	Antrim 1-13	Carlow 2-9	2011
Armagh	Win			
	Loss			
Cavan	Win			
	Loss	Cavan 2-13	Carlow 0-12	2016
Clare	Win			
	Loss	Carlow 2-13	Clare 4-26	2014
Cork	Win			
	Loss			
Derry	Win			
	Loss	Carlow 2-9	Derry 1-18	2010
Donegal	Win			
	Loss	Donegal 2-13	Carlow 1-6	2009
Down	Win			
	Loss	Carlow 1-13	Down 1-19	2004
Dublin	Win	Carlow 2-6	Dublin 1-6	1944
	Loss	Dublin 6-15	Carlow 2-9	1978
Fermanagh	Win			
	Loss			
Galway	Win			
	Loss			
Kerry	Win			
	Loss	Kerry 3-3	Carlow 0-10	1944

Kildare	*Win*	Carlow 3-11	Kildare 2-5	1944
	Loss	Kildare 9-8	Carlow 1-1	1921
Kilkenny	*Win*	Carlow 4-10	Kilkenny 1-4	1963
	Loss	Carlow 0-0	Kilkenny 2-11	1901
Laois	*Win*	Carlow 4-4	Laois 1-7	1948
	Loss	Carlow 0-8	Laois 3-16	2015
Leitrim	*Win*	Carlow 2-14	Leitrim 0-13	2017
	Loss			
Limerick	*Win*			
	Loss	Limerick 2-15	Carlow 0-7	2005
London	*Win*	London 0-12	Carlow 0-13	2017
	Loss			
Longford	*Win*	Carlow 4-15	Longford 1-16	2004
	Loss	Longford 3-15	Carlow 0-13	1983
Louth	*Win*	Louth 0-12	Carlow 2-17	2018
	Loss	Louth 3-19	Carlow 0-11	1994
Mayo	*Win*			
	Loss			
Meath	*Win*			
	Loss	Carlow 0-6	Meath 7-13	2014
Monaghan	*Win*			
	Loss	Carlow 1-7	Monaghan 1-12	2017
New York	*Win*			
	Loss			
Offaly	*Win*	Offaly 0-6	Carlow 1-9	1942
	Loss	Offaly 3-13	Carlow 0-6	1934
Roscommon	*Win*			
	Loss			
Sligo	*Win*			
	Loss	Carlow 2-7	Sligo 2-14	2001
Tipperary	*Win*			
	Loss	Tipperary 1-14	Carlow 0-13	2003
Tyrone	*Win*			
	Loss	Carlow 1-10	Tyrone 3-14	2018
Waterford	*Win*	Waterford 1-10	Carlow 3-11	2001
	Loss			
Westmeath	*Win*	Carlow 3-11	Westmeath 1-4	1985
	Loss	Westmeath 3-15	Carlow 1-10	2013
Wexford	*Win*	Carlow 4-17	Wexford 1-11	1996
	Loss	Wexford 2-24	Carlow 0-5	1898
Wicklow	*Win*	Carlow 4-3	Wicklow 0-1	1918
	Loss	Wicklow 4-12	Carlow 1-4	1956

CAVAN/AN CABHÁN

	Played	387
Overall	Won	214 (55.3%)
Record	Drawn	39
	Lost	134

TITLES

Ulster	1891, 1904, 1905, 1915, 1918, 1919, 1920, 1923, 1924, 1925, 1926, 1928, 1931, 1932, 1933, 1934, 1935, 1936, 1937, 1939, 1940, 1941, 1942, 1943, 1944, 1945, 1947, 1948, 1949, 1952, 1954, 1955, 1962, 1964, 1967, 1969, 1997 (37)
All-Ireland	1933, 1935, 1947, 1948, 1952 (5)

HEAD TO HEAD

(biggest win/loss; blank if counties have never met in championship)

Antrim	Win	Antrim 0-4	Cavan 6-13	1940
	Loss	Antrim 3-4	Cavan 0-1	1911
Armagh	Win	Cavan 4-10	Armagh 0-2	1929
	Loss	Cavan 1-4	Armagh 2-7	1938
Carlow	Win	Cavan 2-13	Carlow 0-12	2016
	Loss			
Clare	Win			
	Loss			
Cork	Win			
	Loss	Cork 1-19	Cavan 0-4	2010
Derry	Win	Cavan 7-7	Derry 4-3	1927
	Loss	Derry 2-14	Cavan 0-5	1999
Donegal	Win	Cavan 5-12	Donegal 0-4	1939
	Loss	Donegal 4-5	Cavan 0-6	1963
Down	Win	Cavan 5-11	Down 1-3	1942
	Loss	Down 2-16	Cavan 0-7	1959
Dublin	Win			
	Loss	Dublin 3-7	Cavan 0-3	1892
Fermanagh	Win	Cavan 8-3	Fermanagh 2-1	1920
	Loss	Fermanagh 2-1	Cavan 0-4	1914
Galway	Win	Cavan 2-5	Galway 1-4	1933
	Loss	Galway 1-12	Cavan 1-4	1941
Kerry	Win	Cavan 2-11	Kerry 2-7	1947
	Loss	Kerry 4-10	Cavan 0-1	1906

Kildare	*Win*	Cavan 3-6	Kildare 2-5	1935
	Loss	Kildare 4-15	Cavan 1-6	1906
Kilkenny	*Win*			
	Loss			
Laois	*Win*			
	Loss	Laois 2-6	Cavan 1-5	1936
Leitrim	*Win*			
	Loss			
Limerick	*Win*			
	Loss	Cavan 0-11	Limerick 2-8	2002
London	*Win*	London 0-11	Cavan 2-22	2015
	Loss			
Longford	*Win*			
	Loss	Cavan 0-11	Longford 2-16	2011
Louth	*Win*	Cavan 1-14	Louth 4-2	1948
	Loss	Louth 2-4	Cavan 0-4	1918
Mayo	*Win*	Cavan 2-5	Mayo 1-7	1937
	Loss	Mayo 1-19	Cavan 3-7	2007
Meath	*Win*	Cavan 0-9	Meath 0-5	1952
	Loss	Meath 1-9	Cavan 1-1	1939
Monaghan	*Win*	Cavan 5-10	Monaghan 1-1	1923
	Loss	Monaghan 3-1	Cavan 0-2	1917
New York	*Win*			
	Loss			
Offaly	*Win*	Offaly 0-16	Cavan 0-17	2017
	Loss	Offaly 3-8	Cavan 1-10	1969
Roscommon	*Win*	Cavan 2-4	Roscommon 0-6	1947
	Loss	Roscommon 5-8	Cavan 1-3	1944
Sligo	*Win*	Cavan 2-5	Sligo 0-4	1928
	Loss			
Tipperary	*Win*	Cavan 1-7	Tipperary 0-8	1935
	Loss	Cavan 0-18	Tipperary 2-15	2017
Tyrone	*Win*	Cavan 8-13	Tyrone 2-3	1946
	Loss	Tyrone 3-19	Cavan 0-7	2005
Waterford	*Win*			
	Loss			
Westmeath	*Win*	Cavan 1-15	Westmeath 1-14	2014
	Loss			
Wexford	*Win*	Cavan 1-14	Wexford 0-5	1945
	Loss	Wexford 3-7	Cavan 2-2	1915
Wicklow	*Win*	Wicklow 1-5	Cavan 2-16	2018
	Loss	Wicklow 1-12	Cavan 0-8	2009

CLARE/AN CLÁR

Overall Record		
	Played	220
	Won	74 (33.6%)
	Drawn	14
	Lost	132

TITLES

Munster 1917, 1992 (2)

All-Ireland none

HEAD TO HEAD

(biggest win/loss; blank if counties have never met in championship)

Antrim	*Win*	Antrim 2-9	Clare 1-13	2006
	Loss			
Armagh	*Win*			
	Loss	Armagh 2-16	Clare 1-15	2018
Carlow	*Win*	Carlow 2-13	Clare 4-26	2014
	Loss			
Cavan	*Win*			
	Loss			
Cork	*Win*	Clare 5-4	Cork 0-1	1917
	Loss	Cork 4-9	Clare 1-1	1951
Derry	*Win*			
	Loss			
Donegal	*Win*			
	Loss	Donegal 0-13	Clare 1-7	2009
Down	*Win*			
	Loss	Clare 1-12	Down 1-13	2011
Dublin	*Win*			
	Loss	Dublin 3-14	Clare 2-12	1992
Fermanagh	*Win*			
	Loss	Clare 0-10	Fermanagh 0-15	2006
Galway	*Win*	Clare 2-1	Galway 0-5	1917
	Loss			
Kerry	*Win*	Clare 3-7	Kerry 1-8	1949
	Loss	Clare 1-9	Kerry 9-21	1979

38

Kildare	Win			
	Loss	Clare 0-12	Kildare 0-13	2014
Kilkenny	Win			
	Loss			
Laois	Win	Laois 0-14	Clare 2-18	2017
	Loss	Clare 0-10	Laois 3-17	2013
Leitrim	Win	Leitrim 0-17	Clare 3-17	2019
	Loss			
Limerick	Win	Clare 4-10	Limerick 0-2	1948
	Loss	Limerick 6-2	Clare 3-3	1945
London	Win			
	Loss			
Longford	Win			
	Loss	Clare 1-12	Longford 2-12	2015
Louth	Win			
	Loss			
Mayo	Win			
	Loss	Clare 0-13	Mayo 2-14	2017
Meath	Win			
	Loss	Clare 1-18	Meath 2-16	2019
Monaghan	Win			
	Loss			
New York	Win			
	Loss			
Offaly	Win	Offaly 2-14	Clare 1-19	2018
	Loss	Offaly 1-12	Clare 1-8	2003
Roscommon	Win	Roscommon 1-9	Clare 2-12	2016
	Loss			
Sligo	Win	Clare 1-15	Sligo 1-7	2004
	Loss	Sligo 1-13	Clare 0-11	2005
Tipperary	Win	Tipperary 0-9	Clare 3-14	1981
	Loss	Tipperary 4-8	Clare 1-2	1923
Tyrone	Win			
	Loss			
Waterford	Win	Clare 4-16	Waterford 0-5	1983
	Loss	Waterford 2-9	Clare 0-2	1911
Westmeath	Win	Clare 0-12	Westmeath 0-9	2005
	Loss			
Wexford	Win			
	Loss	Wexford 0-9	Clare 0-5	1917
Wicklow	Win			
	Loss			

CORK/CORCAIGH

Overall Record		
Played	361	
Won	202 (56%)	
Drawn	20	
Lost	139	

TITLES

Munster
1890, 1891, 1893, 1894, 1897, 1899, 1901, 1906, 1907, 1911, 1916, 1928, 1943, 1945, 1949, 1952, 1956, 1957, 1966, 1967, 1971, 1973, 1974, 1983, 1987, 1988, 1989, 1990, 1993, 1994, 1995, 1999, 2002, 2006, 2008, 2009, 2012 (37)

All-Ireland
1890, 1911, 1945, 1973, 1989, 1990, 2010 (7)

HEAD TO HEAD

(biggest win/loss; blank if counties have never met in championship)

Antrim	Win	Cork 6-6	Antrim 1-2	1912
	Loss			
Armagh	Win	Cork 1-15	Armagh 0-0	1890
	Loss			
Carlow	Win			
	Loss			
Cavan	Win	Cork 1-19	Cavan 0-4	2010
	Loss	Cavan 0-10	Cork 0-3	1952
Clare	Win	Cork 4-9	Clare 1-1	1951
	Loss	Clare 5-4	Cork 0-1	1917
Derry	Win			
	Loss	Derry 1-14	Cork 2-8	1993
Donegal	Win	Cork 1-27	Donegal 2-10	2009
	Loss	Donegal 0-21	Cork 1-15	2016
Down	Win	Down 0-14	Cork 2-20	2011
	Loss	Down 1-13	Cork 0-11	1994
Dublin	Win	Cork 2-10	Dublin 1-9	1989
	Loss	Cork 1-17	Dublin 5-18	2019
Fermanagh	Win			
	Loss	Cork 0-11	Fermanagh 0-18	2004
Galway	Win	Cork 3-4	Galway 0-2	1911
	Loss	Galway 1-14	Cork 1-10	2001
Kerry	Win	Cork 2-23	Kerry 1-11	1990
	Loss	Kerry 6-7	Cork 0-4	1937

40

Kildare	Win	Cork 2-19	Kildare 0-12	2012
	Loss	Kildare 3-7	Cork 0-2	1928
Kilkenny	Win			
	Loss			
Laois	Win	Cork 4-20	Laois 1-15	2019
	Loss			
Leitrim	Win			
	Loss			
Limerick	Win	Cork 5-19	Limerick 1-6	1980
	Loss	Limerick 0-16	Cork 0-6	2003
London	Win	Cork 1-14	London 1-5	1908
	Loss			
Longford	Win	Longford 1-6	Cork 2-9	2016
	Loss			
Louth	Win	Louth 0-14	Cork 0-16	2007
	Loss	Louth 1-9	Cork 1-7	1957
Mayo	Win	Cork 4-16	Mayo 0-1	1903
	Loss	Mayo 1-13	Cork 2-6	2011
Meath	Win	Cork 1-16	Meath 0-9	2007
	Loss	Meath 1-14	Cork 0-11	1987
Monaghan	Win	Cork 1-14	Monaghan 0-6	1988
	Loss			
New York	Win			
	Loss			
Offaly	Win			
	Loss	Offaly 1-16	Cork 1-11	1971
Roscommon	Win	Roscommon 0-10	Cork 1-16	2010
	Loss	Cork 3-9	Roscommon 4-9	2019
Sligo	Win	Cork 3-13	Sligo 0-11	2005
	Loss			
Tipperary	Win	Cork 3-11	Tipperary 0-1	1901
	Loss	Tipperary 2-8	Cork 1-2	1935
Tyrone	Win	Cork 5-10	Tyrone 2-4	1973
	Loss	Cork 0-13	Tyrone 3-20	2018
Waterford	Win	Cork 3-23	Waterford 0-4	1999
	Loss	Waterford 1-11	Cork 1-3	1899
Westmeath	Win			
	Loss			
Wexford	Win	Cork 2-4	Wexford 0-1	1892
	Loss	Wexford 1-1	Cork 0-1	1894
Wicklow	Win			
	Loss			

DERRY/DOIRE

Overall Record		
Played	227
Won	114 (50.2%)
Drawn	9
Lost	104

TITLES

Ulster 1958, 1970. 1975, 1976, 1987, 1993, 1998 (7)

All-Ireland 1993 (1)

HEAD TO HEAD

(biggest win/loss; blank if counties have never met in championship)

Antrim	*Win*	Derry 4-14	Antrim 0-8	1957
	Loss	Antrim 5-10	Derry 0-5	1950
Armagh	*Win*	Derry 1-19	Armagh 2-1	1976
	Loss	Armagh 4-11	Derry 1-5	1953
Carlow	*Win*	Carlow 2-9	Derry 1-18	2010
	Loss			
Cavan	*Win*	Derry 2-14	Cavan 0-5	1999
	Loss	Cavan 7-7	Derry 4-3	1927
Clare	*Win*			
	Loss			
Cork	*Win*	Derry 1-14	Cork 2-8	1993
	Loss			
Donegal	*Win*	Derry 0-18	Donegal 0-2	1906
	Loss	Donegal 1-15	Derry 0-8	1990
Down	*Win*	Down 0-9	Derry 3-11	1993
	Loss	Down 1-12	Derry 0-7	1974
Dublin	*Win*	Derry 0-15	Dublin 0-14	1993
	Loss	Dublin 2-12	Derry 1-9	1958
Fermanagh	*Win*	Fermanagh 1-7	Derry 4-15	1989
	Loss	Fermanagh 1-11	Derry 1-9	2008
Galway	*Win*			
	Loss	Galway 1-11	Derry 0-8	2015
Kerry	*Win*	Derry 2-6	Kerry 2-5	1958
	Loss	Kerry 5-14	Derry 1-10	1976

Kildare	Win	Derry 1-17	Kildare 0-11	2006
	Loss	Derry 1-9	Kildare 2-17	2010
Kilkenny	Win			
	Loss			
Laois	Win	Laois 2-11	Derry 1-18	2007
	Loss	Derry 0-12	Laois 1-13	2019
Leitrim	Win			
	Loss			
Limerick	Win	Derry 0-13	Limerick 0-9	2005
	Loss			
London	Win			
	Loss			
Longford	Win	Longford 0-9	Derry 2-13	2002
	Loss	Longford 0-17	Derry 2-8	2012
Louth	Win	Derry 1-18	Louth 2-10	2016
	Loss			
Mayo	Win	Derry 2-13	Mayo 1-6	2007
	Loss	Mayo 2-21	Derry 1-13	2017
Meath	Win	Derry 1-14	Meath 1-11	2016
	Loss	Meath 0-15	Derry 0-8	1987
Monaghan	Win	Derry 2-15	Monaghan 0-10	1997
	Loss	Monaghan 2-5	Derry 0-1	1916
New York	Win			
	Loss			
Offaly	Win			
	Loss			
Roscommon	Win			
	Loss			
Sligo	Win	Derry 0-15	Sligo 0-8	2013
	Loss			
Tipperary	Win			
	Loss	Tipperary 1-21	Derry 2-17	2016
Tyrone	Win	Derry 3-12	Tyrone 0-7	1970
	Loss	Tyrone 7-3	Derry 2-3	1928
Waterford	Win	Waterford 0-13	Derry 1-17	2017
	Loss			
Westmeath	Win	Westmeath 1-7	Derry 0-13	2010
	Loss			
Wexford	Win	Wexford 0-10	Derry 4-16	2019
	Loss			
Wicklow	Win	Wicklow 1-10	Derry 1-15	2004
	Loss			

43

DONEGAL/DÚN NA NGALL

		Played	242
Overall		Won	114 (47.1%)
Record		Drawn	15
		Lost	113

TITLES

Ulster 1972, 1974, 1983, 1990, 1992, 2011, 2012, 2014, 2018, 2019 (10)

All-Ireland 1992, 2012 (2)

HEAD TO HEAD
(biggest win/loss; blank if counties have never met in championship)

Antrim	*Win*	Donegal 3-19	Antrim 1-9	2017
	Loss	Antrim 2-8	Donegal 0-3	1947
Armagh	*Win*	Donegal 2-16	Armagh 1-7	1993
	Loss	Armagh 3-15	Donegal 0-11	2004
Carlow	*Win*	Donegal 2-13	Carlow 1-6	2009
	Loss			
Cavan	*Win*	Donegal 4-5	Cavan 0-6	1963
	Loss	Cavan 5-12	Donegal 0-4	1939
Clare	*Win*	Donegal 0-13	Clare 1-7	2009
	Loss			
Cork	*Win*	Donegal 0-21	Cork 1-15	2016
	Loss	Cork 1-27	Donegal 2-10	2009
Derry	*Win*	Donegal 1-15	Derry 0-8	1990
	Loss	Derry 0-18	Donegal 0-2	1906
Down	*Win*	Down 1-12	Donegal 2-22	2018
	Loss	Down 2-14	Donegal 0-8	1968
Dublin	*Win*	Donegal 3-14	Dublin 0-17	2014
	Loss	Dublin 1-14	Donegal 0-7	2002
Fermanagh	*Win*	Fermanagh 1-8	Donegal 4-17	1966
	Loss	Fermanagh 2-5	Donegal 1-3	1934
Galway	*Win*	Donegal 3-12	Galway 0-11	2015
	Loss	Galway 4-17	Donegal 0-14	2017
Kerry	*Win*	Donegal 1-12	Kerry 1-10	2012
	Loss	Kerry 2-9	Donegal 0-12	2014

Kildare	*Win*	Donegal 1-12	Kildare 0-14	2011
	Loss	Kildare 1-17	Donegal 1-16	2001
Kilkenny	*Win*			
	Loss			
Laois	*Win*	Laois 0-8	Donegal 0-14	2013
	Loss			
Leitrim	*Win*	Leitrim 1-14	Donegal 1-16	2007
	Loss			
Limerick	*Win*			
	Loss			
London	*Win*			
	Loss			
Longford	*Win*	Donegal 1-17	Longford 1-11	2003
	Loss			
Louth	*Win*			
	Loss			
Mayo	*Win*	Donegal 0-13	Mayo 0-9	1992
	Loss	Mayo 4-17	Donegal 1-10	2013
Meath	*Win*	Donegal 2-19	Meath 1-13	2019
	Loss	Meath 3-9	Donegal 1-7	1990
Monaghan	*Win*	Donegal 4-5	Monaghan 1-9	1946
	Loss	Monaghan 2-8	Donegal 0-1	1929
New York	*Win*			
	Loss			
Offaly	*Win*			
	Loss	Offaly 1-17	Donegal 2-10	1972
Roscommon	*Win*	Donegal 3-11	Roscommon 1-9	2008
	Loss			
Sligo	*Win*	Donegal 0-16	Sligo 0-11	2003
	Loss			
Tipperary	*Win*	Donegal 2-19	Tipperary 0-15	2003
	Loss			
Tyrone	*Win*	Donegal 4-3	Tyrone 1-0	1919
	Loss	Tyrone 8-7	Donegal 0-3	1953
Waterford	*Win*			
	Loss			
Westmeath	*Win*	Westmeath 1-8	Donegal 1-13	2007
	Loss			
Wexford	*Win*			
	Loss			
Wicklow	*Win*	Wicklow 0-12	Donegal 0-16	2005
	Loss			

DOWN/AN DÚN

Overall Record		
Played	264	
Won	123 (46.6%)	
Drawn	18	
Lost	123	

TITLES

Ulster | 1959, 1960, 1961, 1963, 1965, 1966, 1968, 1971, ,1978, 1981, 1991, 1994 (12)

All-Ireland | 1960, 1961, 1968, 1991,1994 (5)

HEAD TO HEAD

(biggest win/loss; blank if counties have never met in championship)

Antrim	Win	Down 5-4	Antrim 0-4	1941
	Loss	Antrim 4-10	Down 0-1	1932
Armagh	Win	Down 5-7	Armagh 2-3	1948
	Loss	Armagh 0-15	Down 0-1	1905
Carlow	Win	Carlow 1-13	Down 1-19	2004
	Loss			
Cavan	Win	Down 2-16	Cavan 0-7	1959
	Loss	Cavan 5-11	Down 1-3	1942
Clare	Win	Clare 1-12	Down 1-13	2011
	Loss			
Cork	Win	Down 1-13	Cork 0-11	1994
	Loss	Down 0-14	Cork 2-20	2011
Derry	Win	Down 1-12	Derry 0-7	1974
	Loss	Down 0-9	Derry 3-11	1993
Donegal	Win	Down 2-14	Donegal 0-8	1968
	Loss	Down 1-12	Donegal 2-22	2018
Dublin	Win	Down 1-12	Dublin 0-13	1994
	Loss	Dublin 1-16	Down 0-8	1978
Fermanagh	Win	Fermanagh 1-8	Down 4-10	1962
	Loss	Fermanagh 0-13	Down 0-10	2009
Galway	Win	Down 2-10	Galway 2-8	1968
	Loss	Galway 1-11	Down 1-4	1959
Kerry	Win	Down 2-10	Kerry 0-8	1960
	Loss			

Kildare	Win	Kildare 1-14	Down 1-16	2010
	Loss	Down 0-11	Kildare 1-18	2014
Kilkenny	Win			
	Loss			
Laois	Win	Laois 0-7	Down 2-9	2009
	Loss			
Leitrim	Win	Down 4-18	Leitrim 0-9	2014
	Loss			
Limerick	Win			
	Loss			
London	Win	London 1-7	Down 1-16	2009
	Loss			
Longford	Win	Down 1-14	Longford 1-10	2010
	Loss	Longford 1-16	Down 0-14	2002
Louth	Win			
	Loss			
Mayo	Win			
	Loss	Mayo 3-18	Down 2-9	2012
Meath	Win	Down 1-16	Meath 1-14	1991
	Loss	Meath 2-16	Down 1-9	1966
Monaghan	Win	Down 6-11	Monaghan 1-3	1963
	Loss	Monaghan 7-8	Down 1-3	1930
New York	Win			
	Loss			
Offaly	Win	Offaly 2-10	Down 5-19	2008
	Loss	Down 0-6	Offaly 0-12	1981
Roscommon	Win			
	Loss			
Sligo	Win	Sligo 0-10	Down 3-20	2010
	Loss	Sligo 1-7	Down 0-4	2006
Tipperary	Win	Down 1-13	Tipperary 0-11	2012
	Loss			
Tyrone	Win	Down 3-13	Tyrone 1-6	1965
	Loss	Down 1-5	Tyrone 0-23	2003
Waterford	Win			
	Loss			
Westmeath	Win			
	Loss			
Wexford	Win			
	Loss	Wexford 2-13	Down 0-12	2008
Wicklow	Win	Wicklow 1-15	Down 0-17	2009
	Loss			

DUBLIN/ÁTHA CLIATH

Overall Record		
Played	489	
Won	343 (70.1%)	
Drawn	37	
Lost	109	

TITLES

Leinster
1891, 1892, 1894, 1896, 1897, 1898, 1899, 1901, 1902, 1904, 1906, 1907, 1908, 1920, 1921, 1922, 1923, 1924, 1932, 1933, 1934, 1941, 1942, 1955, 1958, 1959, 1962, 1963, 1965, 1974, 1975, 1976, 1977, 1978, 1979, 1983, 1984, 1985, 1989, 1992, 1993, 1994, 1995, 2002, 2005, 2006, 2007, 2008, 2009, 2011, 2012, 2013, 2014, 2015, 2016, 2017, 2018, 2019 (58)

All-Ireland
1891, 1892, 1894, 1897, 1898, 1899, 1901, 1902, 1906, 1907, 1908, 1921, 1922, 1923, 1942, 1958, 1963, 1974, 1976, 1977, 1983, 1995, 2011, 2013, 2015, 2016, 2017, 2018, 2019 (29)

HEAD TO HEAD

(biggest win/loss; blank if counties have never met in championship)

Antrim	Win	Dublin 2-12	Antrim 0-2	1903
	Loss			
Armagh	Win	Dublin 4-16	Armagh 1-6	1904
	Loss	Dublin 0-11	Armagh 0-15	2003
Carlow	Win	Dublin 6-15	Carlow 2-9	1978
	Loss	Carlow 2-6	Dublin 1-6	1944
Cavan	Win	Dublin 3-7	Cavan 0-3	1892
	Loss			
Clare	Win	Dublin 3-14	Clare 2-12	1992
	Loss			
Cork	Win	Dublin 5-18	Cork 1-17	2019
	Loss	Cork 2-10	Dublin 1-9	1989
Derry	Win	Dublin 2-12	Derry 1-9	1958
	Loss	Derry 0-15	Dublin 0-14	1993
Donegal	Win	Dublin 1-14	Donegal 0-7	2002
	Loss	Donegal 3-14	Dublin 0-17	2014
Down	Win	Dublin 1-16	Down 0-8	1978
	Loss	Down 1-12	Dublin 0-13	1994
Fermanagh	Win	Dublin 2-23	Fermanagh 2-15	2015
	Loss			
Galway	Win	Dublin 1-24	Galway 2-12	2018
	Loss	Galway 3-5	Dublin 1-9	1934
Kerry	Win	Dublin 3-8	Kerry 0-6	1934
	Loss	Kerry 5-11	Dublin 0-9	1978

Kildare	*Win*	Dublin 2-15	Kildare 0-2	1898
	Loss	Dublin 1-3	Kildare 3-11	1904
Kilkenny	*Win*	Dublin 3-13	Kilkenny 1-2	1902
	Loss			
Laois	*Win*	Dublin 7-17	Laois 0-3	1900
	Loss	Laois 3-8	Dublin 0-13	1971
Leitrim	*Win*	Dublin 3-15	Leitrim 1-9	1994
	Loss			
Limerick	*Win*			
	Loss	Limerick 1-5	Dublin 0-7	1898
London	*Win*	Dublin 3-24	London 0-6	2004
	Loss			
Longford	*Win*	Dublin 4-25	Longford 0-10	2015
	Loss	Longford 1-12	Dublin 0-12	1968
Louth	*Win*	Dublin 5-21	Louth 0-10	2019
	Loss	Louth 4-5	Dublin 1-6	1943
Mayo	*Win*	Dublin 1-9	Mayo 0-2	1923
	Loss	Dublin 0-16	Mayo 0-19	2012
Meath	*Win*	Dublin 5-12	Meath 0-7	1955
	Loss	Meath 3-8	Dublin 0-4	1930
Monaghan	*Win*	Dublin 2-22	Monaghan 0-11	2014
	Loss			
New York	*Win*			
	Loss			
Offaly	*Win*	Offaly 1-0	Dublin 3-7	1910
	Loss	Offaly 3-9	Dublin 0-9	1960
Roscommon	*Win*	Dublin 2-26	Roscommon 0-14	2019
	Loss			
Sligo	*Win*	Dublin 3-17	Sligo 0-12	2001
	Loss			
Tipperary	*Win*	Dublin 1-21	Tipperary 1-13	2010
	Loss	Tipperary 1-6	Dublin 1-2	1922
Tyrone	*Win*	Dublin 2-17	Tyrone 0-11	2017
	Loss	Dublin 1-8	Tyrone 3-14	2008
Waterford	*Win*	Dublin 2-8	Waterford 0-4	1900
	Loss			
Westmeath	*Win*	Dublin 4-29	Westmeath 0-10	2017
	Loss	Westmeath 2-4	Dublin 1-4	1931
Wexford	*Win*	Wexford 0-9	Dublin 3-23	2008
	Loss	Wexford 4-6	Dublin 1-1	1914
Wicklow	*Win*	Dublin 4-25	Wicklow 1-11	2018
	Loss			

FERMANAGH/FEAR MANACH

Overall Record		
Played	177	
Won	51 (28.8%)	
Drawn	12	
Lost	114	

TITLES

Ulster | none

All-Ireland | none

HEAD TO HEAD

(biggest win/loss; blank if counties have never met in championship)

Antrim	Win	Fermanagh 1-21	Antrim 0-11	2015
	Loss	Antrim 1-6	Fermanagh 1-3	1913
Armagh	Win	Fermanagh 3-8	Armagh 0-8	1966
	Loss	Armagh 2-13	Fermanagh 0-5	1985
Carlow	Win			
	Loss			
Cavan	Win	Fermanagh 2-1	Cavan 0-4	1914
	Loss	Cavan 8-3	Fermanagh 2-1	1920
Clare	Win	Clare 0-10	Fermanagh 0-15	2006
	Loss			
Cork	Win	Cork 0-11	Fermanagh 0-18	2004
	Loss			
Derry	Win	Fermanagh 1-11	Derry 1-9	2008
	Loss	Fermanagh 1-7	Derry 4-15	1989
Donegal	Win	Fermanagh 2-5	Donegal 1-3	1934
	Loss	Fermanagh 1-8	Donegal 4-17	1966
Down	Win	Fermanagh 0-13	Down 0-10	2009
	Loss	Fermanagh 1-8	Down 4-10	1962
Dublin	Win			
	Loss	Dublin 2-23	Fermanagh 2-15	2015
Galway	Win			
	Loss			
Kerry	Win			
	Loss	Kerry 2-15	Fermanagh 0-4	2002
Kildare	Win			
	Loss	Fermanagh 0-18	Kildare 3-20	2018
Kilkenny	Win			
	Loss			

Laois	*Win*			
	Loss	Laois 1-19	Fermanagh 2-15	2014
Leitrim	*Win*			
	Loss			
Limerick	*Win*			
	Loss			
London	*Win*			
	Loss	London 0-15	Fermanagh 0-9	2011
Longford	*Win*			
	Loss			
Louth	*Win*			
	Loss			
Mayo	*Win*	Fermanagh 0-12	Mayo 1-8	2003
	Loss	Mayo 2-14	Fermanagh 1-12	2016
Meath	*Win*	Meath 0-9	Fermanagh 1-12	2003
	Loss	Meath 0-11	Fermanagh 0-9	2007
Monaghan	*Win*	Fermanagh 4-13	Monaghan 0-5	1945
	Loss	Monaghan 5-2	Fermanagh 2-0	1915
New York	*Win*			
	Loss			
Offaly	*Win*			
	Loss			
Roscommon	*Win*	Fermanagh 1-14	Roscommon 0-16	2015
	Loss			
Sligo	*Win*			
	Loss			
Tipperary	*Win*			
	Loss			
Tyrone	*Win*	Fermanagh 2-8	Tyrone 0-8	1968
	Loss	Tyrone 5-8	Fermanagh 0-4	1948
Waterford	*Win*			
	Loss			
Westmeath	*Win*	Westmeath 0-7	Fermanagh 1-13	2015
	Loss			
Wexford	*Win*	Fermanagh 2-12	Wexford 0-11	2006
	Loss			
Wicklow	*Win*			
	Loss	Wicklow 0-17	Fermanagh 1-11	2009

GALWAY/GAILLIMH

	Played	346
Overall	Won	196 (56.7%)
Record	Drawn	26
	Lost	124

TITLES

Connacht
1889, 1890, 1901, 1902, 1911, 1913, 1917, 1919, 1922, 1925, 1926, 1933, 1934, 1938, 1940, 1941, 1942, 1945, 1954, 1956, 1957, 1958, 1959, 1960, 1963, 1964, 1965, 1966, 1968, 1970, 1971, 1973, 1974, 1976, 1982, 1983, 1984, 1986, 1987, 1995, 1998, 2000, 2002, 2003, 2005, 2008, 2016, 2019 (48)

All-Ireland 1925, 1934, 1938, 1956, 1964, 1965, 1966, 1998, 2001 (9)

HEAD TO HEAD

(biggest win/loss; blank if counties have never met in championship)

Antrim	Win			
	Loss	Antrim 0-11	Galway 0-10	2012
Armagh	Win	Galway 1-11	Armagh 0-9	2013
	Loss	Armagh 0-12	Galway 1-12	2015
Carlow	Win			
	Loss			
Cavan	Win	Galway 1-12	Cavan 1-4	1941
	Loss	Cavan 2-5	Galway 1-4	1933
Clare	Win			
	Loss	Clare 2-1	Galway 0-5	1917
Cork	Win	Galway 1-14	Cork 1-10	2001
	Loss	Cork 3-4	Galway 0-2	1911
Derry	Win	Galway 1-11	Derry 0-8	2015
	Loss	Derry 1-8	Galway 0-16	1998
Donegal	Win	Galway 4-17	Donegal 0-14	2017
	Loss	Donegal 3-12	Galway 0-11	2015
Down	Win	Galway 1-11	Down 1-4	1959
	Loss	Down 2-10	Galway 2-8	1968
Dublin	Win	Galway 3-5	Dublin 1-9	1934
	Loss	Dublin 1-24	Galway 2-12	2018
Fermanagh	Win			
	Loss			
Kerry	Win	Galway 4-2	Kerry 2-2	1919
	Loss	Kerry 2-17	Galway 0-11	1984

Kildare	*Win*	Galway 1-14	Kildare 1-10	1998
	Loss	Kildare 2-5	Galway 0-1	1919
Kilkenny	*Win*			
	Loss			
Laois	*Win*			
	Loss			
Leitrim	*Win*	Leitrim 0-8	Galway 3-21	1976
	Loss	Leitrim 2-4	Galway 0-3	1927
Limerick	*Win*			
	Loss			
London	*Win*	London 0-8	Galway 8-14	2004
	Loss			
Longford	*Win*			
	Loss			
Louth	*Win*	Galway 2-8	Louth 0-9	2004
	Loss			
Mayo	*Win*	Galway 5-13	Mayo 2-5	1956
	Loss	Mayo 2-16	Galway 0-1	1907
Meath	*Win*	Galway 0-17	Meath 0-8	2001
	Loss	Galway 0-11	Meath 0-15	1970
Monaghan	*Win*	Galway 2-10	Monaghan 2-3	1938
	Loss	Galway 0-8	Monaghan 0-16	2018
New York	*Win*	Galway 3-14	New York 0-6	2005
	Loss			
Offaly	*Win*	Galway 0-16	Offaly 2-8	1973
	Loss	Offaly 1-14	Galway 2-8	1971
Roscommon	*Win*	Galway 2-18	Roscommon 0-6	2008
	Loss	Roscommon 4-3	Galway 0-1	1914
Sligo	*Win*	Galway 6-18	Sligo 0-4	1990
	Loss	Sligo 1-13	Galway 0-6	1975
Tipperary	*Win*	Galway 4-17	Tipperary 4-12	2014
	Loss	Tipperary 2-17	Galway 0-1	1902
Tyrone	*Win*	Galway 0-8	Tyrone 0-6	1956
	Loss	Galway 0-11	Tyrone 1-16	2004
Waterford	*Win*	Galway 1-12	Waterford 0-14	2013
	Loss			
Westmeath	*Win*			
	Loss	Galway 0-10	Westmeath 1-8	2006
Wexford	*Win*	Galway 3-4	Wexford 1-1	1925
	Loss	Galway 0-13	Wexford 1-11	2010
Wicklow	*Win*	Wicklow 1-9	Galway 3-12	2001
	Loss			

KERRY/CIARRAÍ

Overall Record	Played	481
	Won	358 (74.4%)
	Drawn	37
	Lost	86

TITLES

Munster
1892, 1903, 1904, 1905, 1908, 1909, 1910, 1912, 1913, 1914, 1915, 1919, 1923, 1924, 1925, 1926, 1927, 1929, 1930, 1931, 1932, 1933, 1934, 1936, 1937, 1938, 1939, 1940, 1941, 1942, 1944, 1946, 1947, 1948, 1950, 1951, 1953, 1954, 1955, 1958, 1959, 1960, 1961, 1962, 1963, 1964, 1965, 1968, 1969, 1970, 1972, 1975, 1976, 1977, 1978, 1979, 1980, 1981, 1982, 1984, 1985, 1986, 1991, 1996, 1997, 1998, 2000, 2001, 2003, 2004, 2005, 2007, 2010, 2011, 2013, 2014, 2015, 2016, 2017, 2018, 2019 (81)

All-Ireland
1903, 1904, 1909, 1913, 1914, 1924, 1926, 1929, 1930, 1931, 1932, 1937, 1939, 1940, 1941, 1946, 1953, 1955, 1959, 1962, 1969, 1970, 1975, 1978, 1979, 1980, 1981, 1984, 1985, 1986, 1997, 2000, 2004, 2006, 2007, 2009, 2014 (37)

HEAD TO HEAD *(biggest win/loss; blank if counties have never met in championship)*

Antrim	*Win*	Antrim 1-10	Kerry 2-12	2009
	Loss	Antrim 3-5	Kerry 0-2	1912
Armagh	*Win*	Armagh 1-11	Kerry 3-15	1982
	Loss	Armagh 1-12	Kerry 0-14	2002
Carlow	*Win*	Kerry 3-3	Carlow 0-10	1944
	Loss			
Cavan	*Win*	Kerry 4-10	Cavan 0-1	1906
	Loss	Cavan 2-11	Kerry 2-7	1947
Clare	*Win*	Clare 1-9	Kerry 9-21	1979
	Loss	Clare 3-7	Kerry 1-8	1949
Cork	*Win*	Kerry 6-7	Cork 0-4	1937
	Loss	Cork 2-23	Kerry 1-11	1990
Derry	*Win*	Kerry 5-14	Derry 1-10	1976
	Loss	Derry 2-6	Kerry 2-5	1958
Donegal	*Win*	Kerry 2-9	Donegal 0-12	2014
	Loss	Donegal 1-12	Kerry 1-10	2012
Down	*Win*			
	Loss	Down 2-10	Kerry 0-8	1960
Dublin	*Win*	Kerry 5-11	Dublin 0-9	1978
	Loss	Dublin 3-8	Kerry 0-6	1934
Fermanagh	*Win*	Kerry 2-15	Fermanagh 0-4	2002
	Loss			
Galway	*Win*	Kerry 2-17	Galway 0-11	1984
	Loss	Galway 4-2	Kerry 2-2	1919

Kildare	Win	Kerry 7-16	Kildare 0-10	2015
	Loss	Kildare 1-7	Kerry 0-5	1907
Kilkenny	Win			
	Loss			
Laois	Win	Kerry 2-6	Laois 2-4	1938
	Loss			
Leitrim	Win	Kerry 0-4	Leitrim 0-2	1927
	Loss			
Limerick	Win	Kerry 7-7	Limerick 1-4	1936
	Loss	Limerick 5-6	Kerry 1-1	1895
London	Win	Kerry 0-11	London 0-3	1905
	Loss			
Longford	Win	Kerry 4-11	Longford 1-11	2006
	Loss			
Louth	Win	Kerry 1-9	Louth 0-6	1909
	Loss	Louth 1-7	Kerry 0-8	1950
Mayo	Win	Mayo 1-6	Kerry 2-19	1981
	Loss	Mayo 0-13	Kerry 0-3	1948
Meath	Win	Kerry 1-11	Meath 0-5	1947
	Loss	Meath 2-14	Kerry 0-5	2001
Monaghan	Win	Kerry 5-14	Monaghan 0-7	1979
	Loss			
New York	Win			
	Loss			
Offaly	Win	Kerry 1-12	Offaly 0-8	1981
	Loss	Offaly 1-19	Kerry 0-13	1972
Roscommon	Win	Kerry 3-11	Roscommon 0-8	1978
	Loss	Roscommon 1-9	Kerry 2-4	1944
Sligo	Win	Kerry 3-13	Sligo 0-5	1975
	Loss			
Tipperary	Win	Kerry 4-21	Tipperary 0-8	2013
	Loss	Tipperary 1-13	Kerry 1-2	1902
Tyrone	Win	Kerry 1-16	Tyrone 1-6	2012
	Loss	Kerry 0-6	Tyrone 0-13	2003
Waterford	Win	Kerry 7-16	Waterford 0-8	1974
	Loss	Waterford 1-2	Kerry 0-1	1911
Westmeath	Win	Kerry 2-10	Westmeath 1-12	2012
	Loss			
Wexford	Win	Kerry 2-2	Wexford 0-3	1913
	Loss	Kerry 2-1	Wexford 2-4	1915
Wicklow	Win	Kerry 5-14	Wicklow 0-7	2002
	Loss			

KILDARE/CILL DARA

Overall Record		
Played	366	
Won	194 (53%)	
Drawn	32	
Lost	140	

TITLES

Leinster 1903, 1905, 1919, 1926, 1927, 1928, 1929, 1930, 1931, 1935, 1956, 1998, 2000 (13)

All-Ireland 1905, 1919, 1927, 1928 (4)

HEAD TO HEAD

(biggest win/loss; blank if counties have never met in championship)

Antrim	Win	Antrim 0-14	Kildare 1-25	2019
	Loss			
Armagh	Win			
	Loss	Kildare 0-17	Armagh 1-17	2017
Carlow	Win	Kildare 9-8	Carlow 1-1	1921
	Loss	Carlow 3-11	Kildare 2-5	1944
Cavan	Win	Kildare 4-15	Cavan 1-6	1906
	Loss	Cavan 3-6	Kildare 2-5	1935
Clare	Win	Clare 0-12	Kildare 0-13	2014
	Loss			
Cork	Win	Kildare 3-7	Cork 0-2	1928
	Loss	Cork 2-19	Kildare 0-12	2012
Derry	Win	Derry 1-9	Kildare 2-17	2010
	Loss	Derry 1-17	Kildare 0-11	2006
Donegal	Win	Kildare 1-17	Donegal 1-16	2001
	Loss	Donegal 1-12	Kildare 0-14	2011
Down	Win	Down 0-11	Kildare 1-18	2014
	Loss	Kildare 1-14	Down 1-16	2010
Dublin	Win	Dublin 1-3	Kildare 3-11	1904
	Loss	Dublin 2-15	Kildare 0-2	1898
Fermanagh	Win	Fermanagh 0-18	Kildare 3-20	2018
	Loss			
Galway	Win	Kildare 2-5	Galway 0-1	1919
	Loss	Galway 1-14	Kildare 1-10	1998
Kerry	Win	Kildare 1-7	Kerry 0-5	1907
	Loss	Kerry 7-16	Kildare 0-10	2015

Kilkenny	*Win*	Kildare 4-10	Kilkenny 1-2	1982
	Loss	Kildare 0-3	Kilkenny 0-7	1903
Laois	*Win*	Kildare 5-15	Laois 1-1	1902
	Loss	Laois 0-21	Kildare 0-9	2005
Leitrim	*Win*	Leitrim 0-6	Kildare 1-12	2010
	Loss			
Limerick	*Win*	Kildare 0-19	Limerick 0-12	2012
	Loss			
London	*Win*			
	Loss			
Longford	*Win*	Longford 0-11	Kildare 2-24	2015
	Loss	Longford 3-8	Kildare 0-5	1952
Louth	*Win*	Kildare 6-7	Louth 1-5	1926
	Loss	Louth 3-12	Kildare 0-10	1910
Mayo	*Win*	Kildare 2-6	Mayo 0-7	1935
	Loss	Mayo 2-17	Kildare 0-14	2016
Meath	*Win*	Meath 0-13	Kildare 2-16	2017
	Loss	Meath 2-12	Kildare 0-8	1964
Monaghan	*Win*	Kildare 2-10	Monaghan 1 3	1907
	Loss	Monaghan 1-6	Kildare 1-4	1930
New York	*Win*			
	Loss			
Offaly	*Win*	Offaly 0-1	Kildare 2-13	1908
	Loss	Offaly 2-15	Kildare 0-6	1983
Roscommon	*Win*	Roscommon 1-13	Kildare 2-13	2007
	Loss	Kildare 0-19	Roscommon 1-18	2003
Sligo	*Win*	Kildare 0-13	Sligo 0-4	2012
	Loss	Sligo 0-16	Kildare 0-15	2001
Tipperary	*Win*			
	Loss			
Tyrone	*Win*			
	Loss	Kildare 1-15	Tyrone 2-22	2019
Waterford	*Win*			
	Loss			
Westmeath	*Win*	Kildare 4-11	Westmeath 2-5	1992
	Loss	Kildare 2-8	Westmeath 2-9	1960
Wexford	*Win*	Kildare 5-12	Wexford 1-6	1962
	Loss	Wexford 5-5	Kildare 0-6	1945
Wicklow	*Win*	Kildare 5-11	Wicklow 1-7	1937
	Loss	Wicklow 1-7	Kildare 0-6	1990

KILKENNY/CILL CHAINNIGH

Overall Record		
Played	87	
Won	30 (34.5%)	
Drawn	6	
Lost	51	

TITLES

Leinster ▌ 1888, 1900, 1911 (3)

All-Ireland ▌ none

HEAD TO HEAD
(biggest win/loss; blank if counties have never met in championship)

Antrim	*Win*	Antrim 3-1	Kilkenny 1-1	1911
	Loss			
Armagh	*Win*			
	Loss			
Carlow	*Win*	Carlow 0-0	Kilkenny 2-11	1901
	Loss	Carlow 4-10	Kilkenny 1-4	1963
Cavan	*Win*			
	Loss			
Clare	*Win*			
	Loss			
Cork	*Win*			
	Loss			
Derry	*Win*			
	Loss			
Donegal	*Win*			
	Loss			
Down	*Win*			
	Loss			
Dublin	*Win*			
	Loss	Dublin 3-13	Kilkenny 1-2	1902
Fermanagh	*Win*			
	Loss			
Galway	*Win*			
	Loss			
Kerry	*Win*			
	Loss			

Kildare	*Win*	Kildare 0-3	Kilkenny 0-7	1903
	Loss	Kildare 4-10	Kilkenny 1-2	1982
Laois	*Win*	Laois 0-5	Kilkenny 3-17	1909
	Loss	Kilkenny 0-3	Laois 2-1	1920
Leitrim	*Win*			
	Loss			
Limerick	*Win*			
	Loss			
London	*Win*			
	Loss			
Longford	*Win*	Longford 0-3	Kilkenny 2-4	1925
	Loss			
Louth	*Win*	Kilkenny 0-12	Louth 0-0	1901
	Loss	Louth 2-9	Kilkenny 0-4	1909
Mayo	*Win*	Meath 1-2	Kilkenny 4-4	1922
	Loss	Meath 6-19	Kilkenny 0-3	1979
Meath	*Win*			
	Loss			
Monaghan	*Win*			
	Loss			
New York	*Win*			
	Loss			
Offaly	*Win*			
	Loss	Offaly 1-9	Kilkenny 0-5	1910
Roscommon	*Win*			
	Loss			
Sligo	*Win*			
	Loss			
Tipperary	*Win*	Tipperary 0-7	Kilkenny 1-6	1902
	Loss			
Tyrone	*Win*			
	Loss			
Waterford	*Win*			
	Loss			
Westmeath	*Win*	Kilkenny 1-13	Westmeath 0-0	1904
	Loss	Westmeath 8-5	Kilkenny 1-5	1931
Wexford	*Win*	Kilkenny 3-0	Wexford 0-1	1911
	Loss	Wexford 4-12	Kilkenny 0-2	1944
Wicklow	*Win*	Wicklow 0-2	Kilkenny 1-2	1914
	Loss	Wicklow 2-16	Kilkenny 0-3	1978

LAOIS

	Overall Record	
Played	287	
Won	131 (45.6%)	
Drawn	14	
Lost	141	

TITLES

Leinster 1889, 1936, 1937, 1938, 1946, 2003 (6)

All-Ireland none

HEAD TO HEAD
(biggest win/loss; blank if counties have never met in championship)

Antrim	Win			
	Loss	Laois 1-16	Antrim 2-15	2015
Armagh	Win	Laois 1-10	Armagh 0-10	2016
	Loss	Armagh 2-17	Laois 1-11	2005
Carlow	Win	Carlow 0-8	Laois 3-16	2015
	Loss	Carlow 4-4	Laois 1-7	1948
Cavan	Win	Laois 2-6	Cavan 1-5	1936
	Loss			
Clare	Win	Clare 0-10	Laois 3-17	2013
	Loss	Laois 0-14	Clare 2-18	2017
Cork	Win			
	Loss	Laois 1-15	Cork 4-20	2019
Derry	Win	Derry 0-12	Laois 1-13	2019
	Loss	Laois 2-11	Derry 1-18	2007
Donegal	Win			
	Loss	Laois 0-8	Donegal 0-14	2013
Down	Win			
	Loss	Laois 0-7	Down 2-9	2009
Dublin	Win	Laois 3-8	Dublin 0-13	1971
	Loss	Dublin 7-17	Laois 0-3	1900
Fermanagh	Win	Laois 1-19	Fermanagh 2-15	2014
	Loss			
Galway	Win			
	Loss			

60

Kerry	*Win*			
	Loss	Kerry 2-6	Laois 2-4	1938
Kildare	*Win*	Laois 0-21	Kildare 0-9	2005
	Loss	Kildare 5-15	Laois 1-1	1902
Kilkenny	*Win*	Kilkenny 0-3	Laois 2-1	1920
	Loss	Laois 0-5	Kilkenny 3-17	1909
Leitrim	*Win*	Laois 1-13	Leitrim 1-11	2012
	Loss			
Limerick	*Win*			
	Loss			
London	*Win*			
	Loss			
Longford	*Win*	Laois 4-15	Longford 2-4	1994
	Loss	Longford 3-9	Laois 1-4	1968
Louth	*Win*	Laois 2-7	Louth 0-3	1930
	Loss	Louth 2-18	Laois 0-4	1907
Mayo	*Win*			
	Loss	Mayo 4-11	Laois 0-5	1936
Meath	*Win*	Laois 2-11	Meath 0-7	1985
	Loss	Meath 4-14	Laois 0-6	1990
Monaghan	*Win*	Laois 2-12	Monaghan 0 12	2012
	Loss	Laois 1-11	Monaghan 0-19	2018
New York	*Win*			
	Loss			
Offaly	*Win*	Offaly 0-4	Laois 5-11	1947
	Loss	Offaly 6-5	Laois 2-7	1942
Roscommon	*Win*			
	Loss	Roscommon 3-5	Laois 2-6	1946
Sligo	*Win*			
	Loss			
Tipperary	*Win*	Laois 2-16	Tipperary 0-11	2011
	Loss	Tipperary 3-6	Laois 0-0	1889
Tyrone	*Win*	Laois 0-9	Tyrone 0-6	2006
	Loss	Tyrone 3-15	Laois 2-4	2004
Waterford	*Win*			
	Loss			
Westmeath	*Win*	Laois 1-17	Westmeath 0-6	1991
	Loss	Westmeath 2-12	Laois 1-5	1966
Wexford	*Win*	Laois 1-19	Wexford 0-10	2003
	Loss	Wexford 2-11	Laois 0-2	1910
Wicklow	*Win*	Laois 3-6	Wicklow 0-2	1974
	Loss	Wicklow 3-6	Laois 1-6	1957

LEITRIM/LIATROIM

Overall Record		
Played	180	
Won	48 (26.7%)	
Drawn	12	
Lost	120	

TITLES

Connacht | 1927, 1994 (2)

All-Ireland | none

HEAD TO HEAD

(biggest win/loss; blank if counties have never met in championship)

Antrim	Win			
	Loss	Antrim 0-13	Leitrim 1-8	2001
Armagh	Win			
	Loss	Leitrim 0-10	Armagh 8-13	2013
Carlow	Win			
	Loss	Carlow 2-14	Leitrim 0-13	2017
Cavan	Win			
	Loss			
Clare	Win			
	Loss	Leitrim 0-17	Clare 3-17	2019
Cork	Win			
	Loss			
Derry	Win			
	Loss			
Donegal	Win			
	Loss	Leitrim 1-14	Donegal 1-16	2007
Down	Win			
	Loss	Down 4-18	Leitrim 0-9	2014
Dublin	Win			
	Loss	Dublin 3-15	Leitrim 1-9	1994
Fermanagh	Win			
	Loss			
Galway	Win	Leitrim 2-4	Galway 0-3	1927
	Loss	Leitrim 0-8	Galway 3-21	1976

Kerry	*Win*			
	Loss	Kerry 0-4	Leitrim 0-2	1927
Kildare	*Win*			
	Loss	Leitrim 0-6	Kildare 1-12	2010
Kilkenny	*Win*			
	Loss			
Laois	*Win*			
	Loss	Laois 1-13	Leitrim 1-11	2012
Limerick	*Win*			
	Loss			
London	*Win*	London 0-5	Leitrim 1-13	1982
	Loss	Leitrim 0-6	London 0-9	1977
Longford	*Win*			
	Loss	Leitrim 0-10	Longford 0-13	2009
Louth	*Win*	Leitrim 0-25	Louth 1-12	2018
	Loss	Louth 1-16	Leitrim 0-11	2015
Mayo	*Win*	Leitrim 2-8	Mayo 0-10	1976
	Loss	Leitrim 0-3	Mayo 7-6	1973
Meath	*Win*			
	Loss	Meath 1-12	Leitrim 1-8	2005
Monaghan	*Win*			
	Loss	Leitrim 0-9	Monaghan 1-19	2018
New York	*Win*	New York 0-7	Leitrim 4-19	2013
	Loss			
Offaly	*Win*			
	Loss			
Roscommon	*Win*	Leitrim 3-3	Roscommon 0-2	1920
	Loss	Roscommon 5-6	Leitrim 0-1	1931
Sligo	*Win*	Leitrim 5-7	Sligo 0-2	1914
	Loss	Sligo 6-10	Leitrim 0-6	1946
Tipperary	*Win*			
	Loss			
Tyrone	*Win*			
	Loss	Tyrone 1-22	Leitrim 0-7	2002
Waterford	*Win*	Leitrim 0-12	Waterford 0-8	2016
	Loss			
Westmeath	*Win*			
	Loss			
Wexford	*Win*			
	Loss			
Wicklow	*Win*	Leitrim 0-13	Wicklow 0-10	2012
	Loss			

LIMERICK/LUIMNEACH

	Played	181
Overall	Won	48 (26.5%)
Record	Drawn	12
	Lost	121

TITLES

Munster 1896 (1)

All-Ireland 1887, 1896 (2)

HEAD TO HEAD
(biggest win/loss; blank if counties have never met in championship)

Antrim	*Win*	Limerick 3-11	Antrim 0-15	2014
	Loss			
Armagh	*Win*			
	Loss	Armagh 4-10	Limerick 0-11	2003
Carlow	*Win*	Limerick 2-15	Carlow 0-7	2005
	Loss			
Cavan	*Win*	Cavan 0-11	Limerick 2-8	2002
	Loss			
Clare	*Win*	Limerick 6-2	Clare 3-3	1945
	Loss	Clare 4-10	Limerick 0-2	1948
Cork	*Win*	Limerick 0-16	Cork 0-6	2003
	Loss	Cork 5-19	Limerick 1-6	1980
Derry	*Win*			
	Loss	Derry 0-13	Limerick 0-9	2005
Donegal	*Win*			
	Loss			
Down	*Win*			
	Loss			
Dublin	*Win*	Limerick 1-5	Dublin 0-7	1898
	Loss			
Fermanagh	*Win*			
	Loss			
Galway	*Win*			
	Loss			
Kerry	*Win*	Limerick 5-6	Kerry 1-1	1895
	Loss	Kerry 7-7	Limerick 1-4	1936

Kildare	Win			
	Loss	Kildare 0-19	Limerick 0-12	2012
Kilkenny	Win			
	Loss			
Laois	Win			
	Loss			
Leitrim	Win			
	Loss			
London	Win	Limerick 1-16	London 1-13	2014
	Loss			
Longford	Win	Limerick 1-21	Longford 1-15	2012
	Loss	Longford 2-14	Limerick 0-8	2013
Louth	Win			
	Loss	Limerick 0-13	Louth 0-14	2007
Mayo	Win			
	Loss	Limerick 3-7	Mayo 5-19	2018
Meath	Win	Limerick 4-12	Meath 4-3	2008
	Loss	Limerick 2-9	Meath 1-13	2009
Monaghan	Win			
	Loss			
New York	Win			
	Loss			
Offaly	Win	Limerick 3-13	Offaly 0-15	2011
	Loss			
Roscommon	Win			
	Loss			
Sligo	Win			
	Loss	Sligo 0-12	Limerick 0-10	2014
Tipperary	Win	Limerick 4-10	Tipperary 2-5	1967
	Loss	Tipperary 7-18	Limerick 1-5	1975
Tyrone	Win			
	Loss	Tyrone 1-14	Limerick 0-8	2015
Waterford	Win	Limerick 4-10	Waterford 0-6	1965
	Loss	Waterford 1-11	Limerick 0-5	1974
Westmeath	Win			
	Loss	Limerick 0-7	Westmeath 0-17	2001
Wexford	Win	Limerick 1-18	Wexford 1-17	2011
	Loss	Limerick 0-11	Wexford 0-12	2017
Wicklow	Win			
	Loss			

LONDON/LONDAIN

	Played	75
Overall	Won	4 (5.3%)
Record	Drawn	1
	Lost	70

TITLES

Connacht | none

All-Ireland | none

HEAD TO HEAD
(biggest win/loss; blank if counties have never met in championship)

Antrim	*Win*			
	Loss	Antrim 2-11	London 2-9	2012
Armagh	*Win*			
	Loss			
Carlow	*Win*			
	Loss	London 0-12	Carlow 0-13	2017
Cavan	*Win*			
	Loss	London 0-11	Cavan 2-22	2015
Clare	*Win*			
	Loss			
Cork	*Win*			
	Loss	Cork 1-14	London 1-5	1908
Derry	*Win*			
	Loss			
Donegal	*Win*			
	Loss			
Down	*Win*			
	Loss	London 1-7	Down 1-16	2009
Dublin	*Win*			
	Loss	Dublin 3-24	London 0-6	2004
Fermanagh	*Win*	London 0-15	Fermanagh 0-9	2011
	Loss			
Galway	*Win*			
	Loss	London 0-8	Galway 8-14	2004
Kerry	*Win*			
	Loss	Kerry 0-11	London 0-3	1905

County	W/L			
Kildare	*Win*			
	Loss			
Kilkenny	*Win*			
	Loss			
Laois	*Win*			
	Loss			
Leitrim	*Win*	Leitrim 0-6	London 0-9	1977
	Loss	London 0-5	Leitrim 1-13	1982
Limerick	*Win*			
	Loss	Limerick 1-16	London 1-13	2014
Longford	*Win*			
	Loss			
Louth	*Win*			
	Loss	Louth 3-6	London 1-2	1913
Mayo	*Win*			
	Loss	London 0-4	Mayo 3-14	1986
Meath	*Win*			
	Loss			
Monaghan	*Win*			
	Loss	Monaghan 2-18	London 1-9	2005
New York	*Win*			
	Loss			
Offaly	*Win*			
	Loss	Offaly 4-15	London 0-10	2003
Roscommon	*Win*			
	Loss	Roscommon 9-19	London 1-10	1980
Sligo	*Win*	London 1-12	Sligo 0-14	2013
	Loss	London 0-7	Sligo 2-17	2008
Tipperary	*Win*			
	Loss	Tipperary 3-7	London 0-2	1902
Tyrone	*Win*			
	Loss			
Waterford	*Win*			
	Loss	London 0-13	Waterford 1-17	2011
Westmeath	*Win*			
	Loss	Westmeath 0-20	London 0-8	2006
Wexford	*Win*			
	Loss	London 0-9	Wexford 4-22	2010
Wicklow	*Win*			
	Loss	Wicklow 2-22	London 2-6	2002

LONGFORD/LONGFORT

Overall Record		
	Played	190
	Won	65 (34.2%)
	Drawn	13
	Lost	112

TITLES

Leinster 1968 (1)

All-Ireland none

HEAD TO HEAD
(biggest win/loss; blank if counties have never met in championship)

Antrim	Win			
	Loss			
Armagh	Win			
	Loss			
Carlow	Win	Longford 3-15	Carlow 0-13	1983
	Loss	Carlow 4-15	Longford 1-16	2004
Cavan	Win	Cavan 0-11	Longford 2-16	2011
	Loss			
Clare	Win	Clare 1-12	Longford 2-12	2015
	Loss			
Cork	Win			
	Loss	Longford 1-6	Cork 2-9	2016
Derry	Win	Longford 0-17	Derry 2-8	2012
	Loss	Longford 0-9	Derry 2-13	2002
Donegal	Win			
	Loss	Donegal 1-17	Longford 1-11	2003
Down	Win	Longford 1-16	Down 0-14	2002
	Loss	Down 1-14	Longford 1-10	2010
Dublin	Win	Longford 1-12	Dublin 0-12	1968
	Loss	Dublin 4-25	Longford 0-10	2015
Fermanagh	Win			
	Loss			
Galway	Win			
	Loss			
Kerry	Win			
	Loss	Kerry 4-11	Longford 1-11	2006

Kildare	*Win*	Longford 3-8	Kildare 0-5	1952
	Loss	Longford 0-11	Kildare 2-24	2015
Kilkenny	*Win*			
	Loss	Longford 0-3	Kilkenny 2-4	1925
Laois	*Win*	Longford 3-9	Laois 1-4	1968
	Loss	Laois 4-15	Longford 2-4	1994
Leitrim	*Win*	Leitrim 0-10	Longford 0-13	2009
	Loss			
Limerick	*Win*	Longford 2-14	Limerick 0-8	2013
	Loss	Limerick 1-21	Longford 1-15	2012
London	*Win*			
	Loss			
Louth	*Win*	Louth 1-10	Longford 2-15	2017
	Loss	Louth 2-14	Longford 1-2	1948
Mayo	*Win*	Longford 1-12	Mayo 0-14	2010
	Loss			
Meath	*Win*	Longford 2-7	Meath 1-5	1959
	Loss	Longford 0-10	Meath 4-15	1995
Monaghan	*Win*	Monaghan 1-16	Longford 4-15	2004
	Loss			
New York	*Win*			
	Loss			
Offaly	*Win*	Longford 4-3	Offaly 1-4	1944
	Loss	Offaly 5-17	Longford 0-13	1997
Roscommon	*Win*			
	Loss			
Sligo	*Win*			
	Loss	Sligo 0-18	Longford 0-16	2005
Tipperary	*Win*	Longford 1-23	Tipperary 1-10	2006
	Loss	Tipperary 2-17	Longford 0-6	2014
Tyrone	*Win*			
	Loss	Longford 0-15	Tyrone 1-17	2011
Waterford	*Win*	Waterford 1-5	Longford 1-14	2004
	Loss			
Westmeath	*Win*	Longford 3-10	Westmeath 0-8	1961
	Loss	Westmeath 3-17	Longford 2-9	1999
Wexford	*Win*	Longford 2-15	Wexford 0-11	1999
	Loss	Wexford 7-10	Longford 6-2	1927
Wicklow	*Win*	Longford 4-9	Wicklow 0-5	1972
	Loss	Longford 2-8	Wicklow 2-18	1992

LOUTH/AN LÚ

Overall Record	Played	313
	Won	147 (47%)
	Drawn	21
	Lost	145

TITLES

Leinster ▌1909, 1910, 1912, 1943, 1948, 1950, 1953, 1957 (8)

All-Ireland ▌1910, 1912, 1957 (3)

HEAD TO HEAD
(biggest win/loss; blank if counties have never met in championship)

Antrim	Win	Louth 1-17	Antrim 1-11	2013
	Loss	Louth 1-11	Antrim 2-16	2019
Armagh	Win			
	Loss			
Carlow	Win	Louth 3-19	Carlow 0-11	1994
	Loss	Louth 0-12	Carlow 2-17	2018
Cavan	Win	Louth 2-4	Cavan 0-4	1918
	Loss	Cavan 1-14	Louth 4-2	1948
Clare	Win			
	Loss			
Cork	Win	Louth 1-9	Cork 1-7	1957
	Loss	Louth 0-14	Cork 0-16	2007
Derry	Win			
	Loss	Derry 1-18	Louth 2-10	2016
Donegal	Win			
	Loss			
Down	Win			
	Loss			
Dublin	Win	Louth 4-5	Dublin 1-6	1943
	Loss	Dublin 5-21	Louth 0-10	2019
Fermanagh	Win			
	Loss			
Galway	Win			
	Loss	Galway 2-8	Louth 0-9	2004
Kerry	Win	Louth 1-7	Kerry 0-8	1950
	Loss	Kerry 1-9	Louth 0-6	1909

Kildare	*Win*	Louth 3-12	Kildare 0-10	1910
	Loss	Kildare 6-7	Louth 1-5	1926
Kilkenny	*Win*	Louth 2-9	Kilkenny 0-4	1909
	Loss	Kilkenny 0-12	Louth 0-0	1901
Laois	*Win*	Louth 2-18	Laois 0-4	1907
	Loss	Laois 2-7	Louth 0-3	1930
Leitrim	*Win*	Louth 1-16	Leitrim 0-11	2015
	Loss	Leitrim 0-25	Louth 1-12	2018
Limerick	*Win*	Limerick 0-13	Louth 0-14	2007
	Loss			
London	*Win*	Louth 3-6	London 1-2	1913
	Loss			
Longford	*Win*	Louth 2-14	Longford 1-2	1948
	Loss	Louth 1-10	Longford 2-15	2017
Mayo	*Win*			
	Loss	Mayo 2-5	Louth 1-6	1950
Meath	*Win*	Meath 0-5	Louth 6-19	1901
	Loss	Meath 2-7	Louth 0-0	1927
Monaghan	*Win*	Monaghan 1-8	Louth 2-11	2002
	Loss	Monaghan 1-12	Louth 0-14	2005
New York	*Win*			
	Loss			
Offaly	*Win*	Louth 6-14	Offaly 0-1	1901
	Loss	Offaly 5-12	Louth 0-7	1955
Roscommon	*Win*	Louth 0-11	Roscommon 0-10	2005
	Loss	Roscommon 3-10	Louth 3-6	1943
Sligo	*Win*			
	Loss			
Tipperary	*Win*	Tipperary 1-8	Louth 0-13	2001
	Loss	Tipperary 3-21	Louth 0-7	2015
Tyrone	*Win*	Louth 0-13	Tyrone 0-7	1957
	Loss	Louth 0-10	Tyrone 2-21	2014
Waterford	*Win*	Louth 1-12	Waterford 1-8	2005
	Loss			
Westmeath	*Win*	Louth 4-4	Westmeath 0-1	1921
	Loss	Westmeath 2-11	Louth 0-9	1965
Wexford	*Win*	Louth 3-5	Wexford 1-1	1934
	Loss	Wexford 3-6	Louth 0-1	1914
Wicklow	*Win*	Louth 2-22	Wicklow 2-6	1975
	Loss	Louth 1-4	Wicklow 1-7	1889

MAYO/MAIGH EO

Overall Record	Played	359
	Won	203 (56.6%)
	Drawn	28
	Lost	128

TITLES

Connacht	1901, 1904, 1906, 1907, 1908, 1909, 1910, 1915, 1916, 1918, 1920, 1921, 1923, 1924, 1929, 1930, 1931, 1932, 1935, 1936, 1937, 1939, 1948, 1949, 1950, 1951, 1955, 1967, 1969, 1981, 1985, 1988, 1989, 1992, 1993, 1996, 1997, 1999, 2004, 2006, 2009, 2011, 2012, 2013, 2014, 2015 (46)
All-Ireland	1936, 1950, 1951 (3)

HEAD TO HEAD

(biggest win/loss; blank if counties have never met in championship)

Antrim	Win			
	Loss			
Armagh	Win	Mayo 3-9	Armagh 0-6	1950
	Loss			
Carlow	Win			
	Loss			
Cavan	Win	Mayo 1-19	Cavan 3-7	2007
	Loss	Cavan 2-5	Mayo 1-7	1937
Clare	Win	Clare 0-13	Mayo 2-14	2017
	Loss			
Cork	Win	Mayo 1-13	Cork 2-6	2011
	Loss	Cork 4-16	Mayo 0-1	1903
Derry	Win	Mayo 2-21	Derry 1-13	2017
	Loss	Derry 2-13	Mayo 1-6	2007
Donegal	Win	Mayo 4-17	Donegal 1-10	2013
	Loss	Donegal 0-13	Mayo 0-9	1992
Down	Win	Mayo 3-18	Down 2-9	2012
	Loss			
Dublin	Win	Dublin 0-16	Mayo 0-19	2012
	Loss	Dublin 1-9	Mayo 0-2	1923
Fermanagh	Win	Mayo 2-14	Fermanagh 1-12	2016
	Loss	Fermanagh 0-12	Mayo 1-8	2003
Galway	Win	Mayo 2-16	Galway 0-1	1907
	Loss	Galway 5-13	Mayo 2-5	1956

Kerry	*Win*	Mayo 0-13	Kerry 0-3	1948
	Loss	Mayo 1-6	Kerry 2-19	1981
Kildare	*Win*	Mayo 2-17	Kildare 0-14	2016
	Loss	Kildare 2-6	Mayo 0-7	1935
Kilkenny	*Win*			
	Loss			
Laois	*Win*	Mayo 4-11	Laois 0-5	1936
	Loss			
Leitrim	*Win*	Leitrim 0-3	Mayo 7-6	1973
	Loss	Leitrim 2-8	Mayo 0-10	1976
Limerick	*Win*	Limerick 3-7	Mayo 5-19	2018
	Loss			
London	*Win*	London 0-4	Mayo 3-14	1986
	Loss			
Longford	*Win*			
	Loss	Longford 1-12	Mayo 0-14	2010
Louth	*Win*	Mayo 2-5	Louth 1-6	1950
	Loss			
Meath	*Win*	Mayo 2-17	Meath 0-14	2019
	Loss	Meath 3-14	Mayo 1-14	1967
Monaghan	*Win*			
	Loss			
New York	*Win*	New York 1-8	Mayo 3-28	2004
	Loss			
Offaly	*Win*	Mayo 0-13	Offaly 0-7	1997
	Loss			
Roscommon	*Win*	Mayo 6-6	Roscommon 0-0	1921
	Loss	Roscommon 3-13	Mayo 0-8	1980
Sligo	*Win*	Mayo 7-10	Sligo 0-2	1949
	Loss	Sligo 3-8	Mayo 2-5	1923
Tipperary	*Win*	Tipperary 1-11	Mayo 1-19	2018
	Loss	Tipperary 1-5	Mayo 1-0	1922
Tyrone	*Win*	Mayo 1-16	Tyrone 0-13	2013
	Loss	Mayo 1-9	Tyrone 0-13	2008
Waterford	*Win*			
	Loss			
Westmeath	*Win*	Westmeath 1-14	Mayo 3-15	2016
	Loss	Mayo 0-16	Westmeath 1-14	2001
Wexford	*Win*	Mayo 2-4	Wexford 1-4	1925
	Loss	Wexford 3-4	Mayo 1-2	1916
Wicklow	*Win*			
	Loss			

MEATH/AN MHÍ

Overall Record	Played	363
	Won	198 (54.6%)
	Drawn	30
	Lost	135

TITLES

Leinster 1939, 1940, 1947, 1949, 1951, 1952, 1954, 1964, 1966, 1967, 1970, 1986, 1987, 1988, 1990, 1991, 1996, 1999, 2001, 2010 (20)

All-Ireland 1949, 1954, 1967, 1987, 1988, 1996, 1999 (7)

HEAD TO HEAD

(biggest win/loss; blank if counties have never met in championship)

Antrim	*Win*	Antrim 0-13	Meath 5-12	2005
	Loss			
Armagh	*Win*	Meath 0-15	Armagh 2-5	1999
	Loss	Meath 0-13	Armagh 0-18	2014
Carlow	*Win*	Carlow 0-6	Meath 7-13	2014
	Loss			
Cavan	*Win*	Meath 1-9	Cavan 1-1	1939
	Loss	Cavan 0-9	Meath 0-5	1952
Clare	*Win*	Meath 2-16	Clare 1-18	2019
	Loss			
Cork	*Win*	Meath 1-14	Cork 0-11	1987
	Loss	Cork 1-16	Meath 0-9	2007
Derry	*Win*	Meath 0-15	Derry 0-8	1987
	Loss	Derry 1-14	Meath 1-11	2016
Donegal	*Win*	Meath 3-9	Donegal 1-7	1990
	Loss	Meath 1-13	Donegal 2-19	2019
Down	*Win*	Meath 2-16	Down 1-9	1966
	Loss	Down 1-16	Meath 1-14	1991
Dublin	*Win*	Meath 3-8	Dublin 0-4	1930
	Loss	Dublin 5-12	Meath 0-7	1955
Fermanagh	*Win*	Meath 0-11	Fermanagh 0-9	2007
	Loss	Meath 0-9	Fermanagh 1-12	2003
Galway	*Win*	Galway 0-11	Meath 0-15	1970
	Loss	Galway 0-17	Meath 0-8	2001

Kerry	*Win*	Meath 2-14	Kerry 0-5	2001
	Loss	Meath 0-12	Kerry 2-13	1986
Kildare	*Win*	Meath 2-12	Kildare 0-8	1964
	Loss	Meath 0-13	Kildare 2-16	2017
Kilkenny	*Win*	Meath 6-19	Kilkenny 0-3	1979
	Loss	Meath 1-2	Kilkenny 4-4	1922
Laois	*Win*	Meath 4-14	Laois 0-6	1990
	Loss	Laois 2-11	Meath 0-7	1985
Leitrim	*Win*	Meath 1-12	Leitrim 1-8	2005
	Loss			
Limerick	*Win*	Limerick 2-9	Meath 1-13	2009
	Loss	Limerick 4-12	Meath 4-3	2008
London	*Win*			
	Loss			
Longford	*Win*	Longford 0-10	Meath 4-15	1995
	Loss	Longford 2-7	Meath 1-5	1959
Louth	*Win*	Meath 2-7	Louth 0 0	1927
	Loss	Meath 0-5	Louth 6-19	1901
Mayo	*Win*	Meath 3-10	Mayo 1-10	1949
	Loss	Meath 0-14	Mayo 2-17	2019
Monaghan	*Win*	Meath 2-10	Monaghan 0 12	2003
	Loss			
New York	*Win*			
	Loss			
Offaly	*Win*	Meath 2-13	Offaly 0-7	1991
	Loss	Offaly 3-21	Meath 2-12	1973
Roscommon	*Win*	Meath 1-19	Roscommon 0-9	2006
	Loss			
Sligo	*Win*	Meath 0-14	Sligo 1-9	2017
	Loss			
Tipperary	*Win*	Tipperary 0-4	Meath 0-3	1896
	Loss			
Tyrone	*Win*	Meath 2-15	Tyrone 0-12	1996
	Loss	Meath 2-9	Tyrone 0-17	2013
Waterford	*Win*	Meath 1-20	Waterford 0-8	2009
	Loss			
Westmeath	*Win*	Meath 4-12	Westmeath 1-5	1980
	Loss	Westmeath 3-19	Meath 2-18	2015
Wexford	*Win*	Meath 4-15	Wexford 0-3	1966
	Loss	Wexford 4-9	Meath 0-2	1925
Wicklow	*Win*	Meath 6-8	Wicklow 0-4	1950
	Loss	Wicklow 3-7	Meath 1-11	1957

MONAGHAN/MUINEACHÁN

Overall Record	Played	290
	Won	129 (44.5%)
	Drawn	28
	Lost	133

TITLES

Ulster 1888, 1906, 1914, 1916, 1917, 1921, 1922, 1927, 1929, 1930, 1938, 1979, 1985, 1988, 2013, 2015 (16)

All-Ireland none

HEAD TO HEAD

(biggest win/loss; blank if counties have never met in championship)

Antrim	Win	Monaghan 2-18	Antrim 0-4	1983
	Loss	Antrim 2-7	Monaghan 0-2	1962
Armagh	Win	Monaghan 2-9	Armagh 0-2	1922
	Loss	Armagh 5-9	Monaghan 0-5	1961
Carlow	Win	Carlow 1-7	Monaghan 1-12	2017
	Loss			
Cavan	Win	Monaghan 3-1	Cavan 0-2	1917
	Loss	Cavan 5-10	Monaghan 1-1	1923
Clare	Win			
	Loss			
Cork	Win			
	Loss	Cork 1-14	Monaghan 0-6	1988
Derry	Win	Monaghan 2-5	Derry 0-1	1916
	Loss	Derry 2-15	Monaghan 0-10	1997
Donegal	Win	Monaghan 2-8	Donegal 0-1	1929
	Loss	Donegal 1-14	Monaghan 1-9	1983
Down	Win	Monaghan 7-8	Down 1-3	1930
	Loss	Down 6-11	Monaghan 1-3	1963
Dublin	Win			
	Loss	Dublin 2-22	Monaghan 0-11	2014
Fermanagh	Win	Monaghan 5-2	Fermanagh 2-0	1915
	Loss	Fermanagh 4-13	Monaghan 0-5	1945
Galway	Win	Galway 0-8	Monaghan 0-16	2018
	Loss	Galway 2-10	Monaghan 2-3	1938
Kerry	Win	Kerry 5-14	Monaghan 0-7	1979
	Loss			
Kildare	Win	Monaghan 1-6	Kildare 1-4	1930
	Loss	Kildare 2-10	Monaghan 1-3	1907

Kilkenny	Win				
	Loss				
Laois	Win	Laois 1-11	Monaghan 0-19	2018	
	Loss	Laois 2-12	Monaghan 0-12	2012	
Leitrim	Win	Leitrim 0-9	Monaghan 1-19	2018	
	Loss				
Limerick	Win				
	Loss				
London	Win	Monaghan 2-18	London 1-9	2005	
	Loss				
Longford	Win				
	Loss	Monaghan 1-16	Longford 4-15	2004	
Louth	Win	Monaghan 1-12	Louth 0-14	2005	
	Loss	Monaghan 1-8	Louth 2-11	2002	
Mayo	Win				
	Loss				
Meath	Win				
	Loss	Meath 2-10	Monaghan 0-12	2003	
New York	Win				
	Loss				
Offaly	Win				
	Loss	Offaly 1-18	Monaghan 1-10	2011	
Roscommon	Win				
	Loss				
Sligo	Win				
	Loss				
Tipperary	Win				
	Loss				
Tyrone	Win	Monaghan 4-12	Tyrone 0-8	1937	
	Loss	Tyrone 2-14	Monaghan 1-7	2005	
Waterford	Win	Waterford 0-9	Monaghan 5-21	2018	
	Loss				
Westmeath	Win	Monaghan 0-14	Westmeath 1-9	2003	
	Loss				
Wexford	Win	Wexford 1-11	Monaghan 3-23	2017	
	Loss	Wexford 6-6	Monaghan 1-3	1917	
Wicklow	Win	Monaghan 2-19	Wicklow 3-6	2006	
	Loss				

NEW YORK/NUA EABHRAC

	Played	21
Overall	Won	0 (0%)
Record	Drawn	0
	Lost	21

TITLES

Connacht none

All-Ireland none

HEAD TO HEAD

(biggest win/loss; blank if counties have never met in championship)

Antrim	Win			
	Loss			
Armagh	Win			
	Loss			
Carlow	Win			
	Loss			
Cavan	Win			
	Loss			
Clare	Win			
	Loss			
Cork	Win			
	Loss			
Derry	Win			
	Loss			
Donegal	Win			
	Loss			
Down	Win			
	Loss			
Dublin	Win			
	Loss			
Fermanagh	Win			
	Loss			
Galway	Win			
	Loss	Galway 3-14	New York 0-6	2005
Kerry	Win			
	Loss			

Kildare	*Win*			
	Loss			
Kilkenny	*Win*			
	Loss			
Laois	*Win*			
	Loss			
Leitrim	*Win*			
	Loss	New York 0-7	Leitrim 4-19	2013
Limerick	*Win*			
	Loss			
London	*Win*			
	Loss			
Longford	*Win*			
	Loss			
Louth	*Win*			
	Loss			
Mayo	*Win*			
	Loss	New York 1-8	Mayo 3-28	2004
Meath	*Win*			
	Loss			
Monaghan	*Win*			
	Loss			
Offaly	*Win*			
	Loss			
Roscommon	*Win*			
	Loss	New York 1-11	Roscommon 3-21	2011
Sligo	*Win*			
	Loss	New York 0-6	Sligo 3-21	2012
Tipperary	*Win*			
	Loss			
Tyrone	*Win*			
	Loss			
Waterford	*Win*			
	Loss			
Westmeath	*Win*			
	Loss			
Wexford	*Win*			
	Loss			
Wicklow	*Win*			
	Loss			

OFFALY/UÍBH FHAILÍ

	Overall Record	
Played	269
Won	118 (43.9%)
Drawn	23
Lost	128

TITLES

Leinster 1960, 1961, 1969, 1971, 1972, 1973, 1980, 1981, 1982, 1997 (10)

All-Ireland 1971, 1972, 1982 (3)

HEAD TO HEAD
(biggest win/loss; blank if counties have never met in championship)

Antrim	Win	Offaly 2-30	Antrim 1-15	2018
	Loss			
Armagh	Win			
	Loss			
Carlow	Win	Offaly 3-13	Carlow 0-6	1934
	Loss	Offaly 0-6	Carlow 1-9	1942
Cavan	Win	Offaly 3-8	Cavan 1-10	1969
	Loss	Offaly 0-16	Cavan 0-17	2017
Clare	Win	Offaly 1-12	Clare 1-8	2003
	Loss	Offaly 2-14	Clare 1-19	2018
Cork	Win	Offaly 1-16	Cork 1-11	1971
	Loss			
Derry	Win			
	Loss			
Donegal	Win	Offaly 1-17	Donegal 2-10	1972
	Loss			
Down	Win	Down 0-6	Offaly 0-12	1981
	Loss	Offaly 2-10	Down 5-19	2008
Dublin	Win	Offaly 3-9	Dublin 0-9	1960
	Loss	Offaly 1-0	Dublin 3-7	1910
Fermanagh	Win			
	Loss			
Galway	Win	Offaly 1-14	Galway 2-8	1971
	Loss	Galway 0-16	Offaly 2-8	1973
Kerry	Win	Offaly 1-19	Kerry 0-13	1972
	Loss	Kerry 1-12	Offaly 0-8	1981

Kildare	Win	Offaly 2-15	Kildare 0-6	1983
	Loss	Offaly 0-1	Kildare 2-13	1908
Kilkenny	Win	Offaly 1-9	Kilkenny 0-5	1910
	Loss			
Laois	Win	Offaly 6-5	Laois 2-7	1942
	Loss	Offaly 0-4	Laois 5-11	1947
Leitrim	Win			
	Loss			
Limerick	Win			
	Loss	Limerick 3-13	Offaly 0-15	2011
London	Win	Offaly 4-15	London 0-10	2003
	Loss			
Longford	Win	Offaly 5-17	Longford 0-13	1997
	Loss	Longford 4-3	Offaly 1-4	1944
Louth	Win	Offaly 5-12	Louth 0-7	1955
	Loss	Louth 6-14	Offaly 0-1	1901
Mayo	Win			
	Loss	Mayo 0-13	Offaly 0-7	1997
Meath	Win	Offaly 3-21	Meath 2-12	1973
	Loss	Meath 2-13	Offaly 0-7	1991
Monaghan	Win	Offaly 1-18	Monaghan 1-10	2011
	Loss			
New York	Win			
	Loss			
Roscommon	Win	Offaly 3-6	Roscommon 0-6	1961
	Loss	Offaly 1-15	Roscommon 1-20	2003
Sligo	Win	Offaly 3-17	Sligo 0-15	2019
	Loss			
Tipperary	Win			
	Loss	Tipperary 1-12	Offaly 0-10	2012
Tyrone	Win			
	Loss	Offaly 0-8	Tyrone 1-27	2013
Waterford	Win	Waterford 1-7	Offaly 0-20	2015
	Loss			
Westmeath	Win	Offaly 6-5	Westmeath 0-11	1936
	Loss	Westmeath 4-4	Offaly 1-2	1918
Wexford	Win	Offaly 1-17	Wexford 0-2	1907
	Loss	Offaly 0-1	Wexford 3-6	1904
Wicklow	Win	Offaly 0-19	Wicklow 0-7	1977
	Loss	Offaly 0-4	Wicklow 1-11	1899

ROSCOMMON/ROS COMÁIN

Overall Record	Played	279
	Won	125 (44.8%)
	Drawn	24
	Lost	130

TITLES

Connacht | 1892, 1903, 1905, 1912, 1914, 1943, 1944, 1946, 1947, 1952, 1953, 1961, 1962, 1972, 1977, 1978, 1979, 1980, 1990, 1991, 2001, 2010, 2017, 2019 (24)

All-Ireland | 1943, 1944 (2)

HEAD TO HEAD
(biggest win/loss; blank if counties have never met in championship)

Antrim	Win			
	Loss			
Armagh	Win	Roscommon 2-20	Armagh 3-11	1980
	Loss	Roscommon 1-12	Armagh 1-17	2014
Carlow	Win			
	Loss			
Cavan	Win	Roscommon 5-8	Cavan 1-3	1944
	Loss	Cavan 2-4	Roscommon 0-6	1947
Clare	Win			
	Loss	Roscommon 1-9	Clare 2-12	2016
Cork	Win	Roscommon 4-9	Cork 3-9	2019
	Loss	Roscommon 0-10	Cork 1-16	2010
Derry	Win			
	Loss			
Donegal	Win			
	Loss	Donegal 3-11	Roscommon 1-9	2008
Down	Win			
	Loss			
Dublin	Win			
	Loss	Roscommon 0-14	Dublin 2-26	2019
Fermanagh	Win			
	Loss	Fermanagh 1-14	Roscommon 0-16	2015
Galway	Win	Roscommon 4-3	Galway 0-1	1914
	Loss	Galway 2-18	Roscommon 0-6	2008

Kerry	Win	Roscommon 1-9	Kerry 2-4	1944
	Loss	Kerry 3-11	Roscommon 0-8	1978
Kildare	Win	Kildare 0-19	Roscommon 1-18	2003
	Loss	Roscommon 1-13	Kildare 2-13	2007
Kilkenny	Win			
	Loss			
Laois	Win	Roscommon 3-5	Laois 2-6	1946
	Loss			
Leitrim	Win	Roscommon 5-6	Leitrim 0-1	1931
	Loss	Leitrim 3-3	Roscommon 0-2	1920
Limerick	Win			
	Loss			
London	Win	Roscommon 9-19	London 1-10	1980
	Loss			
Longford	Win			
	Loss			
Louth	Win	Roscommon 3-10	Louth 3-6	1943
	Loss	Louth 0-11	Roscommon 0-10	2005
Mayo	Win	Roscommon 3-13	Mayo 0-8	1980
	Loss	Mayo 6-6	Roscommon 0-0	1921
Meath	Win			
	Loss	Meath 1-19	Roscommon 0-9	2006
Monaghan	Win			
	Loss			
New York	Win	New York 1-11	Roscommon 3-21	2011
	Loss			
Offaly	Win			
	Loss			
Sligo	Win	Offaly 1-15	Roscommon 1-20	2003
	Loss	Offaly 3-6	Roscommon 0-6	1961
Tipperary	Win	Roscommon 4-11	Sligo 1-8	1989
	Loss	Sligo 2-7	Roscommon 0-5	1930
Tyrone	Win			
	Loss	Tyrone 4-24	Roscommon 2-12	2018
Waterford	Win	Waterford 3-11	Roscommon 3-19	2002
	Loss			
Westmeath	Win			
	Loss			
Wexford	Win	Roscommon 0-11	Wexford 0-8	2009
	Loss			
Wicklow	Win			
	Loss			

SLIGO/SLIGEACH

Overall Record	Played	223
	Won	71 (31.8%)
	Drawn	20
	Lost	132

TITLES

Connacht 1888, 1928, 1975, 2007 (4)

All-Ireland none

HEAD TO HEAD

(biggest win/loss; blank if counties have never met in championship)

Antrim	Win	Sligo 0-22	Antrim 3-7	2017
	Loss			
Armagh	Win			
	Loss	Sligo 1-13	Armagh 1-19	2018
Carlow	Win	Carlow 2-7	Sligo 2-14	2001
	Loss			
Cavan	Win			
	Loss	Cavan 2-5	Sligo 0-4	1928
Clare	Win	Sligo 1-13	Clare 0-11	2005
	Loss	Clare 1-15	Sligo 1-7	2004
Cork	Win			
	Loss	Cork 3-13	Sligo 0-11	2005
Derry	Win			
	Loss	Derry 0-15	Sligo 0-8	2013
Donegal	Win			
	Loss	Donegal 0-16	Sligo 0-11	2003
Down	Win	Sligo 1-7	Down 0-4	2006
	Loss	Sligo 0-10	Down 3-20	2010
Dublin	Win			
	Loss	Dublin 3-17	Sligo 0-12	2001
Fermanagh	Win			
	Loss			
Galway	Win	Sligo 1-13	Galway 0-6	1975
	Loss	Galway 6-18	Sligo 0-4	1990
Kerry	Win			
	Loss	Kerry 3-13	Sligo 0-5	1975

Kildare	Win	Sligo 0-16	Kildare 0-15	2001
	Loss	Kildare 0-13	Sligo 0-4	2012
Kilkenny	Win			
	Loss			
Laois	Win			
	Loss			
Leitrim	Win	Sligo 6-10	Leitrim 0-6	1946
	Loss	Leitrim 5-7	Sligo 0-2	1914
Limerick	Win	Sligo 0-12	Limerick 0-10	2014
	Loss			
London	Win	London 0-7	Sligo 2-17	2008
	Loss	London 1-12	Sligo 0-14	2013
Longford	Win	Sligo 0-18	Longford 0-16	2005
	Loss			
Louth	Win			
	Loss			
Mayo	Win	Sligo 3-8	Mayo 2-5	1923
	Loss	Mayo 7-10	Sligo 0-2	1949
Meath	Win			
	Loss	Meath 0-14	Sligo 1-9	2017
Monaghan	Win			
	Loss			
New York	Win	New York 0-6	Sligo 3-21	2012
	Loss			
Offaly	Win			
	Loss	Offaly 3-17	Sligo 0-15	2019
Roscommon	Win	Sligo 2-7	Roscommon 0-5	1930
	Loss	Roscommon 4-11	Sligo 1-8	1989
Tipperary	Win	Sligo 1-8	Tipperary 0-7	1923
	Loss			
Tyrone	Win	Sligo 1-14	Tyrone 0-12	2002
	Loss	Sligo 0-14	Tyrone 0-21	2015
Waterford	Win			
	Loss			
Westmeath	Win			
	Loss	Sligo 0-14	Westmeath 1-12	2006
Wexford	Win			
	Loss			
Wicklow	Win	Wicklow 0-10	Sligo 0-12	2014
	Loss	Wicklow 1-18	Sligo 0-16	2011

TIPPERARY/TIOBRAID ÁRANN

Overall Record	Played	274
	Won	116 (42.3%)
	Drawn	14
	Lost	144

TITLES

Munster 1888, 1889, 1895, 1900, 1902, 1918, 1920, 1922, 1935 (9)

All-Ireland 1889, 1895, 1900, 1920 (4)

HEAD TO HEAD
(biggest win/loss; blank if counties have never met in championship)

Antrim	Win	Tipperary 0-10	Antrim 0-8	2012
	Loss			
Armagh	Win			
	Loss	Tipperary 1-15	Armagh 1-17	2017
Carlow	Win	Tipperary 1-14	Carlow 0-13	2003
	Loss			
Cavan	Win	Cavan 0-18	Tipperary 2-15	2017
	Loss	Cavan 1-7	Tipperary 0-8	1935
Clare	Win	Tipperary 4-8	Clare 1-2	1923
	Loss	Tipperary 0-9	Clare 3-14	1981
Cork	Win	Tipperary 2-8	Cork 1-2	1935
	Loss	Cork 3-11	Tipperary 0-1	1901
Derry	Win	Tipperary 1-21	Derry 2-17	2016
	Loss			
Donegal	Win			
	Loss	Donegal 2-19	Tipperary 0-15	2003
Down	Win	Down 1-13	Tipperary 0-11	2012
	Loss	Tipperary 1-6	Dublin 1-2	1922
Dublin	Win	Dublin 1-21	Tipperary 1-13	2010
	Loss			
Fermanagh	Win			
	Loss			
Galway	Win	Tipperary 2-17	Galway 0-1	1902
	Loss	Galway 4-17	Tipperary 4-12	2014
Kerry	Win	Tipperary 1-13	Kerry 1-2	1902
	Loss	Kerry 4-21	Tipperary 0-8	2013
Kildare	Win			
	Loss			

86

Kilkenny	*Win*			
	Loss	Tipperary 0-7	Kilkenny 1-6	1902
Laois	*Win*	Tipperary 3-6	Laois 0-0	1889
	Loss	Laois 2-16	Tipperary 0-11	2011
Leitrim	*Win*			
	Loss			
Limerick	*Win*	Tipperary 7-18	Limerick 1-5	1975
	Loss	Limerick 4-10	Tipperary 2-5	1967
London	*Win*	Tipperary 3-7	London 0-2	1902
	Loss			
Longford	*Win*	Tipperary 2-17	Longford 0-6	2014
	Loss	Longford 1-23	Tipperary 1-10	2006
Louth	*Win*	Tipperary 3-21	Louth 0-7	2015
	Loss	Tipperary 1-8	Louth 0-13	2001
Mayo	*Win*	Tipperary 1-5	Mayo 1-0	1922
	Loss	Tipperary 1-11	Mayo 1-19	2018
Meath	*Win*	Tipperary 0-4	Meath 0-3	1896
	Loss			
Monaghan	*Win*			
	Loss			
New York	*Win*			
	Loss			
Offaly	*Win*	Tipperary 1-12	Offaly 0-10	2012
	Loss			
Roscommon	*Win*			
	Loss			
Sligo	*Win*			
	Loss	Sligo 1-8	Tipperary 0-7	1923
Tyrone	*Win*			
	Loss	Tipperary 0-7	Tyrone 0-19	2015
Waterford	*Win*	Waterford 0-5	Tipperary 1-24	2015
	Loss	Waterford 5-11	Tipperary 1-11	1976
Westmeath	*Win*			
	Loss	Tipperary 0-6	Westmeath 0-15	2008
Wexford	*Win*	Tipperary 1-13	Wexford 0-15	2012
	Loss	Wexford 0-5	Tipperary 0-4	1919
Wicklow	*Win*			
	Loss			

TYRONE/TÍR EOGHAIN

Overall Record	Played	285
	Won	143 (50.2%)
	Drawn	23
	Lost	119

TITLES

Ulster 1956, 1957, 1973, 1984, 1986, 1989, 1995, 1996, 2001, 2003, 2007, 2009, 2010, 2016, 2017 (15)

All-Ireland 2003, 2005, 2008 (3)

HEAD TO HEAD

(biggest win/loss; blank if counties have never met in championship)

Antrim	*Win*	Antrim 2-9	Tyrone 2-23	2019
	Loss	Antrim 2-9	Tyrone 0-3	1963
Armagh	*Win*	Armagh 0-1	Tyrone 3-13	1941
	Loss	Armagh 7-13	Tyrone 2-3	1951
Carlow	*Win*	Carlow 1-10	Tyrone 3-14	2018
	Loss			
Cavan	*Win*	Tyrone 3-19	Cavan 0-7	2005
	Loss	Cavan 8-13	Tyrone 2-3	1946
Clare	*Win*			
	Loss			
Cork	*Win*	Cork 0-13	Tyrone 3-20	2018
	Loss	Cork 5-10	Tyrone 2-4	1973
Derry	*Win*	Tyrone 7-3	Derry 2-3	1928
	Loss	Derry 3-12	Tyrone 0-7	1970
Donegal	*Win*	Tyrone 8-7	Donegal 0-3	1953
	Loss	Donegal 4-3	Tyrone 1-0	1919
Down	*Win*	Down 1-5	Tyrone 0-23	2003
	Loss	Down 3-13	Tyrone 1-6	1965
Dublin	*Win*	Dublin 1-8	Tyrone 3-14	2008
	Loss	Dublin 2-17	Tyrone 0-11	2017
Fermanagh	*Win*	Tyrone 5-8	Fermanagh 0-4	1948
	Loss	Fermanagh 2-8	Tyrone 0-8	1968
Galway	*Win*	Galway 0-11	Tyrone 1-16	2004
	Loss	Galway 0-8	Tyrone 0-6	1956
Kerry	*Win*	Kerry 0-6	Tyrone 0-13	2003
	Loss	Kerry 1-16	Tyrone 1-6	2012
Kildare	*Win*	Tyrone 2-22	Kildare 1-15	2019
	Loss			

Kilkenny	*Win*			
	Loss			
Laois	*Win*	Tyrone 3-15	Laois 2-4	2004
	Loss	Laois 0-9	Tyrone 0-6	2006
Leitrim	*Win*	Tyrone 1-22	Leitrim 0-7	2002
	Loss			
Limerick	*Win*	Tyrone 1-14	Limerick 0-8	2015
	Loss			
London	*Win*			
	Loss			
Longford	*Win*	Longford 0-15	Tyrone 1-17	2011
	Loss			
Louth	*Win*	Louth 0-10	Tyrone 2-21	2014
	Loss	Louth 0-13	Tyrone 0-7	1957
Mayo	*Win*	Mayo 1-9	Tyrone 0-13	2008
	Loss	Mayo 1-16	Tyrone 0-13	2013
Meath	*Win*	Tyrone 1-10	Meath 0-11	2015
	Loss	Meath 2-15	Tyrone 0-12	1996
Monaghan	*Win*	Tyrone 2-14	Monaghan 1-7	2005
	Loss	Monaghan 4-12	Tyrone 0-8	1937
New York	*Win*			
	Loss			
Offaly	*Win*	Offaly 0-8	Tyrone 1-27	2013
	Loss			
Roscommon	*Win*	Tyrone 4-24	Roscommon 2-12	2018
	Loss			
Sligo	*Win*	Sligo 0-14	Tyrone 0-21	2015
	Loss	Sligo 1-14	Tyrone 0-12	2002
Tipperary	*Win*	Tipperary 0-7	Tyrone 0-19	2015
	Loss			
Waterford	*Win*			
	Loss			
Westmeath	*Win*	Tyrone 0-14	Westmeath 1-7	2008
	Loss			
Wexford	*Win*	Tyrone 0-23	Wexford 1-14	2008
	Loss			
Wicklow	*Win*			
	Loss			

WATERFORD/PORT LÁIRGE

Overall Record	Played	181
	Won	31 (17.1%)
	Drawn	9
	Lost	141

TITLES

Munster 1898 (1)

All-Ireland none

HEAD TO HEAD

(biggest win/loss; blank if counties have never met in championship)

Antrim	Win			
	Loss			
Armagh	Win			
	Loss	Waterford 0-8	Armagh 2-21	2003
Carlow	Win			
	Loss	Waterford 1-10	Carlow 3-11	2001
Cavan	Win			
	Loss			
Clare	Win	Waterford 2-9	Clare 0-2	1911
	Loss	Clare 4-16	Waterford 0-5	1983
Cork	Win	Waterford 1-11	Cork 1-3	1899
	Loss	Cork 3-23	Waterford 0-4	1999
Derry	Win			
	Loss	Waterford 0-13	Derry 1-17	2017
Donegal	Win			
	Loss			
Down	Win			
	Loss			
Dublin	Win			
	Loss	Dublin 2-8	Waterford 0-4	1900
Fermanagh	Win			
	Loss			
Galway	Win			
	Loss	Galway 1-12	Waterford 0-14	2013
Kerry	Win	Waterford 1-2	Kerry 0-1	1911
	Loss	Kerry 7-16	Waterford 0-8	1974
Kildare	Win			
	Loss			

Kilkenny	*Win*	
	Loss	
Laois	*Win*	
	Loss	
Leitrim	*Win*	
	Loss	Leitrim 0-12 — Waterford 0-8 — 2016
Limerick	*Win*	Waterford 1-11 — Limerick 0-5 — 1974
	Loss	Limerick 4-10 — Waterford 0-6 — 1965
London	*Win*	London 0-13 — Waterford 1-17 — 2011
	Loss	
Longford	*Win*	
	Loss	Waterford 1-5 — Longford 1-14 — 2004
Louth	*Win*	
	Loss	Louth 1-12 — Waterford 1-8 — 2005
Mayo	*Win*	
	Loss	
Meath	*Win*	
	Loss	Meath 1-20 — Waterford 0-8 — 2009
Monaghan	*Win*	
	Loss	Waterford 0-9 — Monaghan 5-21 — 2018
New York	*Win*	
	Loss	
Offaly	*Win*	
	Loss	Waterford 1-7 — Offaly 0-20 — 2015
Roscommon	*Win*	
	Loss	Waterford 3-11 — Roscommon 3-19 — 2002
Sligo	*Win*	
	Loss	
Tipperary	*Win*	Waterford 5-11 — Tipperary 1-11 — 1976
	Loss	Waterford 0-5 — Tipperary 1-24 — 2015
Tyrone	*Win*	
	Loss	
Westmeath	*Win*	
	Loss	Westmeath 1-22 — Waterford 0-7 — 2019
Wexford	*Win*	Wexford 1-18 — Waterford 3-14 — 2018
	Loss	
Wicklow	*Win*	
	Loss	Wicklow 1-17 — Waterford 0-15 — 2012

WESTMEATH/IAR MHÍ

	Played	200
Overall	Won	72 (36%)
Record	Drawn	13
	Lost	115

TITLES

Leinster 2004 (1)

All-Ireland none

HEAD TO HEAD
(biggest win/loss; blank if counties have never met in championship)

Antrim	*Win*	Antrim 1-10	Westmeath 0-14	2002
	Loss	Antrim 0-16	Westmeath 1-7	2011
Armagh	*Win*			
	Loss	Westmeath 1-11	Armagh 3-16	2018
Carlow	*Win*	Westmeath 3-15	Carlow 1-10	2013
	Loss	Carlow 3-11	Westmeath 1-4	1985
Cavan	*Win*	Cavan 1-15	Westmeath 1-14	2014
	Loss			
Clare	*Win*			
	Loss	Clare 0-12	Westmeath 0-9	2005
Cork	*Win*			
	Loss			
Derry	*Win*			
	Loss	Westmeath 1-7	Derry 0-13	2010
Donegal	*Win*			
	Loss	Westmeath 1-8	Donegal 1-13	2007
Down	*Win*			
	Loss			
Dublin	*Win*	Westmeath 2-4	Dublin 1-4	1931
	Loss	Dublin 4-29	Westmeath 0-10	2017
Fermanagh	*Win*			
	Loss	Westmeath 0-7	Fermanagh 1-13	2015
Galway	*Win*	Galway 0-10	Westmeath 1-8	2006
	Loss			
Kerry	*Win*			
	Loss	Kerry 2-10	Westmeath 1-12	2012
Kildare	*Win*	Westmeath 1-12	Kildare 1-11	2016
	Loss	Kildare 4-11	Westmeath 2-5	1992

Kilkenny	Win	Westmeath 8-5	Kilkenny 1-5	1931
	Loss	Kilkenny 1-13	Westmeath 0-0	1904
Laois	Win	Westmeath 2-12	Laois 1-5	1966
	Loss	Laois 1-17	Westmeath 0-6	1991
Leitrim	Win			
	Loss			
Limerick	Win	Limerick 0-7	Westmeath 0-17	2001
	Loss			
London	Win	Westmeath 0-20	London 0-8	2006
	Loss			
Longford	Win	Westmeath 3-17	Longford 2-9	1999
	Loss	Longford 3-10	Westmeath 0-8	1961
Louth	Win	Westmeath 2-11	Louth 0-9	1965
	Loss	Louth 4-4	Westmeath 0-1	1921
Mayo	Win	Mayo 0-16	Westmeath 1-14	2001
	Loss	Westmeath 1-14	Mayo 3-15	2016
Meath	Win	Westmeath 3-19	Meath 2-18	2015
	Loss	Meath 4-12	Westmeath 1-5	1980
Monaghan	Win			
	Loss	Monaghan 0-14	Westmeath 1-9	2003
New York	Win			
	Loss			
Offaly	Win	Westmeath 4-4	Offaly 1-2	1918
	Loss	Offaly 6-5	Westmeath 0-11	1936
Roscommon	Win			
	Loss			
Sligo	Win	Sligo 0-14	Westmeath 1-12	2006
	Loss			
Tipperary	Win	Tipperary 0-6	Westmeath 0-15	2008
	Loss			
Tyrone	Win			
	Loss	Tyrone 0-14	Westmeath 1-7	2008
Waterford	Win	Westmeath 1-22	Waterford 0-7	2019
	Loss			
Wexford	Win	Westmeath 1-21	Wexford 0-15	2015
	Loss	Wexford 1-24	Westmeath 0-15	2011
Wicklow	Win	Westmeath 3-7	Wicklow 2-5	1982
	Loss	Wicklow 0-15	Westmeath 1-5	1986

WEXFORD/LOCH GARMAN

Overall Record		
Played	299	
Won	129 (43.1%)	
Drawn	25	
Lost	145	

TITLES

Leinster | 1890, 1893, 1913, 1914, 1915, 1916, 1917, 1918, 1925, 1945 (10)

All-Ireland | 1893, 1915, 1916, 1917, 1918 (5)

HEAD TO HEAD

(biggest win/loss; blank if counties have never met in championship)

Antrim	Win	Wexford 4-4	Antrim 0-1	1913
	Loss			
Armagh	Win	Armagh 0-12	Wexford 1-14	2008
	Loss			
Carlow	Win	Wexford 2-24	Carlow 0-5	1898
	Loss	Carlow 4-17	Wexford 1-11	1996
Cavan	Win	Wexford 3-7	Cavan 2-2	1915
	Loss	Cavan 1-14	Wexford 0-5	1945
Clare	Win	Wexford 0-9	Clare 0-5	1917
	Loss			
Cork	Win	Wexford 1-1	Cork 0-1	1894
	Loss	Cork 2-4	Wexford 0-1	1892
Derry	Win			
	Loss	Wexford 0-10	Derry 4-16	2019
Donegal	Win			
	Loss			
Down	Win	Wexford 2-13	Down 0-12	2008
	Loss			
Dublin	Win	Wexford 4-6	Dublin 1-1	1914
	Loss	Wexford 0-9	Dublin 3-23	2008
Fermanagh	Win			
	Loss	Fermanagh 2-12	Wexford 0-11	2006
Galway	Win	Galway 0-13	Wexford 1-11	2010
	Loss	Galway 3-4	Wexford 1-1	1925
Kerry	Win	Wexford 2-4	Kerry 2-1	1915
	Loss	Kerry 2-2	Wexford 0-3	1913

Opponent	Result			Year
Kildare	Win	Wexford 5-5	Kildare 0-6	1945
	Loss	Kildare 5-12	Wexford 1-6	1962
Kilkenny	Win	Wexford 4-12	Kilkenny 0-2	1944
	Loss	Kilkenny 3-0	Wexford 0-1	1911
Laois	Win	Wexford 2-11	Laois 0-2	1910
	Loss	Laois 1-19	Wexford 0-10	2003
Leitrim	Win			
	Loss			
Limerick	Win	Limerick 0-11	Wexford 0-12	2017
	Loss	Limerick 1-18	Wexford 1-17	2011
London	Win	London 0-9	Wexford 4-22	2010
	Loss			
Longford	Win	Wexford 7-10	Longford 6-2	1927
	Loss	Longford 2-15	Wexford 0-11	1999
Louth	Win	Wexford 3-6	Louth 0-1	1914
	Loss	Louth 3-5	Wexford 1-1	1934
Mayo	Win	Wexford 3-4	Mayo 1-2	1916
	Loss	Mayo 2-4	Wexford 1-4	1925
Meath	Win	Wexford 4-9	Meath 0-2	1925
	Loss	Meath 4-15	Wexford 0-3	1966
Monaghan	Win	Wexford 6-6	Monaghan 1-3	1917
	Loss	Wexford 1-11	Monaghan 3-23	2017
New York	Win			
	Loss			
Offaly	Win	Offaly 0-1	Wexford 3-6	1904
	Loss	Offaly 1-17	Wexford 0-2	1907
Roscommon	Win			
	Loss	Roscommon 0-11	Wexford 0-8	2009
Sligo	Win			
	Loss			
Tipperary	Win			
	Loss	Wexford 0-5	Tipperary 0-4	1919
Tyrone	Win	Tipperary 1-13	Wexford 0-15	2012
	Loss	Tyrone 0-23	Wexford 1-14	2008
Waterford	Win			
	Loss	Wexford 1-18	Waterford 3-14	2018
Westmeath	Win	Wexford 1-24	Westmeath 0-15	2011
	Loss	Westmeath 1-21	Wexford 0-15	2015
Wicklow	Win	Wexford 6-4	Wicklow 0-2	1917
	Loss	Wicklow 4-15	Wexford 1-8	1978

WICKLOW/CILL MHANTÁIN

	Overall Record	
Played	173	
Won	42 (24.3%)	
Drawn	10	
Lost	121	

TITLES

Leinster | none

All-Ireland | none

HEAD TO HEAD
(biggest win/loss; blank if counties have never met in championship)

Antrim	Win			
	Loss			
Armagh	Win			
	Loss	Armagh 2-21	Wicklow 0-2	2013
Carlow	Win	Wicklow 4-12	Carlow 1-4	1956
	Loss	Carlow 4-3	Wicklow 0-1	1918
Cavan	Win	Wicklow 1-12	Cavan 0-8	2009
	Loss	Wicklow 1-5	Cavan 2-16	2018
Clare	Win			
	Loss			
Cork	Win			
	Loss			
Derry	Win			
	Loss	Wicklow 1-10	Derry 1-15	2004
Donegal	Win			
	Loss	Wicklow 0-12	Donegal 0-16	2005
Down	Win			
	Loss	Wicklow 1-15	Down 0-17	2009
Dublin	Win			
	Loss	Dublin 4-25	Wicklow 1-11	2018
Fermanagh	Win	Wicklow 0-17	Fermanagh 1-11	2009
	Loss			
Galway	Win			
	Loss	Wicklow 1-9	Galway 3-12	2001
Kerry	Win			
	Loss	Kerry 5-15	Wicklow 0-7	2002

Kildare	*Win*	Wicklow 1-7	Kildare 0-6	1990
	Loss	Kildare 5-11	Wicklow 1-7	1937
Kilkenny	*Win*	Wicklow 2-16	Kilkenny 0-3	1978
	Loss	Wicklow 0-2	Kilkenny 1-2	1914
Laois	*Win*	Wicklow 3-6	Laois 1-6	1957
	Loss	Laois 3-6	Wicklow 0-2	1974
Leitrim	*Win*			
	Loss	Leitrim 0-13	Wicklow 0-10	2012
Limerick	*Win*			
	Loss			
London	*Win*	Wicklow 2-22	London 2-6	2002
	Loss			
Longford	*Win*	Longford 2-8	Wicklow 2-18	1992
	Loss	Longford 4-9	Wicklow 0-5	1972
Louth	*Win*	Louth 1-4	Wicklow 1-7	1889
	Loss	Louth 2-22	Wicklow 2-6	1975
Mayo	*Win*			
	Loss			
Meath	*Win*	Wicklow 3-7	Meath 1-11	1957
	Loss	Meath 6-8	Wicklow 0-4	1950
Monaghan	*Win*			
	Loss	Monaghan 2-19	Wicklow 3-6	2006
New York	*Win*			
	Loss			
Offaly	*Win*	Offaly 0-4	Wicklow 1-11	1899
	Loss	Offaly 0-19	Wicklow 0-7	1977
Roscommon	*Win*			
	Loss			
Sligo	*Win*	Wicklow 1-18	Sligo 0-16	2011
	Loss	Wicklow 0-10	Sligo 0-12	2014
Tipperary	*Win*			
	Loss			
Tyrone	*Win*			
	Loss			
Waterford	*Win*	Wicklow 1-17	Waterford 0-15	2012
	Loss			
Westmeath	*Win*	Wicklow 0-15	Westmeath 1-5	1986
	Loss	Westmeath 3-7	Wicklow 2-5	1982
Wexford	*Win*	Wicklow 4-15	Wexford 1-8	1978
	Loss	Wexford 6-4	Wicklow 0-2	1917

RECORDS BY YEAR

1887

The 1887 Championship was played-off as an open draw knockout competition. Counties were represented by an individual club (either the county champions or a club nominated by the county board). Only clubs that had paid their affiliation fees to the Gaelic Athletic Association were eligible. Games were twenty-one a side. The winner was determined by the team that scored the greater number of goals, if goals were equal then the greater number of points and forfeit points. A 'forfeit' point was awarded where a team played the ball over its own end-line. Five forfeit points equalled one point. Scores are given in the format G-P-F where G is goals, P is points and F is forfeit points.

All-Ireland

First Round

19/7/1887 **Clare** w/o **Wicklow** Athlone

24/7/1887 **Kilkenny 0-4-1 Cork 0-0-0** Dungarvan
Kilmacow v Lee

24/7/1887 **Limerick 3-2-0 Meath 0-2-0** Elm Park, Dublin
Commercials v Dowdstown

24/7/1887 **Louth 1-8-2 Waterford 0-3-1** Elm Park, Dublin
Young Irelands v Ballyduff Lower

24/7/1887 **Wexford** w/o **Galway**
Castlebridge v Meelick

30/7/1887 **Tipperary** w/o **Dublin** Mountrath

Second Round

28/8/1887 **Kilkenny 1-10-0 Limerick 1-10-0** Kilmainham
Kilmacow v Commercials

9/10/1887 **Kilkenny 0-5-2 Limerick 1-3-1** Bansha
Kilmacow v Commercials

28/8/1887 **Louth 0-7-3 Wexford 0-5-3** Kilmainham
Young Irelands v Castlebridge

25/9/1887 **Clare 1-1-0 Tipperary 1-1-1** Nenagh
Newmarket-on-Fergus v Templemore

Semi-final

11/3/1888 **Limerick 1-1-8 Tipperary 0-0-4** Bohercrowe
Commercials v Templemore
Louth *bye*
Dundalk Young Irelands

Final

29/4/1888 **Limerick 1-4-0 Louth 0-3-0** Clonskeagh
Commercials v Dundalk Young Irelands

99

The 1888 Championship was the first played-off as provincial knockout competitions organised by Central Council of the GAA. Due to the GAA tour of America the All-Ireland semi-finals and final never took place. In terms of scoring, 'forfeit points' were no longer recorded for games after 1887. Games were still to be decided on goals scored. If there was a tie on the number of goals scored, the team with more points scored was deemed the winner. As noted in the introduction, there is no record of a replay of the Connacht final but Sligo were subsequently referred to as the 1888 champions.

Connacht

First Round   16/9/1888   **Sligo** w/o **Galway** Mullingar
Black and Blues v Woodford

Final   10/11/1888   **Mayo** 0-5 **Sligo** 0-5 Charlestown
Castlebar v Black and Blues
Mayo   **Sligo** w/o
Castlebar v Black and Blues

Leinster

First Round
   3/6/1888   **Dublin** 1-6 **Kildare** 0-1 Donnybrook
Feagh McHughs v Clane

   10/6/1888   **Kilkenny** 1-3 **Laois** 0-0 Maryborough
Killmacow v Ballinakill

   1/7/1888   **Wexford** 0-1 **Wicklow** 0-2 D'brook
Blues and Whites v Annacurra

   19/8/1888   **Wexford** 1-3 **Wicklow** 1-2 Clonskeagh
Blues and Whites v Annacurra

   19/8/1888   **Louth** 2-3 **Meath** 0-0 Bryanstown
Young Irelands v Dowdstown (Tara) Gaels

Semi-final
   1/7/1888   **Kilkenny** 2-1 **Louth** 0-3 Clonskeagh
Kilmacow v Young Irelands

   2/9/1888   **Wexford** 0-4 **Dublin** 0-3 Clonskeagh
Blues and Whites v Feagh McHughs

Final   23/9/1888   **Kilkenny** 1-4 **Wexford** 0-2 Inchicore
Kilmacow v Blues and Whites

Munster

First Round

27/5/1888	**Cork** 0-1 **Tipperary** 0-2 Buttevant
	Lee v Bohercrowe
8/7/1888	**Clare** 1-2 **Limerick** 1-0 Birdhill
	Newmarket-on-Fergus v Commercials
	Limerick w/o **Clare**
	Commercials v Newmarket-on-Fergus
	Waterford *bye*
	Kilrossenty

Semi-final

22/7/1888	**Tipperary** 0-3 **Waterford** 0-1 Clonmel
	Bohercrowe v Kilrossenty
	Limerick *bye*
	Commercials

Final

| 10/11/1888 | **Tipperary** w/o **Limerick** |
| | *Bohercrowe v Commercials* |

Ulster

Final

19/8/1888	**Cavan** 0-2 **Monaghan** 0-2 Drogheda
	Moch Finns v The Red Hand
9/9/1888	**Cavan** 0-0 **Monaghan** 0-3 Bryanstown
	Moch Finns v The Red Hand

All-Ireland Not played

101

1889

Every county was included in the draw for the 1889 Championship but most did not participate. Wicklow had won the Leinster Championship but, due to objections, the semi-finals and final were replayed. As the Galway and Antrim semi-final didn't come off, the Tipperary/Laois semi-final became the final.

Connacht | *Final* | **Galway** (*Dunmore*) w/o

Leinster

First Round	25/8/1889	**Louth 2-7 Dublin 0-6** Drogheda *Newtown Blues* v *Faugh-a-Ballaghs*
	15/9/1889	**Louth** w/o **Kilkenny** Inchicore *Newtown Blues v Kells*
	15/9/1889	**Laois Wicklow** w/o Inchicore *Maryborough v Bray Emmets*
Semi-final	(re-drawn) 13/10/1889	**Laois 0-9 Wicklow 0-4** Inchicore *Maryborough v Bray Emmets* **Louth** *bye* *Newtown Blues*
	15/9/1889	**Louth 1-4 Wicklow 1-7** Inchicore *Newtown Blues v Bray Emmets*
Final	(re-drawn) 13/10/1889	**Laois 0-3 Louth 0-2** Inchicore *Maryborough v Newtown Blues*

Munster

Semi-final	28/7/1889	**Cork 0-2 Kerry 0-1** Mallow *Midleton v Killorglin*
Final	6/10/1889	**Tipperary 1-2 Cork 0-3** Mallow *Bohercrowe v Midleton*

Ulster | *Final* | **Antrim** (*Belfast Gaelics*) w/o

All-Ireland

Semi-final	20/10/1889	**Antrim Galway** not played *Belfast Gaelics v Dunmore*
Final	20/10/1889	**Tipperary 3-6 Laois 0-0** Inchicore *Bohercrowe v Maryborough*

Only some counties in each province took part in the 1890 Championship.

Connacht

Semi-final	28/9/1890	**Galway** w/o **Mayo** Claremorris	
		Dunmore v	
Final	12/10/1890	**Galway** w/o **Sligo** Mullingar	
		Dunmore v Tubbercurry	

Leinster

First Round	3/8/1890	**Wexford 0-2 Kilkenny 0-1** Ballynaneehagh
		Blues and Whites v Ballyhale
	5/10/1890	**Wexford** w/o **Kilkenny** Ballynaneehagh
		Blues and Whites v Ballyhale
Semi-final	19/10/1890	**Laois 0-1 Dublin 2-8** Clonturk
		Ballyroan v Isles of the Sea
	19/10/1890	**Wexford 0-3 Louth 0-2** Clonturk
		Blues and Whites v Drogheda Davitts
Final	2/11/1890	**Wexford 1-3 Dublin 1-2** Clonturk
		Blues and Whites v Isles of the Sea

Munster

Semi-final	3/8/1890	**Kerry 0-9 Limerick 0-0** Tralee
		Laune Rangers v St. Patricks
	17/8/1890	**Cork 0-6 Waterford 0-0** Youghal
		Midleton v Kinsalebeg
Final	28/9/1890	**Cork 0-0 Kerry 0-0** Raheen
		Midleton v Laune Rangers
	19/10/1890	**Cork 1-4 Kerry 0-1** Banteer
		Midleton v Laune Rangers

Ulster

Semi-final	17/8/1890	**Armagh 3-17 Antrim 0-0** Armagh
		Armagh Harps v Belfast Gaelics
Final	12/10/1890	**Armagh 2-8 Tyrone 1-2** Blaris, Lisburn
		Armagh Harps v Owen Roe O'Neills

All-Ireland

Semi-final	16/11/1890	**Cork 1-15 Armagh 0-0** Clonturk
		Midleton v Armagh Harps
	Nov 1890	**Wexford** w/o **Galway**
		Blues and Whites v Dunmore
Final	26/6/1892	**Cork 2-4 Wexford 0-1** Clonturk
		Midleton v Blues and Whites

There was no Connacht Championship in 1891 and only a limited number of counties entered the provincial championships in 1891.

Connacht | Not played

Leinster

Semi-final
25/10/1891 **Dublin 5-7 Wicklow 0-0** Clonturk
Young Irelands v Annacurra

8/11/1891 **Kildare 0-5 Laois 0-0** Clonturk
Mountrice v Moyanna

Final
8/11/1891 **Dublin** w/o **Kildare** Clonturk
Young Irelands v Mountrice

Munster

Semi-final
20/9/1891 **Cork 2-5 Kerry 0-2** Killarney
Clondrohid v Ballymacelligott

Final
1/11/1891 **Cork 1-5 Waterford 0-4** Youghal
Clondrohid v Dungarvan

Ulster

Semi-final
18/10/1891 **Cavan 3-9 Antrim 0-0** Armagh
Cavan Slashers v Northern Stars

Final
1/11/1891 **Cavan 0-7 Armagh 0-1** Smithborough
Cavan Slashers v Armagh Harps

6/12/1891 **Cavan 1-11 Armagh 0-0** Smithborough
Cavan Slashers v Armagh Harps

All-Ireland

Semi-final
28/2/1892 **Dublin 3-7 Cavan 0-3** Clonturk
Young Irelands v Cavan Slashers

Final
28/2/1892 **Dublin 2-1 Cork 1-1** Clonturk
Young Irelands v Clondrohid

1892

Roscommon was the only entrant from Connacht in 1892 and there were no Ulster entrants. Counties were now officially represented by a 'selection' rather than a club. A number of playing rule changes were introduced; the number of players on each team was reduced from 21 to 17; a goal was worth 5 points; the winner of a match was decided by adding the value of a goal (worth 5) to the number of points (worth 1).

Connacht ▌Roscommon w/o

Leinster ▌

| *Semi-final* | 11/3/1893 | **Dublin 3-5 Kildare 0-1** Clonturk |
| *Final* | 11/3/1893 | **Dublin** w/o **Louth** Clonturk |

Munster ▌

| *Semi-final* | 30/10/1892 | **Cork 0-5 Kerry 3-6** Killarney |
| *Final* | 4/12/1892 | **Kerry 0-11 Waterford 0-0** Fermoy |

Ulster ▌Not played.

All-Ireland ▌

| *Semi-final* | 19/3/1893 | **Dublin 1-9 Roscommon 1-1** Clonturk |
| *Final* | 26/3/1893 | **Dublin 1-4 Kerry 0-3** Clonturk |

There was no Connacht or Ulster Championship in 1893. In Leinster and Munster only a very limited number of counties participated. Wexford won the Leinster title with a walkover as Kilkenny abandoned the final and then refused to play the game.

Connacht	Not played		
Leinster	*Semi-final*	13/5/1894	**Wexford 2-6 Westmeath 0-1** Phoenix Park
	Final	3/6/1894	**Wexford 0-1 Kilkenny 0-5** Wexford
			Wexford w/o **Kilkenny**
Munster	*Final*	1/4/1894	**Cork** w/o **Kerry** Mallow
Ulster	Not played.		
All-Ireland	*Final*	24/6/1894	**Wexford 1-1 Cork 0-1** Phoenix Park

Again, there was no Connacht or Ulster Championship in 1894 and only a very limited number of Leinster and Munster counties participated in the Championship.

Connacht Not played

Leinster	*Semi-final*	9/9/1894	**Meath 1-5 Kilkenny 0-0** Phoenix Park
		23/9/1894	**Dublin 1-11 Wexford 0-0** Clonturk
		14/10/1894	**Dublin 0-4 Meath 0-4** Clonturk
	Final	15/12/1894	**Dublin 0-2 Meath 0-2** Navan
		24/2/1895	**Dublin 1-8 Meath 1-2** Clonturk

Munster	*Semi-final*	19/8/1894	**Tipperary 0-2 Kerry 0-4** Cork Park
		16/9/1894	**Cork 3-5 Limerick 0-0** Cork Park
	Final	2/12/1894	**Cork 0-6 Tipperary 0-2** Limerick
		3/3/1895	**Cork 2-4 Tipperary 0-1** Charleville

Ulster Not played.

All-Ireland	*Final*	24/3/1895	**Dublin 1-1 Cork 0-6** Clonturk
		21/4/1895	**Dublin 0-5 Cork 1-2** Thurles
			Dublin w/o **Cork**

There was no Connacht Championship in 1895. As Cavan were the only Ulster entrant, they were drawn with the Leinster teams. That section of the draw was designated by the GAA's Central Council meeting in August 1895 as the 'Leinster and Ulster' Championship.

Connacht ▌Not played

Leinster and Ulster

First Round	1/9/1895	**Louth 0-5 Cavan 0-1** Clonturk
Second Round	29/9/1895	**Dublin** w/o **Westmeath**
	29/9/1895	**Meath 1-13 Kilkenny 1-0** Clonturk
	29/9/1895	**Wexford 0-4 Kildare 1-4** Clonturk
Third Round	10/11/1895	**Louth 0-2 Kildare 2-10** Jones' Road
		Dublin *bye*
		Meath *bye*
Semi-final	16/2/1896	**Dublin 3-7 Kildare 0-4** Jones' Road
	16/2/1896	**Meath** w/o **Wicklow**
Final	1/3/1896	**Meath 0-6 Dublin 0-2** Jones' Road

Munster

Semi-final	30/11/1895	**Limerick 5-6 Kerry 1-1** Mallow
	1/2/1896	**Tipperary 2-7 Waterford 0-1** Tipperary
Final	23/2/1896	**Tipperary 0-5 Limerick 0-2** Kilmallock

All-Ireland ▌

Final	15/3/1896	**Tipperary 0-4 Meath 0-3** Jones' Road

In 1896 again only Leinster and Munster staged provincial championships while Galway was nominated to represent Connacht. Clare and Kerry had intended to participate in Munster but their non-participation meant Limerick had to play in all three rounds. From 1896 the value of a goal was equivalent to three points.

Connacht ▌Not played

Leinster

First Round	15/11/1896	**Dublin 0-11 Wicklow 1-2** Jones' Road
	29/11/1896	**Louth 1-6 Offaly 1-2** Jones' Road
	6/12/1896	**Kildare 0-6 Wexford 0-2** Jones' Road
		Meath w/o **Laois** Jones' Road
		Kilkenny w/o **Longford**
Second Round	9/5/1897	**Dublin 1-11 Louth 0-4** Navan
		Kildare *bye*
		Kilkenny *bye*
		Meath *bye*
Semi-final	23/5/1897	**Meath 1-10 Kilkenny 0-4** Jones' Road
	31/5/1897	**Dublin 2-15 Kildare 1-11** Navan
Final	24/10/1897	**Dublin 2-4 Meath 1-5** Jones' Road

Munster

First Round	14/3/1897	**Limerick 1-2 Cork 1-1** Tipperary
Semi-final	3/11/1897	**Limerick 2-4 Tipperary 0-6** Mallow
Final	21/11/1897	**Limerick 0-4 Waterford 0-1** Mallow

Ulster ▌Not played

All-Ireland

Semi-final	19/12/1897	**Limerick** w/o **Galway** Tipperary
Final	6/1/1898	**Limerick 1-5 Dublin 0-7** Jones' Road

1897

There was no Connacht or Ulster Championship in 1897. Only Leinster and Munster counties took part in the 1897 Championship.

Connacht | Not played

Leinster

First Round
15/5/1898	**Dublin 0-14 Kilkenny 0-1** Carlow
17/7/1898	**Laois 0-9 Kildare 2-17** Jones' Road
10/7/1898	**Meath 0-3 Louth 1-7** Balbriggan
17/7/1898	**Wexford 2-24 Carlow 0-5** Jones' Road
	Wicklow w/o **Offaly**

Second Round
17/7/1898	**Dublin 2-15 Kildare 0-2** Jones' Road
	Louth *bye*
	Wexford *bye*
	Wicklow *bye*

Semi-final
4/9/1898	**Wicklow 1-6 Louth 1-4** Jones' Road
4/9/1898	**Dublin 1-5 Wexford 1-7** Jones' Road
18/12/1898	**Dublin 0-10 Wexford 0-9** Jones' Road

Final
| 18/12/1898 | **Dublin 1-9 Wicklow 0-3** Jones' Road |

Munster

First Round
| 1/5/1898 | **Cork 1-5 Waterford 1-4** Dungarvan |
| | **Tipperary** w/o **Kerry** |

Semi-final
| 1/8/1898 | **Cork 0-5 Tipperary 1-0** Cork Park |
| | **Limerick** *bye* |

Final
| 25/9/1898 | **Cork 0-5 Limerick 0-3** Tipperary |

Ulster | Not played

All-Ireland

Final
| 5/2/1899 | **Dublin 2-6 Cork 0-2** Jones' Road |

1898

Again, in 1898, only Leinster and Munster counties took part in the Championship.

Connacht Not played

		19/11/1899	**Dublin w/o Kildare** Jones' Road
	First	19/11/1899	**Offaly 0-4 Wicklow 1-11** Jones' Road
	Round	10/12/1899	**Laois Wexford** w/o
Leinster		10/12/1899	**Meath Kilkenny** w/o
	Semi-final	17/12/1899	**Wicklow 0-3 Wexford 3-10** Jones' Road
		17/12/1899	**Dublin 1-16 Kilkenny 0-5** Jones' Road
	Final	4/2/1900	**Dublin 2-6 Wexford 0-0** Jones' Road

	First	1/5/1898	**Cork 1-5 Waterford 1-4** Dungarvan
	Round		**Tipperary** w/o **Kerry**
Munster	*Semi-final*	20/8/1899	**Waterford 0-9 Tipperary 0-0** Waterford
	Final	24/9/1899	**Waterford 1-11 Cork 1-3** Lismore

Ulster Not played

All-Ireland	*Final*	8/4/1900	**Dublin 2-8 Waterford 0-4** Tipperary

1899

In 1899, only a limited number of Leinster and Munster counties took part in the Championship.

Connacht Not played

Leinster
First Round	8/7/1900	**Dublin 7-17 Laois 0-3** Kilkenny
Semi-final	16/9/1900	**Dublin 0-10 Kilkenny 0-2** Kilkenny
Final	13/1/1901	**Dublin 1-7 Wexford 0-3** Jones' Road

Munster *Final*
14/10/1900	**Cork 0-1 Tipperary 2-1** Tipperary
18/11/1900	**Cork 1-2 Tipperary 0-1** Limerick
13/1/1901	**Cork 3-11 Tipperary 0-1** Limerick

Ulster Not played

All-Ireland *Final* 10/2/1901 **Dublin 1-10 Cork 0-6** Jones' Road

Galway and Antrim had walkovers in Connacht and Ulster. From 1900 England was constituted as a province by the GAA and the winner of the All-Ireland Championship would play off for the 'All-Ireland' against English Champions. Thus the Tipperary v Galway and Tipperary v London games are both typically described as the All-Ireland final although the latter fixture was officially organised as the All-Ireland Champions versus the Champions of England.

Connacht | Galway w/o

Leinster

First Round	7/7/1901	**Meath 0-5 Louth 6-19** Drogheda	
	12/5/1901	**Carlow 0-0 Kilkenny 2-11** Borris	
	26/5/1901	**Dublin 0-8 Wexford 1-7** Kilkenny	
	30/6/1901	**Kildare Wicklow** w/o	
	June 1901	**Offaly** w/o **Laois**	
Second Round	18/8/1901	**Louth 6-14 Offaly 0-1** Donnycarney	
		Kilkenny *bye*	
		Wexford *bye*	
		Wicklow *bye*	
Semi-final	28/7/1901	**Kilkenny 1-5 Wexford 0-4** Waterford	
	15/9/1901	**Wicklow 0-7 Louth 1-8** Monkstown	
Final	3/11/1901	**Kilkenny 0-12 Louth 0-0** Wexford	

Munster

First Round	20/10/1901	**Limerick w/o Clare** Market's Field
	3/11/1901	**Tipperary 0-3 Cork 0-1** Dungarvan
Semi-final	16/3/1902	**Tipperary 2-4 Limerick 2-1** Tipperary
	10/11/1901	**Kerry 1-3 Waterford 0-5** Turner's Cross
Final	11/5/1902	**Tipperary 1-13 Kerry 1-2** Market's Field

Ulster | Antrim w/o

All-Ireland

Semi-final	29/6/1902	**Tipperary 0-7 Kilkenny 1-6** Carrick-on-Suir
	24/8/1902	**Tipperary w/o Kilkenny** Carrick-on-Suir
	20/7/1902	**Galway w/o Antrim** Terenure
Final	21/9/1902	**Tipperary 2-17 Galway 0-1** Terenure

All-Ireland v England

Final	26/10/1902	**Tipperary 3-7 London 0-2** Jones' Road

1901

The game that was fixed as the final of the 1901 Ulster Championship was between two Antrim clubs, Tír na nÓg (Belfast) and Lamh Dearg, as no other Ulster county entered. As well as the eight Ulster counties, Clare, Leitrim, Longford, Sligo and Westmeath did not contest the 1901 Championship. The winners of the All-Ireland semi-finals progressed to what the press now dubbed the 'Irish' Final but which was still designated by the GAA as the 'All-Ireland Final' with the winner progressing to a play-off against the Champions of England (which also was designated as the 'All-Ireland Final').

Connacht	*Semi-final*	12/10/1902	**Galway 0-5 Roscommon 0-3** Ball'dereen
	Final	9/11/1902	**Mayo 2-4 Galway 0-3** Claremorris
		2/5/1903	**Galway 0-6 Mayo 2-2** Claremorris
Leinster	*First Round*	19/10/1902	**Kildare 5-15 Laois 1-1** Jones' Road
		19/10/1902	**Louth 2-17 Offaly 0-0** Jones' Road
	Second Round	21/7/1902	**Wexford 0-7 Wicklow 1-1** Wexford
		10/8/1902	**Dublin 3-13 Kilkenny 1-2** Terenure
		28/9/1902	**Carlow 2-4 Meath 3-6** Donnycarney
		9/11/1902	**Kildare 1-7 Louth 3-9** Jones' Road
	Semi-final	2/11/1902	**Wexford 0-8 Meath 0-4** Jones' Road
		14/12/1902	**Dublin 1-5 Louth 0-3** Drogheda
	Final	22/3/1903	**Dublin 1-9 Wexford 0-1** Kilkenny
Munster	*First Round*	31/8/1902	**Cork 0-8 Kerry 0-1** Market's Field
		5/10/1902	**Cork 0-8 Kerry 0-6** Millstreet
		19/10/1902	**Tipperary 0-5 Waterford 0-4** Cork
		15/3/1903	**Tipperary 0-9 Waterford 0-2** Ck-on-Suir
	Semi-final	29/3/1903	**Cork 2-3 Tipperary 0-6** Market's Field
			Limerick *bye*
	Final	19/4/1903	**Cork 1-9 Limerick 1-6** Tipperary
Ulster	*Final*	4/4/1903	**Tir na nOg 3-5 Lamh Dearg 2-5** Celtic Pk
All-Ireland	*Semi-final*	12/4/1903	**Dublin 2-12 Antrim 0-2** Jones' Road
		17/5/1903	**Cork 4-16 Mayo 0-1** Limerick
	'Irish' Final	5/7/1903	**Dublin 1-2 Cork 0-4** Tipperary
	Final	2/8/1903	**Dublin 0-14 London 0-2** Jones' Road

Derry, Donegal, Fermanagh, Longford and Monaghan did not enter the 1902 Championship. In Connacht, Galway was uncontested.

Connacht ▌ Galway w/o

Leinster

First Round	15/11/1903	**Kildare 0-3 Kilkenny 0-7** Carlow
	29/11/1903	**Laois 2-7 Meath 0-5** Jones' Road
	20/12/1903	**Carlow 0-4 Offaly 3-10** Abbeyleix
Second Round	1/11/1903	**Wicklow 1-0 Dublin 1-16** Jones' Road
	22/11/1903	**Louth 2-10 Westmeath 0-2** Jones' Road
	24/1/1904	**Offaly 0-3 Wexford 0-3** Jones' Road
	7/2/1904	**Offaly 0-5 Wexford 0-10** Jones' Road
	6/3/1904	**Offaly 0-1 Wexford 3-6** Jones' Road
	31/1/1904	**Kilkenny 1-8 Laois 0-4** Kilkenny
	6/12/1903	**Dublin 1-6 Louth 0-2** Navan
Semi-final	26/3/1904	**Wexford 0-7 Kilkenny 0-7** Jones' Road
	17/4/1904	**Wexford 0-4 Kilkenny 0-1** Jones' Road
Final	12/6/1904	**Dublin 1-5 Wexford 0-5** Kilkenny

Munster

First Round	10/5/1903	**Kerry 0-4 Waterford 0-** Cork
	7/6/1902	**Tipperary 5-6 Limerick 1-4** Turners Cross
	28/6/1903	**Cork 0-7 Clare 1-2** Tipperary
Semi-final	9/8/1903	**Kerry 2-7 Cork 0-3** Millstreet
		Tipperary bye
Final	4/10/1903	**Tipperary 1-4 Kerry 1-4** Turner's Cross
	1/11/1903	**Tipperary 1-6 Kerry 1-5** Turner's Cross

Ulster

First Round	17/1/1904	**Cavan** w/o **Down**
	3/1/1904	**Armagh 0-3 Tyrone 0-2** Armagh
	30/1/1904	**Armagh 1-6 Tyrone 0-3** Dungannon
Semi-final	7/2/1904	**Antrim 1-3 Cavan 0-1** Belfast
		Armagh bye
Final	4/4/1904	**Armagh 2-2 Antrim 1-4** Belfast

All-Ireland

Semi-final	24/4/1904	**Tipperary 2-5 Galway 0-4** Athenry
	5/6/1904	**Dublin 4-16 Armagh 1-6** Drogheda
'Irish' Final	24/7/1904	**Dublin 0-6 Tipperary 0-5** Kilkenny
Final	11/9/1904	**Dublin 2-8 London 0-4** Cork

Donegal, Galway, Leitrim and Sligo did not enter the 1903 Championship.

Connacht	*Final*	10/4/1904	**Mayo 0-4 Roscommon 1-2** Claremorris

Leinster

First Round
- 24/7/1904 **Wicklow 1-2 Wexford 0-11** Enniscorthy
- 31/7/1904 **Longford 0-6 Westmeath 0-7** Mullingar
- 21/8/1904 **Offaly 0-2 Laois 1-5** Maryborough
- 4/9/1904 **Louth 0-7 Meath 0-2** Dundalk
- 18/9/1904 **Dublin 1-3 Kildare 3-11** Geashill
- **Kilkenny** w/o **Carlow**

Second Round
- 9/10/1904 **Kilkenny 1-13 Westmeath 0-0** Jones' Road
- 15/10/1904 **Louth 1-6 Wexford 0-1** Jones' Road
- 23/10/1904 **Kildare 4-5 Laois 0-1** Maryborough

Semi-final
- 12/11/1904 **Kilkenny 1-4 Louth 0-1** Jones' Road
- **Kildare** *bye*

Final
- 11/12/1904 **Kildare 1-2 Kilkenny 0-5** Wexford
- 26/2/1905 **Kildare 1-6 Kilkenny 1-5** Wexford
- 4/6/1905 **Kildare 0-9 Kilkenny 0-1** Jones' Road

Munster

First Round
- 1/5/1904 **Clare 1-5 Limerick 0-3** Limerick
- 13/6/1904 **Kerry 4-8 Waterford 1-3** Turners Cross
- 19/6/1904 **Cork 1-5 Tipperary 0-4** Killmallock

Semi-final
- 7/8/1904 **Kerry 2-7 Clare 2-0** Market's Field
- **Cork** *bye*

Final
- 30/10/1904 **Kerry 1-7 Cork 0-3** Market's Field

Ulster

First Round
- 1/1/1905 **Tyrone** w/o **Derry** Dungannon
- 6/1/1905 **Monaghan 0-4 Fermanagh 0-1** Enniskillen
- 19/1/1905 **Monaghan** w/o **Fermanagh**
- 22/1/1905 **Cavan 0-5 Antrim 0-2** Cavan
- 17/3/1905 **Antrim 0-3 Cavan 0-5** Cavan
- 29/1/1905 **Armagh 0-15 Down 0-1** Newry
- 19/2/1905 **Armagh 0-12 Tyrone 0-2** Coalisland

Semi-final
- 17/3/1905 **Armagh 3-14 Tyrone 0-1** Armagh
- 17/3/1905 **Cavan 1-8 Monaghan 0-3** Newbliss

Final
- 23/4/1905 **Cavan 0-5 Armagh 0-5** Armagh
- 28/5/1905 **Cavan 0-5 Armagh 0-5** Cavan
- 11/6/1905 **Cavan 0-8 Armagh 0-4** Newbliss

All-Ireland

Semi-final	7/5/1905	**Kerry 2-7 Mayo 0-4** Limerick
	18/6/1905	**Kildare 0-8 Cavan 0-0** Jones' Road
'Irish'	23/7/1905	**Kerry 1-4 Kildare 1-3** Tipperary
	27/8/1905	**Kerry 0-7 Kildare 1-4** Cork
Final	15/10/1905	**Kerry 0-8 Kildare 0-2** Cork
Final	12/11/1905	**Kerry 0-11 London 0-3** Jones' Road

1904

Carlow, Leitrim, Longford, Sligo, Westmeath and Wicklow did not enter the 1904 Championship. Confusion over the format of the Ulster Championship meant that, as the Donegal/Derry tie was initially listed as a semi-final, Derry then refused to travel to meet Monaghan in a play-off for a place in the final.

Connacht	*Semi-final*	26/3/1905	**Mayo 0-7 Galway 0-4** Claremorris
	Final	23/4/1905	**Mayo 3-6 Roscommon 0-1** Claremorris
Leinster	*First Round*	21/1/1906	**Offaly 2-1 Louth 1-5** Jones' Road
		11/2/1906	**Wexford 0-6 Meath 0-5** Jones' Road
		25/3/1906	**Wexford 2-4 Meath 2-4** Athy
		22/4/1906	**Wexford 0-8 Meath 0-3** Athy
		18/2/1906	**Laois 0-5 Kilkenny 0-6** Kilkenny
		18/3/1906	**Dublin 0-9 Kildare 0-5** Jones' Road
	Semi-final	1/4/1906	**Dublin 0-11 Louth 0-6** Dundalk
		20/5/1906	**Wexford 0-3 Kilkenny 0-6** Jones' Road
	Final	17/6/1906	**Dublin 0-5 Kilkenny 0-1** Wexford
Munster	*First Round*	11/6/1905	**Waterford 1-11 Tipperary 0-6** Ck-on-Suir
		30/7/1905	**Limerick 0-6 Clare 0-8** Limerick
	Semi-final	1/10/1905	**Clare 0-6 Waterford 2-10** Tipperary
		29/10/1905	**Kerry 1-4 Cork 0-0** Market's Field
	Final	10/12/1905	**Kerry 0-3 Waterford 0-3** Cork
		7/1/1906	**Kerry 2-3 Waterford 0-2** Dungarvan
Ulster	*First Round*	12/2/1906	**Tyrone 0-2 Derry 1-3** Derry
	Second Round	22/10/1905	**Cavan 0-4 Fermanagh 0-1** Newbliss
		5/11/1905	**Antrim 1-11 Down 1-1** Banbridge
		3/12/1905	**Monaghan 1-13 Armagh 1-2** Monaghan
		17/3/1906	**Derry 0-18 Donegal 0-2** Derry
	Semi-final	11/2/1906	**Antrim 0-1 Cavan 0-10** Cavan
		16/4/1906	**Antrim 0-1 Cavan 1-6** Clones
		6/5/1906	**Monaghan** w/o **Derry** Castleblaney
	Final	24/5/1906	**Cavan 0-7 Monaghan 0-3** Clones
All-Ireland	*Semi-final*	6/5/1906	**Kerry 4-10 Cavan 0-1** Jones' Road
		13/5/1906	**Dublin 0-8 Mayo 1-4** Jones' Road
	Final	1/7/1906	**Kerry 0-5 Dublin 0-2** Cork

1905

Due to the delay in completing the 1904 Ulster Championship, the 1904 and 1905 titles were awarded to Cavan for defeating Monaghan in the 1904 final. Carlow, Longford, Westmeath and Wicklow did not enter the 1905 Championship. The GAA now had the Champions of England join in the first 'All-Ireland' round rather than in the final ('England' was always represented by London). Scotland were also included but Glasgow gave Cavan a walkover.

Connacht

First Round	8/4/1906	**Mayo** w/o **Leitrim** Claremorris
Semi-final	8/4/1906	**Roscommon 0-8 Galway 0-3** Claremorris
	29/4/1906	**Mayo 1-7 Sligo 0-2** Claremorris
Final	27/5/1906	**Roscommon 0-7 Mayo 0-5** Tuam

Leinster

First Round	8/7/1906	**Kilkenny 2-7 Laois 1-4** Athy
	22/7/1906	**Louth 1-8 Wexford 1-1** Jones' Road
	19/8/1906	**Kildare 0-6 Dublin 0-2** Athy
	2/9/1906	**Offaly 0-8 Meath 0-1** Jones' Road
	19/8/1906	**Kilkenny 0-5 Louth 0-5** Jones' Road
Semi-final	28/10/1906	**Kilkenny 0-6 Louth 1-1** Jones' Road
	14/10/1906	**Kildare 1-6 Offaly 0-6** Geashill
Final	6/1/1907	**Kildare 0-12 Louth 1-7** Jones' Road

Munster

First Round	13/5/1906	**Cork 3-8 Waterford 0-5** Dungarvan
	29/7/1906	**Limerick 0-6 Clare 0-4** Tipperary
	27/8/1906	**Kerry 5-8 Tipperary 1-4** Cork
Semi-final	20/1/1907	**Kerry 1-7 Cork 0-5** Cork
		Limerick *bye*
Final	7/4/1907	**Kerry 2-10 Limerick 1-6** Tralee

Ulster

Cavan w/o

All-Ireland

First Round	5/8/1906	**Dublin 1-9 London 1-4** Jones' Road
	5/8/1906	**Cavan** w/o **Glasgow** Belfast
	2/9/1906	**Kerry 2-10 Roscommon 1-3** Limerick
Semi-final	30/9/1906	**Kildare 4-15 Cavan 1-6** Jones' Road
		Kerry *bye*
Final	16/6/1907	**Kildare 1-7 Kerry 0-5** Thurles

1906

Carlow, Longford, Tyrone, Westmeath and Wicklow did not enter the 1906 Championship. As the Leinster-Ulster quarter-final took place before the provincial finals, Kildare represented Leinster and Monaghan was nominated by Ulster. Subsequently Dublin won the Leinster Championship and replaced Kildare for the semi-final.

Connacht

First Round	3/2/1907	**Roscommon 5-6 Leitrim 0-3** Longford
	7/4/1907	**Mayo 2-16 Galway 0-1** Claremorris
Semi-final	21/4/1907	**Roscommon 3-6 Sligo 1-3** Ballaghadereen
		Mayo *bye*
Final	26/5/1907	**Mayo 2-13 Roscommon 0-5** Tuam

Leinster

First Round	3/3/1907	**Dublin 1-9 Kilkenny 0-5** Enniscorthy
	31/3/1907	**Offaly 0-6 Wexford 1-6** Jones' Road
	14/4/1907	**Louth 2-18 Laois 0-4** Jones' Road
	14/4/1907	**Meath 0-2 Kildare 0-8** Jones' Road
Semi-final	29/4/1907	**Kildare 0-13 Wexford 0-1** Athy
	5/5/1907	**Dublin 0-8 Louth 0-6** Navan
Final	7/7/1907	**Dublin 1-9 Kildare 0-8** Kilkenny

Munster

First Round	12/5/1907	**Kerry 2-8 Clare 0-1** Market's Field
	23/6/1907	**Tipperary 0-6 Limerick 0-6** Cork
	7/7/1907	**Tipperary 1-9 Limerick 0-2** Fermoy
Semi-final	19/5/1907	**Cork 2-7 Waterford 1-2** Dungarvan
	21/7/1907	**Kerry 0-7 Tipperary 0-3** Market's Field
Final	18/8/1907	**Cork 1-10 Kerry 0-3** Tipperary

Ulster

First Round	28/4/1907	**Monaghan 2-4 Cavan 0-5** Cootehill
	6/5/1907	**Down 1-6 Armagh 0-4** Newry
	16/6/1907	**Antrim 1-8 Down 0-9** Newry
	23/6/1907	**Derry 0-18 Donegal 0-2** Derry
Semi-final	7/7/1907	**Monaghan 0-10 Fermanagh 1-4** Newbliss
	18/8/1907	**Antrim 1-14 Derry 0-4** Belfast
Final	25/8/1907	**Monaghan 2-10 Antrim 1-2** Clones

All-Ireland

First Round	19/5/1907	**Kildare 2-10 Monaghan 1-3** Shaun's Park
Semi-final	4/8/1907	**Dublin 2-7 London 0-3** Wexford
	8/9/1907	**Cork 0-10 Mayo 0-6** Limerick
Final	20/10/1907	**Dublin 0-5 Cork 0-4** Athy

1907

Carlow, Laois, Longford and Westmeath did not enter the 1907 Championship. The provincial winners for England and Scotland were drawn to play in the first round of the All-Ireland stage. As the Ulster Championship had not been completed Monaghan was nominated to represent Ulster. While the first round of the Ulster Championship for 1907 took place in December 1907, it was not completed until 1908 and was awarded as the 1908 Championship. Technically, then no 1907 Ulster Championship was awarded. Mayo was nominated to represent Connacht in the All-Ireland semi-final.

Connacht

First Round	3/5/1908	**Sligo 0-3 Leitrim 0-1** Mohill	
	12/7/1908	**Mayo 3-6 Galway 0-1** Tuam	
Semi-final	27/9/1908	**Mayo 1-16 Sligo 1-3** Sligo	
		Roscommon *bye*	
Final	31/1/1909	**Mayo 2-5 Roscommon 0-4** Tuam	

Leinster

First Round	22/9/1907	**Louth 1-14 Wicklow 0-5** Jones' Road
	8/12/1907	**Dublin 0-11 Kildare 0-7** Jones' Road
	8/12/1907	**Offaly 1-17 Wexford 0-2** Jones' Road
	15/3/1908	**Kilkenny 1-5 Meath 1-9** Jones' Road
Semi-final	31/1/1908	**Dublin 2-6 Louth 0-6** Jones' Road
	5/4/1908	**Meath 0-4 Offaly 1-6** Jones' Road
Final	26/4/1908	**Dublin 1-11 Offaly 0-4** Athy

Munster

First Round	8/12/1907	**Cork 2-5 Limerick 0-2** Limerick
	15/3/1908	**Kerry 4-6 Clare 0-2** Market's Field
Semi-final	29/3/1908	**Cork 1-9 Kerry 0-6** Market's Field
	29/3/1908	**Tipperary 1-14 Waterford 0-3** Carrick-on-Suir
Final	26/4/1908	**Cork 1-7 Tipperary 1-1** Dungarvan

Ulster

Not awarded

All-Ireland

First Round	15/3/1908	**Dublin 1-5 Monaghan 0-2** Jones' Road	
	19/4/1908	**England** w/o **Scotland** London	
	10/5/1908	**Cork 2-10 Mayo 0-2** Limerick	
Semi-final	7/6/1908	**Cork 1-14 London 1-5** Cork	
		Dublin *bye*	
Final	5/7/1908	**Dublin 0-6 Cork 0-2** Tipperary	

Carlow, Longford, Westmeath and Wicklow did not enter the 1908 Championship. The winners of England and Scotland were now drawn in a 'semi-final' to determine who would play the winner of the 'Irish' final (there was a plan to also include an 'Irish-America' team that never took place). The Connacht Championship had now fallen further behind and the draw for 1908 wasn't made until the Provincial Council meeting in May 1909. Even then there were long delays between games.

Connacht

First Round	20/6/1909	**Mayo** w/o **Roscommon** Claremorris
	20/3/1910	**Sligo 1-3 Leitrim 0-3** Carrick-on-Shannon
Semi-final	28/8/1910	**Sligo 1-7 Galway 2-5** Sligo
		Mayo *bye*
Final	30/10/1910	**Mayo 1-4 Galway 0-3** Ballina

Leinster

	27/9/1908	**Dublin 1-9 Meath 0-1** Jones' Road
	27/9/1908	**Wexford 0-10 Laois 2-9** Jones' Road
First Round	11/10/1908	**Louth 2-7 Kilkenny 1-10** Jones' Road
	1/11/1908	**Louth 0-11 Kilkenny 0-6** Jones' Road
	11/10/1908	**Offaly 0-0 Kildare 0-0** Jones' Road
	1/11/1908	**Offaly 0-1 Kildare 2-13** Jones' Road
Semi-final	18/10/1908	**Dublin 0-13 Laois 0-7** Jones' Road
	15/11/1908	**Kildare 0-5 Louth 0-5** Jones' Road
	29/11/1908	**Kildare 1-6 Louth 1-5** Jones' Road
Final	13/12/1908	**Dublin 1-7 Kildare 0-3** Athy

Munster

First Round	2/8/1908	**Cork 0-16 Limerick 0-3** Ennis
	27/9/1908	**Waterford 0-13 Tipperary 2-4** Fermoy
Semi-final	26/7/1908	**Kerry 1-8 Clare 0-3** Listowel
	18/10/1908	**Cork 1-5 Waterford 1-7** Mallow
Final	6/12/1908	**Kerry 0-7 Waterford 0-2** Cork

Ulster

		Derry Donegal *not played*
	15/12/1907	**Antrim 0-4 Down 0-4** Newry
First Round	2/2/1908	**Antrim 0-9 Down 0-5** Newry
	22/12/1907	**Fermanagh** w/o **Monaghan**
	16/2/1908	**Cavan** w/o **Tyrone**
		Armagh *bye*
Semi-final	6/6/1908	**Antrim 0-12 Armagh 0-6** Armagh
	21/6/1908	**Cavan 0-7 Fermanagh 0-2** Enniskillen
Final	13/9/1908	**Antrim 1-8 Cavan 0-4** Clones

All-Ireland	*'Irish'*	14/2/1909	**Kerry 2-4 Mayo 0-1** Limerick
	Semi-final	21/2/1909	**Dublin 1-8 Antrim 0-2** Jones' Road
	'Irish' Final	9/5/1909	**Dublin 0-10 Kerry 0-3** Thurles
	Semi-final	21/3/1909	**England w/o Scotland** Glasgow **Dublin** *bye*
	Final	1/8/1909	**Dublin 1-10 London 0-4** Jones' Road

1909

Carlow, Donegal, Longford, Westmeath and Wicklow did not enter the 1909 Championship. The Ulster Championship was re-organised after Cavan and Down failed to meet. Down was drawn against the winners of Antrim/Monaghan (but did not field in the end). For the All-Ireland semi-finals Leinster nominated Louth and Ulster nominated Antrim.

Connacht	First Round	20/3/1910	**Sligo 1-3 Leitrim 0-3** Carrick-on-Shannon
	Semi-final	20/6/1909	**Mayo** w/o **Roscommon** Claremorris
		28/8/1910	**Sligo 1-7 Galway 2-5** Sligo
	Final	30/10/1910	**Mayo 1-4 Galway 0-3** Ballina
Leinster	First Round	16/5/1909	**Offaly 1-4 Kildare 1-9** Maryborough
		23/5/1909	**Laois 0-5 Kilkenny 3-17** Kilkenny
		13/6/1909	**Dublin 0-18 Wexford 0-6** Wexford
		11/7/1909	**Louth 0-7 Meath 0-5** Navan
	Semi-final	12/9/1909	**Louth 1-11 Dublin 1-8** Dundalk
		3/10/1909	**Kilkenny** w/o **Kildare**
	Final	24/10/1909	**Louth 2-9 Kilkenny 0-4** Jones' Road
Munster	First Round	20/6/1909	**Limerick 0-12 Clare 0-9** Ennis
		4/7/1909	**Kerry 2-10 Tipperary 0-5** Fermoy
	Semi-final	11/7/1909	**Cork 2-7 Waterford 0-3** Dungarvan
		1/8/1909	**Kerry 2-18 Limerick 1-2** Listowel
	Final	19/9/1909	**Kerry 2-8 Cork 1-7** Market's Field
		7/11/1909	**Kerry 1-6 Cork 0-6** Cork
Ulster	First Round	28 Mar 1909	**Monaghan 2-1 Armagh 0-4** Castleblayney
		1/8/1909	**Monaghan 1-7 Armagh 0-3** Castleblayney
		4/4/1909	**Antrim** w/o **Derry**
		22/8/1909	**Fermanagh 2-4 Tyrone 1-6** Clones
		12/9/1909	**Antrim 0-10 Monaghan 0-6** Clones
	Second Round		**Çavan** *bye*
			Down *bye*
			Fermanagh *bye*
	Semi-final	17/10/1909	**Cavan 0-6 Fermanagh 0-1** Belturbet
		7/11/1909	**Antrim** w/o **Down** Shaun's Park
	Final	28/11/1909	**Antrim 1-9 Cavan 0-5** Clones
All-Ireland	Semi-final	10/10/1909	**Louth 2-13 Antrim 0-15** Shaun's Park
		21/11/1909	**Kerry 2-12 Mayo 0-6** Ennis
	Final	5/12/1909	**Kerry 1-9 Louth 0-6** Jones' Road

Carlow, Donegal, Down, Limerick, Longford, Waterford and Westmeath did not enter the 1910 Championship. The English provincial champions were included and drawn against Leinster for the All–Ireland first round. Scotland were also drawn to face Ulster in the first round (but Glasgow did not field). No score is available for the Clare/Limerick tie. In April 1910 the GAA introduced a number of rule changes: goal posts were now to be 16 feet high and 21 feet apart with a cross bar at 8 feet; nets were to be used; players now had to wear numbered jerseys.

Connacht	First Round	6/11/1910	**Leitrim 0-3 Sligo 0-0** Carrick-on-Shannon
	Semi-final	26/3/1911	**Galway 0-5 Leitrim 0-3** Athlone
		16/7/1911	**Mayo 0-5 Roscommon 0-6** Athlone
	Final	7/10/1911	**Galway 1-3 Roscommon 1-2** Athlone
Leinster	First Round	12/6/1910	**Dublin 1 11 Wicklow 0-5** Jones' Road
		19/6/1910	**Offaly 1-9 Kilkenny 0-5** Maryborough
		3/7/1910	**Louth 3-12 Kildare 0-10** Jones' Road
		3/7/1910	**Wexford 2-11 Laois 0-2** Jones' Road
	Second Round	24/7/1910	**Louth 3-11 Meath 1-3** Dundalk
		4/9/1910	**Dublin 1-6 Wexford 0-10** Jones' Road
			Offaly *bye*
	Semi-final	25/9/1910	**Offaly 1-0 Dublin 3-7** Jones' Road
			Louth *bye*
	Final	16/10/1910	**Louth 0-3 Dublin 0-0** Navan
Munster	First Round	12/6/1910	**Kerry 2-13 Waterford 0-1** Cork
		17/7/1910	**Cork 2-10 Tipperary 0-3** Dungarvan
		28/8/1910	**Clare** w/o **Limerick** Ennis
	Semi-final	2/10/1910	**Kerry 3-1 Clare 0-0** Limerick
			Cork *bye*
	Final	30/10/1910	**Kerry 0-4 Cork 0-2** Cork
Ulster	First Round	1/5/1910	**Cavan 0-2 Fermanagh 0-2** Belturbet
		3/7/1910	**Cavan 1-9 Fermanagh 0-5** Belturbet
		1/5/1910	**Monaghan 0-10 Armagh 1-7** Castleblayney
		3/7/1910	**Monaghan 1-5 Armagh 0-4** Crossmaglen
		3/7/1910	**Tyrone** w/o **Derry** Dungannon
		17/7/1910	**Cavan 1-9 Tyrone 1-4** Bundoran
	Semi-final	4/9/1910	**Antrim 1-4 Monaghan 1-3** Armagh
		27/11/1910	**Antrim 1-2 Monaghan 0-3** Dundalk
	Final	18/6/1911	**Antrim 3-4 Cavan 0-1** Dundalk

All-Ireland	First Round	11/9/1910	**Louth 2-4 London 2-2** Dundalk
			Antrim w/o **Glasgow**
	Semi-final	21/8/1910	**Kerry 1-7 Mayo 0-4** Tuam
		2/10/1910	**Dublin 3-5 Antrim 1-2** Jones' Road
	Final		**Louth** w/o **Kerry**

1911

There was no Connacht or Ulster Championship in 1911 and Longford and Westmeath did not enter the Championship. GAA Congress ruled (in April 1911) that any 1910 provincial championship that hadn't been completed by 1st June 1911 was also to be considered as the 1911 championship. Thus Antrim and Galway, by winning the finals of their 1910 provincial championships after April 1911 were also deemed to have won the 1911 championships.

Connacht — Galway w/o

Leinster

First Round	11/6/1911	Kilkenny 3-0 Wexford 0-1 Waterford
	9/7/1911	Louth 4-10 Offaly 1-1 Jones' Road
	16/7/1911	Meath 2-2 Laois 1-3 Jones' Road
	16/7/1911	Kildare 2-6 Wicklow 1-3 Jones' Road
Second Round	30/7/1911	Dublin 3-2 Louth 1-4 Navan
	13/8/1911	Kilkenny 1-2 Kildare 0-2 Maryborough
		Meath bye
Semi-final	20/8/1911	Meath 1-3 Dublin 0-2 Jones' Road
		Kilkenny bye
Final	22/10/1911	Kilkenny 2-4 Meath 1-2 Jones' Road

Munster

First Round	21/5/1911	Waterford 2-9 Clare 0-2 Tipperary
	2/7/1911	Kerry 2-4 Limerick 0-1 Market's Field
Semi-final	9/7/1911	Cork 3-3 Tipperary 0-1 Kilmallock
	27/8/1911	Waterford 1-2 Kerry 0-1 Mallow
Final	29/10/1911	Cork 2-5 Waterford 0-1 Dungarvan

Ulster — Antrim w/o

All-Ireland

Semi-final	3/12/1911	Cork 3-4 Galway 0-2 Portlaoise
	10/12/1911	Antrim 3-1 Kilkenny 1-1 Jones' Road
Final	14/1/1912	Cork 6-6 Antrim 1-2 Jones' Road

1912

Carlow, Derry, Donegal, Longford, Tyrone and Westmeath did not enter the 1912 Championship. No score is available for the Down/Armagh tie.

Connacht

First Round	9/6/1912	**Leitrim w/o Sligo** Carrick-on-Shannon
	21/7/1912	**Mayo 0-3 Galway 4-4** Roscommon
Semi-final	1/9/1912	**Roscommon 0-3 Leitrim 0-1** Ck-on-Shn
		Galway *bye*
Final	15/9/1912	**Roscommon 0-2 Galway 0-0** Castlerea

Leinster

First Round	16/6/1912	**Laois 0-2 Dublin 2-2** Maryborough
	23/6/1912	**Kildare 0-2 Louth 1-1** Jones' Road
	23/6/1912	**Kilkenny 1-4 Meath 0-3** Jones' Road
	14/7/1912	**Wicklow 4-4 Wexford 1-3** New Ross
		Offaly *bye*
Second Round	14/7/1912	**Dublin 2-3 Kilkenny 2-3** Athy
	11/8/1912	**Dublin 3-4 Kilkenny 0-1** Jones' Road
	4/8/1912	**Louth 1-2 Offaly 0-1** Jones' Road
		Wicklow *bye*
Semi-final	22/9/1912	**Dublin 1-4 Wicklow 0-0** Wexford
		Louth *bye*
Final	20/10/1912	**Louth 1-2 Dublin 1-1** Navan

Munster

First Round	23/6/1912	**Kerry 2-3 Cork 0-1** Tralee
	30/6/1912	**Waterford 0-5 Limerick 0-1** Waterford
Semi-final	21/7/1912	**Clare 2-2 Tipperary 1-0** Tipperary
	15/9/1912	**Kerry 1-4 Waterford 0-1** Fermoy
Final	20/10/1912	**Kerry 0-3 Clare 0-1** Ennis

Ulster

First Round	12/5/1912	**Antrim 3-1 Monaghan 0-5** Clones
	26/5/1912	**Cavan 2-2 Fermanagh 0-2** Wattlebridge
	2/6/1912	**Armagh w/o Down** Crossmaglen
Semi-final	14/7/1912	**Cavan 0-1 Armagh 0-1** Newbliss
	4/8/1912	**Cavan 1-2 Armagh 1-1** Newbliss
		Antrim *bye*
Final	10/11/1912	**Antrim 2-2 Armagh 0-1** Castleblayney

All-Ireland

Semi-final	25/8/1912	**Antrim 3-5 Kerry 0-2** Jones' Road
	29/9/1912	**Dublin 2-4 Roscommon 1-1** Jones' Road
Final	3/11/1912	**Louth 1-7 Antrim 1-2** Jones' Road

1913

Carlow, Derry, Donegal, Kildare, Kilkenny, Longford, Westmeath and Wicklow did not enter the 1913 Championship. Tyrone withdrew from the semi-final of the Ulster Championship.

Connacht

First Round	15/6/1913	**Sligo 2-1 Leitrim 1-1** Boyle
Semi-final	13/7/1913	**Galway 1-6 Roscommon 0-2** Athenry
	10/8/1913	**Sligo 1-2 Mayo 3-4** Sligo
Final	28/9/1913	**Galway 1-2 Mayo 0-3** Castlerea

Leinster

First Round	6/7/1913	**Dublin 2-2 Kildare 2-1** Jones' Road
	6/7/1913	**Laois 1-1 Wicklow 0-2** Jones' Road
	20/7/1913	**Louth 2-5 Kilkenny 0-1** Jones' Road
	20/7/1913	**Meath 1-4 Offaly 0-3** Jones' Road
Second Round	10/8/1913	**Wexford 1-4 Laois 1-3** Jones' Road
	17/8/1913	**Louth 2-3 Meath 0-2** Dundalk
		Dublin bye
Semi final	24/8/1913	**Wexford 2-3 Dublin 1-0** Wexford
		Louth bye
Final	21/9/1913	**Wexford 2-3 Louth 2-2** Jones' Road

Munster

First Round	25/5/1913	**Kerry 2-2 Clare 0-1** Ennis
	22/6/1913	**Tipperary 2-4 Waterford 1-1** Thurles
	24/8/1913	**Cork 3-3 Limerick 0-3** Tipperary
Semi-final	31/8/1913	**Kerry 0-2 Tipperary 0-2** Cork
	12/10/1913	**Kerry 0-5 Tipperary 1-0** Fermoy
Final	26/10/1913	**Kerry 1-6 Cork 0-1** Cork

Ulster

First Round	15/6/1913	**Antrim 1-6 Down 0-3** Belfast
	15/6/1913	**Monaghan 2-0 Cavan 1-3** Cavan
	20/7/1913	**Monaghan 0-3 Cavan 0-2** Cootehill
	22/6/1913	**Fermanagh 1-3 Armagh 1-1** Monaghan
		Tyrone bye
Semi-final	31/8/1913	**Antrim 1-6 Fermanagh 1-3** Clones
		Monaghan bye
Final	21/9/1913	**Antrim 2-1 Monaghan 1-2** Newbliss

All-Ireland

First Round	4/8/1913	**Louth 3-6 London 1-2** Kensal Rise, London
Semi-final	5/10/1913	**Wexford 4-4 Antrim 0-1** Jones' Road
	9/11/1913	**Kerry 1-8 Galway 0-1** Portlaoise
Final	14/12/1913	**Kerry 2-2 Wexford 0-3** Jones' Road

1914

Donegal, Longford and Westmeath did not enter the 1914 Championship.

Connacht

First Round	2/8/1914	**Roscommon 2-3 Mayo 1-3** Castlerea	
Semi-final	12/7/1914	**Leitrim 5-7 Sligo 0-2** Boyle	
	20/9/1914	**Roscommon 4-3 Galway 0-1** Castlebar	
Final	11/10/1914	**Roscommon 1-2 Leitrim 0-1** Boyle	

Leinster

First Round	7/6/1914	**Dublin 0-5 Carlow 0-1** Maryborough
	14/6/1914	**Laois 1-4 Kildare 0-5** Croke Park
	14/6/1914	**Offaly 0-2 Louth 3-9** Croke Park
	21/6/1914	**Wicklow 0-2 Kilkenny 1-2** New Ross
	21/6/1914	**Wexford 2-4 Meath 1-1** Croke Park
Second Round	5/7/1914	**Louth 5-3 Laois 0-3** Croke Park
	12/7/1914	**Wexford 1-5 Kilkenny 0-3** New Ross
		Dublin *bye*
Semi-final	26/7/1914	**Wexford 4-6 Dublin 1-1** Kilkenny
		Louth *bye*
Final	16/8/1914	**Wexford 3-6 Louth 0-1** Croke Park

Munster

First Round	7/6/1914	**Tipperary 4-4 Limerick 0-4** Waterford
	21/6/1914	**Kerry 3-6 Clare 2-0** Ennis
Semi-final	14/6/1914	**Cork 0-3 Waterford 0-2** Cork
	13/9/1914	**Kerry 2-3 Tipperary 0-2** Dungarvan
Final	4/10/1914	**Kerry 0-5 Cork 0-1** Tralee

Ulster

First Round	24/5/1914	**Armagh 2-5 Down 0-0** Newry
	21/6/1914	**Fermanagh 2-4 Tyrone 1-2** Clones
	21/6/1914	**Monaghan 3-2 Derry 0-3** Derry
	4/7/1914	**Cavan 2-3 Antrim 1-2** Clones
Semi-final	26/7/1914	**Fermanagh 2-1 Cavan 0-4** Clones
	2/8/1914	**Monaghan 0-0 Armagh 0-0** Carrickmacross
	16/8/1914	**Monaghan 1-1 Armagh 0-2** Culleville
Final	23/8/1914	**Monaghan 2-4 Fermanagh 0-2** Newbliss

All-Ireland

First Round	19/7/1914	**Wexford w/o London** Wexford
Semi-final	6/9/1914	**Kerry 2-4 Roscommon 0-1** Portlaoise
	13/9/1914	**Wexford 2-6 Monaghan 0-1** Croke Park
Final	14/11/1914	**Kerry 1-3 Wexford 2-0** Croke Park
	29/11/1914	**Kerry 2-3 Wexford 0-6** Croke Park

Derry, Donegal, Longford, Tyrone and Westmeath did not enter the 1915 Championship.

Connacht

First Round	4/7/1915	**Sligo 1-2 Leitrim 1-1** Carrick-on-Shannon
Semi-final	15/8/1915	**Roscommon 1-2 Sligo 0-1** Boyle
	12/9/1915	**Mayo 3-2 Galway 1-3** Athlone
Final	26/9/1915	**Roscommon 0-3 Mayo 3-1** Castlerea

Leinster

First Round	23/5/1915	**Kildare 1-6 Wicklow 1-2** Croke Park
	6/6/1915	**Dublin 1-2 Laois 1-2** Tullamore
	4/7/1915	**Dublin 1-8 Laois 0-2** Newbridge
	20/6/1915	**Offaly 2-5 Meath 0-4** Croke Park
	20/6/1915	**Louth 0-4 Carlow 0-1** Croke Park
	27/6/1915	**Wexford 0-9 Kilkenny 0-1** Waterford
Second Round	18/7/1915	**Wexford 1-7 Offaly 0-2** Croke Park
	8/8/1915	**Dublin 1-2 Kildare 0-1** Croke Park
		Louth *bye*
Semi-final	29/8/1915	**Dublin 2-2 Louth 0-3** Navan
		Wexford *bye*
Final	12/9/1915	**Wexford 2-2 Dublin 2-2** Croke Park
	10/10/1915	**Wexford 3-5 Dublin 1-3** Croke Park

Munster

First Round	19/4/1915	**Kerry 4-3 Limerick 0-2** Limerick
	9/5/1915	**Tipperary 2-3 Cork 1-1** Waterford
Semi-final	21/5/1915	**Clare 2-4 Waterford 1-2** Fermoy
	1/8/1915	**Kerry 1-6 Tipperary 0-2** Cork
Final	17/10/1915	**Kerry 4-3 Clare 0-1** Tipperary

Ulster

First Round	30/5/1915	**Cavan 1-3 Antrim 0-2** Wattlebridge
	18/7/1915	**Cavan 0-3 Antrim 0-1** Wattlebridge
	13/6/1915	**Fermanagh 1-2 Monaghan 1-1** Clones
	8/8/1915	**Monaghan 5-2 Fermanagh 2-0** Belturbet
	11/7/1915	**Armagh 1-7 Down 1-3** Newry
Semi-final	1/8/1915	**Cavan 0-9 Armagh 0-4** Newbliss
		Monaghan *bye*
Final	22/8/1915	**Cavan 2-5 Monaghan 3-2** Belturbet
	2/9/1915	**Cavan 0-4 Monaghan 0-3** Clones

All-Ireland

Semi-final	19/9/1915	**Kerry 2-3 Roscommon 1-1** Portlaoise
	17/10/1915	**Wexford 3-7 Cavan 2-2** Croke Park
Final	7/11/1915	**Wexford 2-4 Kerry 2-1** Croke Park

1916

Carlow, Donegal, Longford, Offaly, Tyrone and Wicklow did not enter the 1916 Championship. No score is available for the Antrim/Armagh game.

Connacht

First Round	13/8/1916	**Leitrim 2-2 Sligo 0-3** Boyle
Semi-final	27/8/1916	**Leitrim 0-2 Roscommon 1-2** Elphin
	3/9/1916	**Mayo 2-6 Galway 2-2** Athlone
Final	1/10/1916	**Mayo 1-5 Roscommon 0-3** Castlerea

Leinster

First Round	23/7/1916	**Meath 1-2 Laois 0-4** Croke Park
	23/7/1916	**Kildare 3-3 Louth 1-4** Croke Park
	6/8/1916	**Kilkenny 2-2 Westmeath 0-5** Maryborough
	3/9/1916	**Wexford** w/o **Dublin** Wexford
Semi-final	10/9/1916	**Kildare 1-6 Kilkenny 1-3** New Ross
	24/9/1916	**Wexford 6-5 Meath 1-2** Croke Park
Final	15/10/1916	**Wexford 1-7 Kildare 1-0** Croke Park

Munster

First Round	9/7/1916	**Kerry 2-2 Tipperary 0-1** Cork
	30/7/1916	**Clare 3-1 Limerick 0-0** Listowel
Semi-final	30/7/1916	**Cork 4-3 Waterford 2-4** Cork
		Clare w/o **Kerry**
Final	3/9/1916	**Cork 2-2 Clare 1-4** Clonmel

Ulster

First Round	25/6/1916	**Cavan 2-3 Fermanagh 0-1** Wattlebridge
	7/7/1916	**Monaghan 2-5 Derry 0-1** Clones
	23/7/1916	**Antrim** w/o **Armagh** Camlough
Semi-final	20/8/1916	**Monaghan 4-3 Cavan 1-5** Belturbet
	27/8/1916	**Antrim 1-3 Down 1-0** Portaferry
Final	24/9/1916	**Monaghan 2-3 Antrim 0-2** Clones

All-Ireland

Semi-final	22/10/1916	**Mayo 1-2 Cork 0-2** Athlone
	19/11/1916	**Mayo 1-2 Cork 1-1** Croke Park
	22/10/1916	**Wexford 0-9 Monaghan 1-1** Carrickmacross
Final	17/12/1916	**Wexford 3-4 Mayo 1-2** Croke Park

Donegal did not enter the 1917 Championship. In the Antrim/Down game the recorded score includes the total but does not state the number of goals/points scored.

Connacht

First Round	1/7/1917	**Roscommon 2-3 Leitrim 1-0** Elphin
Semi-final	5/8/1917	**Mayo 0-3 Sligo 0-0** Tubbercurry
	12/8/1917	**Galway 1-4 Roscommon 1-0** Mountbellew
Final	7/10/1917	**Galway 1-4 Mayo 1-1** Castlerea

Leinster

First Round	24/6/1917	**Louth 2-7 Meath 0-0** Navan
	1/7/1917	**Laois 2-7 Offaly 0-0** Tullamore
	1/7/1917	**Kilkenny 0-1 Carlow 1-0** Kilkenny
	8/7/1917	**Dublin 1-6 Kildare 2-1** Newbridge
	16/7/1917	**Wexford 6-4 Wicklow 0-2** Wexford
Second Round	5/8/1917	**Longford 2-2 Westmeath 4-5** Mostrim
	5/8/1917	**Louth 1-4 Dublin 0-14** Drogheda
	26/8/1917	**Laois 0-5 Carlow 0-1** Carlow
		Wexford *bye*
Semi-final	13/8/1917	**Wexford 1-7 Westmeath 0-1** Croke Park
	23/9/1917	**Dublin 0-5 Laois 0-2** Croke Park
Final	14/10/1917	**Wexford 1-3 Dublin 1-1** Croke Park

Munster

First Round	29/6/1917	**Tipperary** w/o **Kerry** Charleville
	15/7/1917	**Clare 2-6 Waterford 0-3** Waterford
Semi-final	8/7/1917	**Cork 1-1 Limerick 0-0** Market's Field
	26/8/1917	**Clare 0-5 Tipperary 0-4** Market's Field
Final	14/10/1917	**Clare 5-4 Cork 0-1** Tipperary

Ulster

First Round	13/5/1917	**Antrim 0-22 Down 0-4** Downpatrick
	13/5/1917	**Armagh 2-3 Tyrone 1-3** Armagh
	13/5/1917	**Cavan 3-5 Derry 2-1** Derry
	13/5/1917	**Monaghan 1-2 Fermanagh 1-0** Wattlebridge
Semi-final	17/6/1917	**Antrim 2-4 Armagh 1-5** Armagh
	12/8/1917	**Armagh 0-5 Antrim 0-3** Belfast
	1/7/1917	**Monaghan 3-1 Cavan 0-2** Cootehill
Final	28/10/1917	**Monaghan 4-2 Armagh 0-4** Clones

All-Ireland

Semi-final	18/11/1917	**Clare 2-1 Galway 0-5** Athlone
	18/11/1917	**Wexford 6-6 Monaghan 1-3** Wexford
Final	9/12/1917	**Wexford 0-9 Clare 0-5** Croke Park

Donegal did not enter the 1918 Championship. Leinster nominated Louth to play in the All-Ireland semi-final, but Wexford (the Leinster champions) took their place in the final.

Connacht	*First Round*	30/6/1918	**Roscommon 0-5 Leitrim 1-4** Elphin
	Semi-final	18/8/1918	**Mayo 1-6 Sligo 1-0** Swinford
		25/8/1918	**Galway 1-5 Leitrim 1-0** Elphin
	Final	22/9/1918	**Mayo 0-4 Galway 0-1** Castlerea
Leinster	*First Round*	26/5/1918	**Westmeath 3-3 Longford 0-3** Longford
	Second Round	26/5/1918	**Carlow 4-3 Wicklow 0-1** Ferns
		2/6/1918	**Wexford 2-6 Kilkenny 0-1** New Ross
		23/6/1918	**Westmeath 4-4 Offaly 1-2** Rochfortbridge
		30/6/1918	**Kildare 2-2 Laois 0-3** Maryborough
		14/7/1918	**Louth 1-4 Meath 1-3** Drogheda
			Dublin *bye*
	Third Round	8/9/1918	**Louth 3-5 Dublin 3-3** Drogheda
		20/10/1918	**Kildare 4-2 Westmeath 0-3** Croke Park
			Wexford *bye*
			Carlow *bye*
	Semi-final	22/9/1918	**Wexford 5-8 Carlow 2-2** Enniscorthy
		27/10/1918	**Louth 0-7 Kildare 0-1** Croke Parke
	Final	19/1/1919	**Wexford 2-5 Louth 1-4** Croke Park
Munster	*First Round*	2/6/1918	**Tipperary 1-5 Cork 0-2** Thurles
			Waterford w/o **Limerick**
	Semi-final	23/6/1918	**Tipperary 4-4 Waterford 0-0** Clonmel
		25/8/1918	**Kerry 5-3 Clare 1-3** Limerick
	Final	22/9/1918	**Tipperary 1-1 Kerry 0-1** Cork
Ulster	*First Round*	28/4/1918	**Antrim 4-1 Derry 2-4** Belfast
		5/5/1918	**Armagh 0-5 Down 0-4** Camlough
		26/5/1918	**Cavan 1-4 Fermanagh 1-2** Belturbet
		10/6/1918	**Monaghan 4-4 Tyrone 1-0** Armagh
	Semi-final	30/6/1918	**Antrim 1-2 Monaghan 0-3** Armagh
		17/8/1918	**Cavan 2-4 Armagh 0-0** Cootehill
	Final	15/9/1918	**Cavan 3-2 Antrim 0-0** Belturbet
All-Ireland	*Semi-final*	20/10/1918	**Louth 2-4 Cavan 0-4** Belturbet
		1/12/1918	**Tipperary 2-2 Mayo 1-4** Croke Park
	Final	16/2/1919	**Wexford 0-5 Tipperary 0-4** Croke Park

For the first time every county participated in the 1919 Championship.

Connacht

First Round	15/6/1919	**Sligo 1-1 Roscommon 3-1** Boyle
Semi-final	5/7/1919	**Galway 1-3 Mayo 1-2** Tuam
	13/7/1919	**Roscommon 1-6 Leitrim 0-1** Castlerea
Final	3/8/1919	**Galway 1-6 Roscommon 0-5** Tuam

Leinster

First Round	25/5/1919	**Westmeath 2-2 Longford 1-0** Edgeworthstn.
	25/5/1919	**Meath 2-5 Louth 2-5** Drogheda
	8/6/1919	**Meath 1-6 Louth 1-6** Navan
	15/6/1919	**Meath 1-5 Louth 1-4** Navan
	1/6/1919	**Wexford 0-6 Kilkenny 0-2** New Ross
	15/6/1919	**Wicklow 2-2 Carlow 2-1** Carlow
Second Round	1/6/1919	**Kildare 3-5 Laois 2-5** Newbridge
	15/6/1919	**Westmeath 0-3 Offaly 0-2** Tullamore
	13/7/1919	**Dublin 0-7 Meath 0-2** Navan
	13/7/1919	**Wicklow 0-1 Wexford 5-3** Enniscorthy
Semi-final	6/7/1919	**Westmeath 1-5 Kildare 4-3** Edenderry
	31/8/1919	**Dublin 0-11 Wexford 1-1** Croke Park
Final	7/9/1919	**Kildare 1-3 Dublin 1-2** Croke Park

Munster

First Round	18/5/1919	**Waterford 2-0 Cork 0-2** Dungarvan
	25/5/1919	**Kerry 2-4 Tipperary 2-3** Cork
Semi-final	22/6/1919	**Limerick 0-2 Clare 1-4** Ennis
	6/7/1919	**Kerry 3-5 Waterford 0-0** Tralee
Final	3/8/1919	**Kerry 6-11 Clare 2-0** Ennis

Ulster

First Round	25/5/1919	**Derry 2-4 Fermanagh 0-3** Wattlebridge
Second Round	18/5/1919	**Armagh 0-4 Monaghan 0-3** Castleblayney
	25/5/1919	**Donegal 4-3 Tyrone 1-0** Strabane
	1/6/1919	**Cavan 0-10 Down 1-0** Cavan
	1/6/1919	**Antrim 1-4 Derry 1-1** Derry
Semi-final	22/6/1919	**Antrim 2-4 Armagh 1-4** Armagh
	6/7/1919	**Cavan 3-11 Donegal 2-3** Bundoran
Final	31/8/1919	**Cavan 5-5 Antrim 0-2** Clones

All-Ireland

Semi-final	24/8/1919	**Galway 2-6 Kerry 3-3** Croke Park
	14/9/1919	**Galway 4-2 Kerry 2-2** Croke Park
	14/9/1919	**Kildare 3-2 Cavan 1-3** Navan
Final	28/9/1919	**Kildare 2-5 Galway 0-1** Croke Park

1920

Wicklow did not enter the 1920 Championship.

Connacht	*First Round*	4/7/1920	**Leitrim 3-3 Roscommon 0-2** Elphin
	Semi-final	18/7/1920	**Galway 0-3 Mayo 2-4** Castlerea
		8/8/1920	**Sligo 1-7 Leitrim 0-2** Elphin
	Final	22/8/1920	**Mayo 2-3 Sligo 1-4** Castlerea
Leinster	*First Round*	2/5/1920	**Westmeath 2-2 Longford 2-1** Mullingar
		9/5/1920	**Meath 0-1 Louth 1-4** Dundalk
		9/5/1920	**Kilkenny 0-3 Laois 2-1** Kilkenny
		9/5/1920	**Wicklow 1-7 Carlow 3-2** Tullow
		16/5/1920	**Dublin 3-3 Offaly 0-3** Maryborough
	Second Round	30/5/1920	**Laois 3-5 Carlow 2-2** Carlow
		13/6/1920	**Westmeath 0-6 Louth 0-3** Navan
		13/6/1920	**Wexford 1-2 Kildare 2-6** Croke Park
			Dublin *bye*
	Semi-final	27/6/1920	**Dublin 2-6 Laois 0-1** Croke Park
		15/8/1920	**Kildare 1-5 Westmeath 0-1** Croke Park
	Final	29/8/1920	**Dublin 1-3 Kildare 0-3** Croke Park
Munster	*First Round*	6/6/1920	**Clare 1-2 Tipperary 1-2** Limerick
		11/7/1920	**Clare 0-2 Tipperary 0-2** Limerick
		15/8/1920	**Clare 0-1 Tipperary 1-7** Clonmel
		13/6/1920	**Waterford 3-2 Limerick 1-1** Dungarvan
		20/6/1920	**Kerry 2-6 Cork 0-4** Cork
	Semi-final	19/2/1922	**Tipperary 3-4 Waterford 0-1** Dungarvan
			Kerry *bye*
	Final	9/4/1922	**Tipperary 2-2 Kerry 0-2** Cork
Ulster	*First Round*	23/5/1920	**Cavan 2-2 Monaghan 1-3** Clones
	Second Round	9/5/1920	**Down 3-1 Antrim 1-2** Newcastle
		16/5/1920	**Armagh 2-1 Tyrone 0-0** Dungannon
		23/5/1920	**Derry 0-11 Donegal 0-7** Derry
		13/6/1920	**Cavan 8-3 Fermanagh 2-1** Wattlebridge
	Semi-final	20/6/1920	**Armagh 0-4 Down 0-3**
		23/7/1920	**Cavan 3-4 Derry 0-1** Belturbet
	Final	8/8/1920	**Cavan 4-6 Armagh 1-4** Cootehill
All-Ireland	*Semi-final*	26/9/1920	**Dublin 3-6 Cavan 1-3** Navan
		7/5/1922	**Tipperary 1-5 Mayo 1-0** Croke Park
	Final	11/6/1922	**Tipperary 1-6 Dublin 1-2** Croke Park

There was no Munster Championship due to the War of Independence and Leitrim, Derry, Longford, Tyrone and Wicklow did not enter the 1921 Championship. The Connacht Championship started in 1921 but was re-drawn in 1922.

Connacht

First Round	20/11/1921	**Mayo 6-6 Roscommon 0-0** Castlerea
(re-drawn) Semi-final	18/6/1922	**Galway 0-1 Mayo 0-6** Tuam
	2/7/1922	**Roscommon w/o Sligo** Tubercurry
Final	25/3/1923	**Mayo 1-4 Roscommon 0-1** Castlerea

Leinster

First Round	1/5/1921	**Dublin 3-6 Meath 0-0** Croke Park
	1/5/1921	**Carlow w/o Offaly** Croke Park
	8/5/1921	**Laois 1-2 Kildare 2-3** Athy
	19/6/1921	**Louth 4-4 Westmeath 0-1** Drogheda
		Kilkenny *bye*
		Wexford *bye*
Second Round	12/6/1921	**Kildare 9-8 Carlow 1-1** Athy
		Wexford w/o Kilkenny
		Dublin *bye*
		Louth *bye*
Semi-final	10/7/1921	**Dublin 1-6 Louth 0-3** Croke Park
	31/7/1921	**Wexford 0-3 Kildare 2-7** Croke Park
Final	28/8/1921	**Dublin 0-6 Kildare 1-3** Croke Park
	18/9/1921	**Dublin 3-3 Kildare 1-2** Croke Park

Munster Not played

Ulster

First Round	13/6/1921	**Antrim 1-5 Down 1-2** Newcastle
	6/11/1921	**Monaghan 0-3 Armagh 0-1** Clones
	13/11/1921	**Derry 2-1 Donegal 0-3** Strabane
	27/11/1921	**Cavan 1-2 Fermanagh 0-0** Wattlebridge
	11/12/1921	**Derry 1-4 Antrim 0-3** Derry
Semi-final	11/12/1921	**Monaghan 0-8 Cavan 0-8** Clones
	22/1/1922	**Monaghan 2-2 Cavan 0-2** Clones
Final	28/10/1923	**Monaghan 2-2 Derry 0-1** Clones

All-Ireland

Semi-final	18/6/1922	**Dublin 2-8 Cavan 2-2** Dundalk
	29/4/1923	**Mayo w/o Tipperary** Croke Park
Final	17/6/1923	**Dublin 1-9 Mayo 0-2** Croke Park

1922

Carlow, Longford, Offaly, Tyrone, Westmeath and Wicklow did not enter the 1922 Championship. Sligo won their All-Ireland semi-final but when a replay of the Connacht Championship was ordered, they lost to Galway who then contested the All-Ireland final.

Connacht	*First Round*	6/5/1923	**Sligo 2-4 Roscommon 0-4** Ballaghadereen
	(re-drawn) Semi-final	22/7/1923	**Galway 3-3 Leitrim 0-3** Boyle
		19/8/1923	**Sligo 3-8 Mayo 2-5** Castlerea
	Final	2/9/1923	**Sligo 3-2 Galway 1-7** Tuam
		30/9/1923	**Galway 2-4 Sligo 1-5** Croke Park

Leinster	*First Round*	9/4/1922	**Dublin 1-5 Louth 0-2** Navan
		30/4/1922	**Kildare 2-5 Wexford 1-1** Croke Park
		28/5/1922	**Kilkenny 4-4 Laois 1-1** Kilkenny
			Meath *bye*
	Semi-final	4/6/1922	**Meath 1-2 Kilkenny 4-4** Croke Park
		1/10/1922	**Kildare 0-2 Dublin 2-5** Croke Park
	Final	5/11/1922	**Dublin 1-7 Kilkenny 0-2** Croke Park

Munster	*First Round*	22/4/1922	**Cork 1-7 Clare 0-2** Market's Field
			Tipperary w/o **Waterford** Clonmel
	Semi-final	20/5/1923	**Tipperary 2-3 Cork 2-2** Cork
			Limerick w/o **Kerry**
	Final	1/7/1923	**Tipperary 1-7 Limerick 0-1** Thurles

Ulster	*First Round*	7/5/1922	**Down 0-1 Armagh 2-4** Warrenpoint
		7/5/1922	**Monaghan 1-4 Antrim 1-3** Clones
		11/6/1922	**Donegal 1-1 Cavan 0-8** Bundoran
			Derry w/o **Fermanagh**
	Semi-final	16/7/1922	**Monaghan 2-9 Armagh 0-2** Ballybay
		13/8/1922	**Cavan 4-4 Derry 1-1** Cavan
	Final	22/4/1923	**Cavan 2-3 Monaghan 2-3** Clones
		20/5/1923	**Cavan 2-6 Monaghan 2-7** Belturbet

All-Ireland	*Semi-final*	15/7/1923	**Dublin 2-5 Monaghan 0-0** Dundalk
		9/9/1923	**Sligo 1-8 Tipperary 0-7** Croke Park
	Final	7/10/1923	**Dublin 0-6 Galway 0-4** Croke Park

1923

Carlow, Fermanagh, Longford, Offaly, Westmeath and Wicklow did not enter the 1923 Championship. Derry were disqualified from the Ulster Championship and Donegal re-instated.

Connacht

First Round	14/10/1923	**Leitrim 2-5 Roscommon 0-2** Boyle
(re-drawn)	28/10/1923	**Mayo 3-5 Sligo 1-2** Castlerea
Semi-final	13/4/1924	**Galway 1-3 Leitrim 1-0** Strokestown
Final	4/5/1924	**Mayo 0-3 Galway 0-2** Tuam

Leinster

First Round	15/4/1923	**Kilkenny 2-3 Kildare 2-1** Portlaoise
	22/4/1923	**Meath 1-4 Louth 0-2** Navan
	6/5/1923	**Laois 2-7 Wexford 1-4** Croke Park
		Dublin *bye*
Semi-final	24/6/1923	**Dublin 3-3 Laois 1 2** Croke Park
	8/7/1923	**Meath 3-1 Kilkenny 0-3** Croke Park
Final	12/8/1923	**Dublin 3-5 Meath 0-0** Croke Park

Munster

First Round	8/7/1923	**Cork 1-5 Waterford 2-1** Cork
	29/7/1923	**Kerry 4-5 Limerick 1-3** Limerick
Semi-final	22/7/1923	**Tipperary 4-8 Clare 1-2** Nenagh
	2/9/1923	**Kerry 3-4 Cork 0-3** Cork
Final	14/10/1923	**Kerry 0-5 Tipperary 0-3** Tralee

Ulster

First Round	8/7/1923	**Monaghan 4-1 Armagh 1-4** Ballybay
	10/6/1923	**Cavan 1-5 Antrim 0-4** Belturbet
	17/6/1923	**Derry 1-3 Donegal 1-2** Letterkenny
		Tyrone w/o **Down**
Semi-final	12/8/1923	**Cavan 4-10 Donegal 3-1** Bundoran
	19/8/1923	**Monaghan 3-6 Tyrone 0-3** Clones
Final	2/9/1923	**Cavan 5-10 Monaghan 1-1** Cavan

All-Ireland

Semi-final	27/4/1924	**Kerry 1-3 Cavan 1-2** Croke Park
	18/5/1924	**Dublin 1-6 Mayo 1-2** Croke Park
Final	28/9/1924	**Dublin 1-5 Kerry 1-3** Croke Park

Derry, Longford, Offaly, Westmeath and Wicklow did not enter the 1924 Championship.

Connacht	*First Round*	25/5/1924	**Roscommon 1-4 Sligo 0-2** Ballaghaderreen
	Semi-final	22/6/1924	**Mayo 0-2 Leitrim 0-2** Ballaghaderreen
		31/8/1924	**Mayo 3-1 Leitrim 1-2** Sligo
		6/7/1924	**Galway 2-4 Roscommon 1-2** Ballinasloe
		21/9/1924	**Galway 4-3 Roscommon 1-1** Castlerea
	Final	19/10/1924	**Mayo 0-1 Galway 0-1** Balla
		9/11/1924	**Mayo 2-6 Galway 0-5** Tuam
Leinster	*First Round*	6/4/1924	**Dublin 2-3 Meath 1-4** Navan
		13/4/1924	**Carlow 1-2 Wexford 4-1** New Ross
		20/4/1924	**Kildare 3-4 Laois 0-2** Athy
		11/5/1924	**Louth 3-4 Kilkenny 0-2** Croke Park
	Semi-final	7/9/1924	**Louth 2-4 Dublin 2-6** Navan
		21/9/1924	**Wexford 1-1 Kildare 0-1** Croke Park
	Final	19/10/1924	**Dublin 1-4 Wexford 1-4** Croke Park
		30/11/1924	**Dublin 3-5 Wexford 2-3** Croke Park
Munster	*First Round*	11/5/1924	**Kerry 5-3 Tipperary 1-5** Clonmel
		18/5/1924	**Cork 2-1 Waterford 0-0** Dungarvan
	Semi-final	11/5/1924	**Clare 0-6 Limerick 0-0** Kilkee
		7/9/1924	**Kerry 4-3 Cork 2-1** Cork
	Final	12/10/1924	**Kerry 5-8 Clare 2-2** Limerick
Ulster	*First Round*	18/5/1924	**Cavan 5-6 Armagh 1-6** Cootehill
		18/5/1924	**Tyrone 0-2 Donegal 0-1** Letterkenny
		25/5/1924	**Monaghan 4-6 Fermanagh 2-1** Clones
		1/6/1924	**Antrim 0-9 Down 0-5** Downpatrick
	Semi-final	22/6/1924	**Monaghan 1-5 Antrim 1-4** Ballybay
		24/8/1924	**Cavan 1-7 Tyrone 0-7** Belturbet
		31/8/1924	**Monaghan 1-4 Antrim 1-1** Carrickmacross
	Final	21/9/1924	**Cavan 1-3 Monaghan 0-6** Belturbet
		2/11/1924	**Cavan 2-3 Monaghan 1-3** Ballybay
All-Ireland	*Semi-final*	7/12/1924	**Kerry 1-4 Mayo 0-1** Croke Park
		18/1/1925	**Dublin 0-6 Cavan 1-1** Croke Park
	Final	16/4/1925	**Kerry 0-4 Dublin 0-3** Croke Park

1925

Derry, Offaly, Westmeath and Wicklow did not enter the 1925 Championship. Connacht nominated Mayo for the All-Ireland semi-final. After Mayo beat Wexford in the semi-final, the Connacht champions, Galway, were to play in the final. Kerry beat Cavan in the other semi-final but both teams were then disqualified. Rather than awarding the All-Ireland title by giving Galway a walkover in the final the GAA proposed then to re-play both semi-finals. However, Kerry refused to replay their semi-final against Cavan, so Cavan advanced to meet Galway in the final.

Connacht	*First Round*	17/5/1925	**Roscommon 2-4 Sligo 2-2** Boyle
		5/7/1925	**Roscommon 1-5 Sligo 1-5** Roscommon
		19/7/1925	**Roscommon 1-3 Sligo 0-6** Sligo
		26/7/1925	**Roscommon 2-0 Sligo 0-6** Boyle
		2/8/1925	**Roscommon 1-5 Sligo 1-3** Roscommon
		13/9/1925	**Roscommon 0-2 Sligo 2-3** Roscommon
		28/6/1925	**Galway 1-1 Leitrim 1-1** Castlerea
		2/8/1925	**Galway 1-4 Leitrim 2-1** Roscommon
		13/9/1925	**Galway 1-4 Leitrim 0-5** Roscommon
	Semi-final	4/10/1925	**Mayo 2-6 Sligo 1-6** Tuam
			Galway *bye*
	Final	18/10/1925	**Galway 1-5 Mayo 1-3** Tuam
Leinster	*First Round*	3/5/1925	**Longford 0-3 Kilkenny 2-4** Croke Park
		17/5/1925	**Kildare 5-8 Carlow 1-0** Athy
		24/5/1925	**Louth 4-2 Laois 3-3** Croke Park
		7/6/1925	**Wexford 4-9 Meath 0-2** Croke Park
	Second Round	5/7/1925	**Dublin 1-6 Wexford 2-4** Kilkenny
		12/7/1925	**Louth 0-7 Kilkenny 0-3** Croke Park
			Kildare *bye*
	Semi-final	2/8/1925	**Louth 0-5 Kildare 3-3** Croke Park
			Wexford *bye*
	Final	23/8/1925	**Wexford 2-7 Kildare 0-3** Croke Park

Munster	*First Round*	31/5/1925	**Kerry 1-2 Tipperary 0-4** Limerick
		28/6/1925	**Kerry 3-1 Tipperary 0-4** Cork
		19/7/1925	**Cork 1-3 Limerick 1-1** Buttevant
	Semi-final	14/6/1925	**Clare 2-2 Waterford 0-1** Miltown Malbay
		16/8/1925	**Kerry 3-8 Cork 1-0** Tralee
	Final	13/9/1925	**Kerry 5-5 Clare 0-0** Killarney

Ulster	*First Round*	3/5/1925	**Monaghan 1-3 Armagh 0-5** Castleblayney
		21/6/1925	**Monaghan 2-2 Armagh 1-4** Castleblayney
		10/5/1925	**Antrim 0-16 Down 0-1** Newry
		24/5/1925	**Cavan 1-5 Tyrone 1-3** Dungannon
		14/6/1925	**Fermanagh 0-1 Donegal 3-6** Ballyshannon
	Semi-final	5/7/1925	**Antrim 2-5 Monaghan 0-4** Newry
		19/7/1925	**Cavan 0-18 Donegal 0-2** Ballyshannon
	Final	2/8/1925	**Cavan 2-3 Antrim 3-0** Monaghan
		16/8/1925	**Cavan 3-6 Antrim 0-1** Belturbet

All-Ireland	*Semi-final*	23/8/1925	**Kerry 1-7 Cavan 2-3** Tralee
		30/8/1925	**Mayo 2-4 Wexford 1-4** Croke Park
	Semi-final	6/12/1925	**Galway 3-4 Wexford 1-1** Croke Park
			Cavan w/o **Kerry**
	Final	10/1/1926	**Galway 3-2 Cavan 1-2** Croke Park

142

1926

Offaly, Westmeath and Wicklow did not enter the 1926 Championship.

Connacht	First Round	30/5/1926	**Sligo 1-3 Mayo 2-6** Castlerea
	Semi-final	2/5/1926	**Galway 2-2 Roscommon 1-1** Roscommon
		13/6/1926	**Mayo 2-3 Leitrim 0-2** Sligo
	Final	11/7/1926	**Galway 3-2 Mayo 1-2** Roscommon

Leinster	First Round	9/5/1926	**Kilkenny 2-5 Longford 1-5** Longford
		9/5/1926	**Laois 2-8 Carlow 0-4** Tullow
		16/5/1926	**Wexford 0-7 Meath 0-3** Croke Park
		23/5/1926	**Kildare 6-7 Louth 1-5** Croke Park
	Second Round	20/6/1926	**Wexford 0-4 Kilkenny 0-1** New Ross
		20/6/1926	**Kildare 0-6 Dublin 1-3** Tullamore
		4/7/1926	**Kildare 2-5 Dublin 1-2** Portlaoise
			Laois *bye*
	Semi-final	18/7/1926	**Wexford 2-6 Laois 1-2** Kilkenny
			Kildare *bye*
	Final	21/8/1926	**Kildare 2-8 Wexford 1-5** Croke Park

Munster	First Round	9/5/1926	**Kerry 0-6 Clare 1-1** Milltown Malbay
		27/6/1926	**Cork 1-6 Waterford 1-1** Cork
	Semi-final	23/5/1926	**Tipperary 6-5 Limerick 0-1** Carrick-on-Suir
		18/7/1926	**Kerry 1-9 Cork 2-1** Listowel
	Final	25/7/1926	**Kerry 0-11 Tipperary 1-4** Cork

Ulster	First Round	9/5/1926	**Tyrone 3-8 Fermanagh 2-1** Omagh
	Second Round	9/5/1926	**Antrim 3-6 Armagh 1-8** Camlough
		16/5/1926	**Cavan 4-7 Donegal 1-5** Cavan
		16/5/1926	**Monaghan 0-4 Down 0-1** Hilltown
		6/6/1926	**Tyrone 3-3 Derry 2-1** Dungannon
	Semi-final	5/7/1926	**Antrim 2-5 Tyrone 0-3** Omagh
		27/6/192	**Cavan 0-7 Monaghan 0-7** Belturbet
		1/8/1926	**Cavan 0-7 Monaghan 1-3** Ballybay
	Final	22/8/1926	**Cavan 5-3 Antrim 0-6** Cavan

All-Ireland	Semi-final	8/8/1926	**Kerry 1-6 Cavan 0-1** Croke Park
		22/8/1926	**Kildare 2-5 Galway 0-2** Croke Park
	Final	5/9/1926	**Kerry 1-3 Kildare 0-6** Croke Park
		17/10/1926	**Kerry 1-4 Kildare 0-4** Croke Park

1927

Carlow, Fermanagh, Offaly, Westmeath and Wicklow did not enter the 1927 Championship.

Connacht

First Round	29/5/1927	**Sligo 1-8 Mayo 2-3** Castlerea
	19/6/1927	**Sligo 0-0 Mayo 1-0** Sligo
Semi-final	22/5/1927	**Leitrim 1-3 Roscommon 0-2** Cck-on-Shn
	26/6/1927	**Leitrim 0-7 Roscommon 1-0** Ballinamore
	17/7/1927	**Mayo 1-4 Galway 1-5** Tuam
Final	7/8/1927	**Leitrim 2-4 Galway 0-3** Roscommon

Leinster

First Round	22/5/1927	**Kildare 1-4 Kilkenny 0-2** Portlaoise
	22/5/1927	**Meath 2-7 Louth 0-0** Navan
	29/5/1927	**Wexford 7-10 Longford 6-2** Croke Park
	19/6/1927	**Dublin 2-5 Laois 0-3** Athy
Semi-final	17/7/1927	**Dublin 0-11 Wexford 2-5** Kilkenny
	31/7/1927	**Dublin 0-8 Wexford 1-1** Kilkenny
	17/7/1927	**Kildare 1-6 Meath 1-2** Drogheda
Final	14/8/1927	**Kildare 0-5 Dublin 0-3** Croke Park

Munster

First Round	8/5/1927	**Kerry 1-7 Cork 0-1** Cork
	12/6/1927	**Tipperary 4-3 Limerick 0-4** Clonmel
Semi-final	15/5/1927	**Clare 2-6 Waterford 1-1** Ennis
	14/8/1927	**Kerry 2-6 Tipperary 1-1** Dungarvan
Final	11/9/1927	**Kerry 4-4 Clare 1-3** Kilrush

Ulster

First Round	22/5/1927	**Antrim 1-9 Tyrone 0-11** Belfast
	22/5/1927	**Armagh 1-5 Donegal 0-4** Armagh
	22/5/1927	**Cavan 7-7 Derry 4-3** Belfast
	22/5/1927	**Monaghan 2-5 Down 1-2** Newry
Semi-final	19/6/1927	**Cavan 1-6 Monaghan 2-6** Castleblayney
	26/6/1927	**Armagh 3-6 Antrim 0-4** Newry
Final	31/7/1927	**Monaghan 3-5 Armagh 2-5** Armagh

All-Ireland

Semi-final	28/8/1927	**Kerry 0-4 Leitrim 0-2** Tuam
	28/8/1927	**Kildare 1-7 Monaghan 0-2** Drogheda
Final	25/9/1927	**Kildare 0-5 Kerry 0-3** Croke Park

1928

Carlow, Donegal, Kilkenny, Limerick, Offaly, Waterford, Westmeath and Wicklow did not enter the 1928 Championship.

Connacht	*First Round*	10/6/1928	**Leitrim 1-0 Galway 1-0** Roscommon
		24/6/1928	**Leitrim 0-7 Galway 0-3** Roscommon
	Semi-final	17/6/1928	**Mayo 1-5 Roscommon 0-3** Ballyhaunis
		15/7/1928	**Sligo 1-5 Leitrim 0-2** Boyle
	Final	5/8/1928	**Sligo 1-4 Mayo 0-6** Tuam

Leinster	*First Round*	22/4/1928	**Meath 0-11 Longford 3-4** Mullingar
		20/5/1928	**Dublin 0-5 Louth 0-3** Navan
		20/5/1928	**Kildare 0-4 Laois 1-0** Athy
		3/6/1928	**Wexford 7-7 Kilkenny 3-4** New Ross
	Semi-final	10/6/1928	**Kildare 3-6 Longford 0-2** Croke Park
		8/7/1928	**Dublin 3-3 Wexford 0-4** Croke Park
	Final	22/7/1928	**Kildare 0-10 Dublin 1-6** Croke Park

Munster	*First Round*	10/6/1928	**Kerry 3-4 Clare 0-5** Kilrush
	Semi-final	8/7/1928	**Tipperary 1-7 Kerry 2-3** Tipperary
			Cork *bye*
	Final	5/8/1928	**Cork 4-3 Tipperary 0-4** Dungarvan

Ulster	*First Round*	27/5/1928	**Monaghan 3-5 Down 1-3** Castleblayney
		27/5/1928	**Tyrone 7-3 Derry 2-3** Dungannon
		10/6/1928	**Armagh 6-3 Fermanagh 1-7** Enniskillen
		17/6/1928	**Cavan 1-5 Antrim 0-2** Belturbet
	Semi-final	1/7/1928	**Armagh 0-4 Monaghan 0-1** Carrickmacross
		8/7/1928	**Cavan 4-3 Tyrone 0-4** Dungannon
	Final	29/7/1928	**Cavan 2-6 Armagh 1-4** Cavan

All-Ireland	*Semi-final*	26/8/1928	**Cavan 2-5 Sligo 0-4** Cavan
		2/9/1928	**Kildare 3-7 Cork 0-2** Croke Park
	Final	30/9/1928	**Kildare 2-6 Cavan 2-5** Croke Park

1929

Carlow, Derry, Limerick, Offaly, Waterford, Westmeath and Wicklow did not enter the 1929 Championship.

Connacht	First Round	16/6/1929	**Leitrim 0-6 Sligo 1-4** Boyle
	Semi-final	9/6/1929	**Mayo 6-6 Roscommon 0-4** Castlerea
		7/7/1929	**Sligo 0-0 Galway 0-7** Roscommon
	Final	21/7/1929	**Mayo 1-6 Galway 0-4** Roscommon

Leinster	First Round	5/5/1929	**Wexford 0-7 Laois 3-3** Kilkenny
		12/5/1929	**Kildare 1-5 Meath 0-8** Drogheda
		9/6/1929	**Kildare 3-5 Meath 0-9** Drogheda
		26/5/1929	**Dublin 3-7 Longford 1-6** Mullingar
		26/5/1929	**Kilkenny 0-10 Louth 0-4** Croke Park
	Semi-final	30/6/1929	**Laois 5-5 Dublin 3-10** Athy
		7/7/1929	**Kildare 2-11 Kilkenny 0-3** Portlaoise
	Final	21/7/1929	**Kildare 2-3 Laois 0-6** Croke Park

Munster	Semi-final	26/5/1929	**Cork 1-3 Kerry 1-7** Cork
		26/5/1929	**Tipperary 1-4 Clare 3-3** Kilrush
	Final	14/7/1929	**Kerry 1-14 Clare 1-2** Killarney

Ulster	First Round	19/5/1929	**Armagh 5-4 Down 3-2** Newry
		19/5/1929	**Tyrone 0-8 Fermanagh 0-2** Enniskillen
		26/5/1929	**Cavan 1-11 Antrim 0-2** Belfast
		2/6/1929	**Monaghan 2-8 Donegal 0-1** Bundoran
	Semi-final	16/6/1929	**Tyrone 1-2 Monaghan 3-7** Monaghan
		30/6/1929	**Cavan 4-10 Armagh 0-2** Belturbet
	Final	28/7/1929	**Monaghan 1-4 Cavan 1-4** Cavan
		11/8/1929	**Monaghan 1-10 Cavan 0-7** Carrickmacross

All-Ireland	Semi-final	18/8/1929	**Kerry 3-8 Mayo 1-1** Roscommon
		25/8/1929	**Kildare 0-9 Monaghan 0-1** Croke Park
	Final	22/9/1929	**Kerry 1-8 Kildare 1-5** Croke Park

1930

Derry, Donegal, Limerick, Waterford and Wicklow did not enter the 1930 Championship. Antrim was disqualified after beating Fermanagh.

Connacht

First Round	18/5/1930	**Mayo 3-4 Leitrim 1-1** Sligo
	1/6/1930	**Galway 1-5 Sligo 2-4** Castlebar
Semi-final	29/6/1930	**Sligo 2-7 Roscommon 0-5** Boyle
		Mayo *bye*
Final	10/8/1930	**Mayo 1-7 Sligo 1-2** Tuam

Leinster

First Round	4/5/1930	**Wexford 4-2 Kilkenny 2-1** New Ross
	11/5/1930	**Kildare 6-7 Offaly 3-3** Tullamore
	1/6/1930	**Dublin 2-8 Westmeath 0-4** Mullingar
	1/6/1930	**Meath 1-12 Longford 1-5** Mullingar
	8/6/1930	**Laois 2-7 Louth 0-3** Croke Park
Second Round	29/6/1930	**Meath 3-8 Dublin 0-4** Drogheda
	06/7/1930	**Kildare 2-11 Wexford 0-5** Croke Park
		Laois *bye*
Semi-final	20/7/1930	**Kildare 4-4 Laois 1-4** Kilkenny
		Meath *bye*
Final	10/8/1930	**Kildare 0-6 Meath 1-3** Croke Park
	17/8/1930	**Kildare 2-6 Meath 1-2** Croke Park

Munster

First Round	1/6/1930	**Cork 3-8 Clare 0-4** Cork
Semi-final	20/7/1930	**Tipperary 2-6 Cork 1-3** Clonmel
		Kerry *bye*
Final	10/8/1930	**Kerry 3-4 Tipperary 1-2** Tipperary

Ulster

First Round	25/5/1930	**Armagh 2-3 Tyrone 2-3** Dungannon
	8/6/1930	**Armagh 1-8 Tyrone 1-3** Armagh
	1/6/1930	**Antrim 3-3 Fermanagh 2-5** Enniskillen
	8/6/1930	**Monaghan 7-8 Down 1-3** Newry
		Cavan *bye*
Semi-final	22/6/1930	**Cavan 2-3 Fermanagh 1-0** Belturbet
	29/6/1930	**Armagh 0-5 Monaghan 2-2** Armagh
Final	27/7/1930	**Monaghan 4-3 Cavan 1-5** Carrickmacross

All-Ireland

Semi-final	24/8/1930	**Kerry 1-9 Mayo 1-4** Roscommon
	24/8/1930	**Monaghan 1-6 Kildare 1-4** Croke Park
Final	28/9/1930	**Kerry 3-11 Monaghan 0-2** Croke Park

Carlow, Derry, Longford and Kilkenny did not enter the 1931 Championship. In Munster, Kerry had a bye into the final. Antrim were awarded the Ulster Championship tie against Donegal despite losing (as Donegal had initially refused to field).

Connacht	First Round	31/5/1931	**Mayo 1-8 Sligo 1-3** Tuam
	Semi-final	5/7/1931	**Mayo 3-5 Galway 1-4** Castlerea
		24/5/1931	**Roscommon 5-6 Leitrim 0-1** Boyle
	Final	9/8/1931	**Mayo 2-10 Roscommon 3-2** Boyle
Leinster	First Round	17/5/1931	**Westmeath 8-5 Kilkenny 1-5** Athlone
		31/5/1931	**Kildare 2-4 Laois 1-6** Portlaoise
		7/6/1931	**Meath 2-1 Offaly 1-1** Navan
		28/6/1931	**Meath 0-8 Offaly 0-3** Navan
		14/6/1931	**Dublin 5-6 Louth 1-5** Drogheda
	Second Round	5/7/1931	**Dublin 4-3 Wexford 1-3** Enniscorthy
			Kildare bye
			Meath bye
			Westmeath bye
	Semi-final	19/7/1931	**Kildare 1-4 Meath 1-4** Croke Park
		2/8/1931	**Kildare 1-5 Meath 0-5** Croke Park
		26/7/1931	**Westmeath 2-4 Dublin 1-4** Tullamore
	Final	9/8/1931	**Kildare 2-9 Westmeath 1-6** Croke Park
Munster	First Round	7/6/1931	**Tipperary 4-4 Limerick 0-1** Newcastlewest
		14/6/1931	**Cork 3-4 Clare 1-2** Cork
	Second Round	21/6/1931	**Tipperary 0-7 Waterford 0-0** Dungarvan
			Cork bye
	Semi-final	5/7/1931	**Cork 3-1 Tipperary 2-11** Clonmel
	Final	9/8/1931	**Kerry 5-8 Tipperary 0-2** Tralee
Ulster	First Round	10/5/1931	**Donegal 2-4 Antrim 0-1** Letterkenny
		17/5/1931	**Monaghan 3-8 Tyrone 1-4** Dungannon
		24/5/1931	**Armagh 0-6 Down 0-2** Newry
		14/6/1931	**Cavan 2-5 Fermanagh 1-2** Belturbet
	Semi-final	21/6/1931	**Armagh 1-9 Monaghan 0-4** Carrickmacross
		5/7/1931	**Cavan 4-9 Antrim 2-3** Corrigan Park
	Final	2/8/1931	**Cavan 0-8 Armagh 2-1** Dundalk
All-Ireland	Semi-final	30/8/1931	**Kerry 1-6 Mayo 1-4** Tuam
		30/8/1931	**Kildare 0-10 Cavan 1-5** Cavan
	Final	27/9/1931	**Kerry 1-11 Kildare 0-8** Croke Park

1932

Carlow, Derry, Donegal, Kilkenny, Longford and Wicklow did not enter the 1932 Championship.

Connacht

First Round	29/5/1932	**Galway 4-7 Roscommon 0-2** Castlerea
Semi-final	22/5/1932	**Sligo 1-7 Leitrim 0-3** Carrick-on-Shannon
	17/7/1932	**Mayo 3-5 Galway 1-3** Castlerea
Final	7/8/1932	**Mayo 2-6 Sligo 0-7** Tuam

Leinster

	1/5/1932	**Kildare 4-5 Louth 0-7** Navan
First Round	22/5/1932	**Westmeath 3-5 Offaly 0-4** Tullamore
	22/5/1932	**Wexford 5-4 Laois 0-4** Kilkenny
	29/5/1932	**Dublin 3-6 Meath 0-4** Newbridge
Semi-final	5/6/1932	**Wexford 2-8 Kildare 2-5** Croke Park
	17/7/1932	**Dublin 3-7 Westmeath 2-5** Tullamore
Final	7/8/1932	**Dublin 0-8 Wexford 1-5** Croke Park
	14/8/1932	**Dublin 4-6 Wexford 1-5** Croke Park

Munster

First Round	15/5/1932	**Clare 3-5 Cork 1-6** Tralee
	15/5/1932	**Tipperary 2-4 Waterford 1-4** Clonmel
Semi-final	22/5/1932	**Kerry 1-11 Limerick 1-3** Newcastlewest
	24/7/1932	**Tipperary 0-9 Clare 0-4** Limerick
Final	7/8/1932	**Kerry 3-10 Tipperary 1-4** Carrick-on-Suir

Ulster

	10/4/1932	**Armagh 1-5 Tyrone 1-4** Armagh
First Round	17/4/1932	**Antrim 4-10 Down 0-1** Corrigan Park
	17/4/1932	**Monaghan 1-7 Fermanagh 1-3** Monaghan
	24/4/1932	**Cavan 8-7 Donegal 1-6** Cavan
Semi-final	8/5/1932	**Armagh 2-6 Antrim 0-6** Corrigan Park
	29/5/1932	**Cavan 8-8 Monaghan 2-6** Belturbet
Final	19/6/1932	**Cavan 2-9 Armagh 0-2** Monaghan

All-Ireland

Semi-final	21/8/1932	**Kerry 1-3 Dublin 1-1** Croke Park
	21/8/1932	**Mayo 2-4 Cavan 0-8** Croke Park
Final	25/9/1932	**Kerry 2-7 Mayo 2-4** Croke Park

1933

Carlow, Derry, Kilkenny, Limerick, Longford and Wicklow did not enter the 1933 Championship. In Munster, due to a US tour, Kerry had a bye directly into the Munster final.

Connacht

First Round	28/5/1933	**Galway 2-10 Roscommon 0-0** Tuam
Semi-final	11/6/1933	**Mayo 4-10 Leitrim 1-0** Tubbercurry
	2/7/1933	**Galway 4-8 Sligo 0-4** Castlerea
Final	23/7/1933	**Galway 1-7 Mayo 1-5** Castlerea

Leinster

	7/5/1933	**Offaly 1-3 Wexford 4-4** Croke Park
First Round	28/5/1933	**Louth 4-7 Westmeath 1-6** Navan
	28/5/1933	**Kildare 1-9 Laois 2-6** Kilkenny
	11/6/1933	**Kildare 2-11 Laois 1-5** Kilkenny
	11/6/1933	**Dublin 1-8 Meath 1-4** Drogheda
Semi-final	25/6/1933	**Dublin 3-6 Louth 1-3** Navan
	2/7/1933	**Kildare 1-8 Wexford 2-8** Croke Park
Final	30/7/1933	**Dublin 0-9 Wexford 1-4** Croke Park

Munster

First Round	14/5/1933	**Tipperary 1-11 Clare 1-2** Limerick
	14/5/1933	**Cork 4-4 Waterford 4-4** Mitchelstown
	2/7/1933	**Cork 2-7 Waterford 0-1** Dungarvan
Semi-final	23/7/1933	**Tipperary 2-9 Cork 2-2** Clonmel
		Kerry *bye*
Final	13/8/1933	**Kerry 2-8 Tipperary 1-4** Clonmel

Ulster

	11/6/1933	**Antrim 0-3 Tyrone 0-3** Coalisland
First Round	25/6/1933	**Antrim 3-5 Tyrone 3-5** Corrigan Park
	9/7/1933	**Antrim 1-2 Tyrone 1-8** Omagh
	18/6/1933	**Armagh 2-1 Down 1-3** Warrenpoint
	25/6/1933	**Fermanagh 2-3 Monaghan 0-3** Belturbet
Semi-final	2/7/1933	**Armagh 0-2 Cavan 1-8** Cavan
	16/7/1933	**Fermanagh 1-3 Tyrone 1-4** Bundoran
Final	6/8/1933	**Cavan 6-13 Tyrone 1-2** Cavan

All-Ireland

Semi-final	20/8/1933	**Galway 0-8 Dublin 1-4** Mullingar
	27/8/1933	**Cavan 1-5 Kerry 0-5** Cavan
Final	24/9/1933	**Cavan 2-5 Galway 1-4** Croke Park

Derry, Kilkenny, Leitrim, Longford, and Wicklow did not enter the 1934 Championship.

Connacht	*Semi-final*	17/6/1934	**Galway 2-7 Roscommon 0-4** Castlerea
		8/7/1934	**Mayo 3-7 Sligo 1-3** Tubbercurry
	Final	22/7/1934	**Galway 2-4 Mayo 0-5** Castlerea

Leinster	*First Round*	20/5/1934	**Offaly 3-13 Carlow 0-6** Athy
		6/5/1934	**Louth 2-5 Laois 1-6** Croke Park
	Second Round	27/5/1934	**Wexford 1-5 Kildare 0-6** Kilkenny
		3/6/1934	**Dublin 2-10 Westmeath 0-4** Kells
		10/6/1934	**Meath 2-13 Offaly 2-6** Newbridge
	Semi-final	1/7/1934	**Louth 3-5 Wexford 1-1** Croke Park
		8/7/1934	**Dublin 2-8 Meath 2-9** Drogheda
	Final	29/7/1934	**Dublin 1-2 Louth 0-5** Croke Park
		5/8/1934	**Dublin 3-2 Louth 2-5** Croke Park
		19/8/1934	**Dublin 2-9 Louth 1-10** Drogheda

Munster	*First Round*	27/5/1934	**Kerry 2-6 Cork 0-3** Fermoy
		3/6/1934	**Tipperary 2-11 Clare 2-2** Tipperary
	Semi-final	24/6/1934	**Limerick 4-7 Waterford 1-6** Clonmel
		15/7/1934	**Kerry 2-8 Tipperary 0-12** Clonmel
	Final	29/7/1934	**Kerry 1-14 Limerick 1-2** Listowel

Ulster		29/4/1934	**Cavan 2-5 Tyrone 2-4** Omagh
	First Round	3/6/1934	**Antrim 0-5 Armagh 0-12** Corrigan Park
		3/6/1934	**Fermanagh 2-5 Donegal 1-3** Carrickmacross
		3/6/1934	**Monaghan 4-7 Down 2-6** Newry
	Semi-final	10/6/1934	**Armagh 2-3 Monaghan 1-3** Armagh
		15/7/1934	**Fermanagh 1-3 Cavan 3-4** Belturbet
	Final	29/7/1934	**Cavan 3-8 Armagh 0-2** Castleblayney

All-Ireland	*Semi-final*	12/8/1934	**Galway 1-8 Cavan 1-4** Tuam
		9/9/1934	**Dublin 3-8 Kerry 0-6** Tuam
	Final	23/9/1934	**Galway 3-5 Dublin 1-9** Croke Park

1935

Derry, Kilkenny, Longford, Waterford and Wicklow did not enter the 1935 Championship.

Connacht

First Round	12/5/1935	**Sligo 3-10 Roscommon 3-3** Tubbercurry	
Semi-final	26/5/1935	**Mayo 9-2 Leitrim 3-3** Sligo	
	2/6/1935	**Galway 5-4 Sligo 0-2** Castlebar	
Final	21/7/1935	**Mayo 0-12 Galway 0-5** Roscommon	

Leinster

First Round	5/5/1935	**Carlow 5-7 Wexford 1-6** Muinebeag	
	5/5/1935	**Westmeath 3-7 Offaly 2-2** Mullingar	
Second Round	12/5/1935	**Carlow 3-6 Westmeath 4-3** Croke Park	
	2/6/1935	**Carlow 2-2 Westmeath 3-6** Portlaoise	
Third Round	9/6/1935	**Dublin 0-3 Louth 0-6** Navan	
	23/6/1935	**Meath 2-7 Westmeath 0-8** Kells	
Semi-final	7/7/1935	**Kildare 1-9 Laois 0-3** Tullamore	
	14/7/1935	**Meath 1-4 Louth 1-5** Croke Park	
Final	28/7/1935	**Kildare 0-8 Louth 0-6** Croke Park	

Munster

First Round	12/5/1935	**Clare 2-4 Waterford 0-6** Dungarvan	
		Tipperary w/o **Kerry**	
Semi-final	26/5/1935	**Cork 2-3 Limerick 0-4** Charleville	
	30/6/1935	**Tipperary 1-8 Clare 0-8** Ennis	
Final	21/7/1935	**Tipperary 2-8 Cork 1-2** Fermoy	

Ulster

First Round	9/6/1935	**Armagh 2-5 Down 0-5** Armagh	
	9/6/1935	**Cavan 1-11 Donegal 1-9** Bundoran	
	16/6/1935	**Fermanagh 0-5 Tyrone 1-2** Omagh	
	30/6/1935	**Fermanagh 1-11 Tyrone 2-6** Irvinestown	
	16/6/1935	**Monaghan 3-8 Antrim 2-2** Castleblayney	
	30/6/1935	**Cavan 2-12 Monaghan 0-1** Cavan	
Semi-final	8/7/1935	**Fermanagh 0-9 Armagh 1-6** Enniskillen	
	14/7/1935	**Fermanagh 3-4 Armagh 2-2** Armagh	
Final	28/7/1935	**Cavan 2-6 Fermanagh 2-1** Belturbet	

All-Ireland

Semi-final	18/8/1935	**Cavan 1-7 Tipperary 0-8** Croke Park	
	25/8/1935	**Kildare 2-6 Mayo 0-7** Croke Park	
Final	22/9/1935	**Cavan 3-6 Kildare 2-5** Croke Park	

1936

Derry, Kilkenny, Leitrim, Longford, Waterford and Wicklow did not enter the 1936 Championship. In Ulster Cavan had a bye directly to the semi-finals.

Connacht

Semi-final	24/5/1936	**Mayo 5-6 Sligo 0-4** Ballina
	7/6/1936	**Galway 2-6 Roscommon 1-4** Castlerea
Final	19/7/1936	**Mayo 2-4 Galway 1-7** Roscommon
	2/8/1936	**Mayo 2-7 Galway 1-4** Roscommon

Leinster

First Round	3/5/1936	**Carlow 2-0 Wexford 2-6** Kilkenny
	3/5/1936	**Offaly 6-5 Westmeath 0-11** Tullamore
	24/5/1936	**Offaly 0-8 Dublin 1-3** Mullingar
Second Round	7/6/1936	**Kildare 0-12 Meath 1-6** Mullingar
	14/6/1936	**Louth 2-5 Wexford 1-5** Wexford
		Laois *bye*
Semi-final	28/6/1936	**Laois 4-5 Offaly 3-4** Athy
	5/7/1936	**Kildare 1-8 Louth 1-4** Navan
Final	19/7/1936	**Laois 3-3 Kildare 0-8** Croke Park

Munster

First Round	24/5/1936	**Kerry 7-7 Limerick 1-4** Foynes
Semi-final	24/5/1936	**Clare 2-6 Cork 1-3** Ennis
	12/7/1936	**Kerry 1-5 Tipperary 0-5** Limerick
Final	26/7/1936	**Kerry 1-11 Clare 2-2** Limerick

Ulster

First Round	14/6/1936	**Armagh 0-11 Antrim 2-1** Belfast
	14/6/1936	**Down 4-6 Tyrone 2-3** Warrenpoint
	21/6/1936	**Donegal 1-8 Fermanagh 0-7** Enniskillen
	28/6/1936	**Monaghan 3-5 Down 2-8** Carrickmacross
Second Round	12/7/1936	**Monaghan 4-9 Down 0-4** Newry
		Armagh *bye*
		Donegal *bye*
Semi-final	19/7/1936	**Armagh 2-1 Cavan 1-8** Armagh
	26/7/1936	**Monaghan 2-8 Donegal 0-11** Carrickmacross
Final	9/8/1936	**Cavan 1-7 Monaghan 0-7** Castleblayney

All-Ireland

Semi-final	9/8/1936	**Mayo 1-5 Kerry 0-6** Roscommon
	23/8/1936	**Laois 2-6 Cavan 1-5** Croke Park
Final	27/9/1936	**Mayo 4-11 Laois 0-5** Croke Park

1937

Derry, Kilkenny, Leitrim and Longford did not enter the 1937 Championship.

Connacht

First Round	16/5/1937	**Sligo 2-10 Roscommon 1-6** Castlerea
Semi-final	13/6/1937	**Galway 3-1 Sligo 0-2** Castlerea
		Mayo *bye*
Final	18/7/1937	**Mayo 3-5 Galway 0-8** Roscommon

Leinster

First Round	9/5/1937	**Kildare 5-11 Wicklow 1-7** Carlow
	16/5/1937	**Laois 2-6 Offaly 1-9** Newbridge
	30/5/1937	**Laois 2-7 Offaly 1-7** Athy
	30/5/1937	**Meath 3-9 Westmeath 2-3** Kells
	23/5/1937	**Dublin 1-7 Louth 0-10** Navan
	20/6/1937	**Dublin 1-4 Louth 2-5** Navan
	6/6/1937	**Wexford 2-7 Carlow 1-4** Kilkenny
	20/6/1937	**Wexford 3-7 Meath 1-8** Croke Park
Second Round		**Kildare** *bye*
		Laois *bye*
		Louth *bye*
Semi-final	4/7/1937	**Wexford 0-6 Louth 1-5** Drogheda
	11/7/1937	**Laois 2-10 Kildare 2-7** Carlow
Final	25/7/1937	**Laois 0-12 Louth 0-4** Croke Park

Munster

First Round	16/5/1937	**Tipperary 1-8 Waterford 1-6** Clonmel
	13/6/1937	**Kerry 6-7 Cork 0-4** Killarney
Semi-final	13/6/1937	**Clare 2-3 Limerick 1-6** Kilrush
	27/6/1937	**Clare 1-8 Limerick 0-6** Foynes
	11/7/1937	**Kerry 2-11 Tipperary 0-4** Mitchelstown
Final	18/7/1937	**Kerry 4-9 Clare 1-1** Limerick

Ulster

First Round	6/6/1937	**Donegal 3-8 Antrim 0-6** Bundoran
	6/6/1937	**Monaghan 4-12 Tyrone 0-8** Coalisland
	13/6/1937	**Armagh 4-14 Down 2-7** Armagh
	13/6/1937	**Cavan 3-11 Fermanagh 2-6** Enniskillen
Semi-final	27/6/1937	**Cavan 2-12 Donegal 1-4** Cavan
	4/7/1937	**Monaghan 1-3 Armagh 2-12** Armagh
Final	2/7/1937	**Cavan 0-13 Armagh 0-3** Castleblayney

All-Ireland

Semi-final

Final

15/8/1937 **Kerry 2-3 Laois 2-3** Cork
22/8/1937 **Kerry 2-2 Laois 1-4** Mullingar
29/8/1937 **Cavan 2-5 Mayo 1-7** Croke Park
26/9/1937 **Kerry 2-5 Cavan 1-8** Croke Park
17/10/1937 **Kerry 4-4 Cavan 1-7** Croke Park

1938

Derry, Down, Kilkenny, Leitrim and Roscommon did not enter the 1938 Championship.

Connacht

Semi-final	19/6/1938	**Galway 3-11 Sligo 2-3** Tuam
		Mayo *bye*
Final	17/7/1938	**Galway 0-8 Mayo 0-5** Roscommon

Leinster

First Round	1/5/1938	**Louth 2-4 Westmeath 0-3** Navan
	8/5/1938	**Carlow 2-5 Wicklow 2-5** Enniscorthy
	5/6/1938	**Carlow 5-9 Wicklow 1-7** Naas
	22/5/1938	**Offaly 1-7 Wexford 2-4** Kilkenny
	12/6/1938	**Offaly 1-9 Wexford 1-5** Carlow
Second Round	29/5/1938	**Kildare 4-7 Dublin 3-5** Portlaoise
	3/7/1938	**Laois 2-5 Louth 2-2** Croke Park
	3/7/1938	**Meath 4-4 Carlow 2-7** Croke Park
	10/7/1938	**Offaly 2-4 Longford 0-8** Mullingar
Semi-final	10/7/1938	**Laois 4-6 Meath 2-3** Croke Park
	24/7/1938	**Offaly 0-6 Kildare 4-8** Carlow
Final	7/8/1938	**Laois 2-8 Kildare 1-3** Croke Park

Munster

First Round	29/5/1938	**Kerry 2-6 Clare 0-1** Ennis
	12/6/1938	**Tipperary 1-10 Waterford 1-8** Dungarvan
Semi-final	29/5/1938	**Cork 2-7 Limerick 2-3** Tipperary
	3/7/1938	**Kerry 2-6 Tipperary 1-3** Mitchelstown
Final	7/8/1938	**Kerry 4-14 Cork 0-6** Clonakilty

Ulster

First Round	19/6/1938	**Armagh 2-5 Antrim 1-4** Corrigan Park
	19/6/1938	**Monaghan 3-3 Tyrone 0-6** Omagh
	3/7/1938	**Cavan 3-10 Fermanagh 1-4** Belturbet
Semi-final	10/7/1938	**Monaghan 0-7 Donegal 0-6** Carndonagh
	17/7/1938	**Cavan 1-4 Armagh 2-7** Armagh
Final	31/7/1938	**Monaghan 2-5 Armagh 2-2** Armagh

All-Ireland

Semi-final	14/8/1938	**Galway 2-10 Monaghan 2-3** Mullingar
	21/8/1938	**Kerry 2-6 Laois 2-4** Croke Park
Final	25/9/1938	**Galway 3-3 Kerry 2-6** Croke Park
	23/10/1938	**Galway 2-4 Kerry 0-7** Croke Park

1939

Derry, Fermanagh, Kilkenny, Leitrim and Roscommon did not enter the 1939 Championship. Kerry had a bye into the Munster final due to a proposed American tour. The Ulster final was abandoned with fifteen minutes left and had to be replayed.

Connacht

Semi-final	25/6/1939	Mayo 2-10 Sligo 0-2 Sligo
		Galway *bye*
Final	16/7/1939	Mayo 2-6 Galway 0-3 Roscommon

Leinster

First Round	14/5/1939	Wicklow 1-3 Carlow 2-8 Enniscorthy
	14/5/1939	Longford 0-17 Westmeath 4-4 Longford
Second Round	28/5/1939	Longford 3-4 Carlow 2-5 Portlaoise
Quarter-final	11/6/1939	Kildare 2-11 Offaly 1-1 Kilkenny
	28/5/1939	Louth 3-4 Dublin 1-6 Navan
	4/6/1939	Meath 1-9 Laois 1-7 Mullingar
	11/6/1939	Wexford 0-6 Longford 0-4 Croke Park
Semi-final	9/7/1939	Meath 2-10 Kildare 2-8 Drogheda
	2/7/1939	Wexford 1-7 Louth 0-7 Croke Park
Final	30/7/1939	Meath 2-7 Wexford 2-3 Croke Park

Munster

First Round	14/5/1939	Cork 0-8 Waterford 0-7 Dungarvan
	14/5/1939	Clare 1-8 Limerick 2-5 Ennis
	18/6/1939	Clare 2-14 Limerick 0-3 Kilrush
Quarter-final	4/6/1939	Tipperary 1-9 Cork 2-2 Mitchelstown
		Clare *bye*
Semi-final	2/7/1939	Tipperary 4-5 Clare 1-6 Limerick
		Kerry *bye*
Final	23/7/1939	Kerry 2-11 Tipperary 0-4 Clonmel

Ulster

First Round	25/6/1939	Down 1-6 Antrim 1-5 Corrigan Park
	25/6/1939	Cavan 4-11 Tyrone 1-2 Omagh
Second Round	2/7/1939	Donegal 0-6 Down 1-1 Magheragallon
		Cavan *bye*
Semi-final	16/7/1939	Monaghan 1-6 Armagh 1-6 Castleblayney
	23/7/1939	Monaghan 0-2 Armagh 1-6 Castleblayney
	23/7/1939	Cavan 5-12 Donegal 0-4 Cavan
Final	6/8/1939	Cavan 2-6 Armagh 2-4 Castleblayney
	15/8/1939	Cavan 2-3 Armagh 1-4 Croke Park

All-Ireland

Semi-final	13/8/1939	**Kerry 0-4 Mayo 0-4** Croke Park
	10/9/1939	**Kerry 3-8 Mayo 1-4** Croke Park
	20/8/1939	**Meath 1-9 Cavan 1-1** Croke Park
Final	24/9/1939	**Kerry 2-5 Meath 2-3** Croke Park

1940

Derry, Fermanagh, Kilkenny, Leitrim, Roscommon and Westmeath did not enter the 1940 Championship.

Connacht

Semi-final	30/6/1940	**Sligo 2-4 Mayo 1-7** Sligo
	14/7/1940	**Sligo 0-7 Mayo 3-2** Sligo
		Galway *bye*
Final	21/7/1940	**Galway 1-7 Mayo 0-5** Roscommon

Leinster

First Round	5/5/1940	**Laois 1-7 Carlow 1-6** Athy
	12/5/1940	**Meath 3-11 Longford 1-7** Mullingar
	19/5/1940	**Offaly 1-13 Wicklow 1-5** Naas
	19/5/1940	**Dublin 1-9 Louth 2-5** Navan
Quarter-final	2/6/1940	**Laois 3-4 Wexford 0-4** Carlow
	23/6/1940	**Offaly 2-6 Kildare 0-8** Portlaoise
		Dublin *bye*
		Meath *bye*
Semi-final	7/7/1940	**Meath 1-7 Dublin 0-4** Newbridge
	14/7/1940	**Offaly 0-7 Laois 2-7** Athy
Final	28/7/1940	**Meath 2-7 Laois 1-7** Croke Park

Munster

First Round	19/5/1940	**Kerry 4-9 Limerick 1-2** Glin
	19/5/1940	**Tipperary 2-7 Cork 1-5** Mitchelstown
	19/5/1940	**Clare 1-6 Waterford 2-3** Kilrush
	30/6/1940	**Clare 1-3 Waterford 2-5** Dungarvan
Semi-final	30/6/1940	**Kerry 4-8 Tipperary 1-5** Cork
		Waterford *bye*
Final	21/7/1940	**Kerry 1-10 Waterford 0-6** Waterford

Ulster

First Round	23/6/1940	**Antrim 3-3 Cavan 0-12** Corrigan Park
	7/7/1940	**Antrim 0-4 Cavan 6-13** Cavan
	23/6/1940	**Donegal 0-6 Armagh 0-5** Armagh
	30/6/1940	**Down 3-8 Tyrone 2-5** Newcastle
Semi-final	14/7/1940	**Cavan 0-12 Donegal 2-3** Bundoran
	14/7/1940	**Monaghan 2-3 Down 2-3** Castleblayney
	21/7/1940	**Monaghan 1-3 Down 0-8** Newcastle
Final	28/7/1940	**Cavan 4-10 Down 1-5** Cavan

All-Ireland

Semi-final	18/8/1940	**Galway 3-8 Meath 2-5** Croke Park
	18/8/1940	**Kerry 3-4 Cavan 0-8** Croke Park
Final	22/9/1940	**Kerry 0-7 Galway 1-3** Croke Park

1941

Derry, Fermanagh, Kilkenny, Leitrim and Limerick did not enter the 1941 Championship. The Leinster final was delayed until November due to the prevalence of foot and mouth disease in Carlow (Dublin was nominated to represent Leinster in the All-Ireland semi-final). Foot and mouth also forced the withdrawal of Tipperary in Munster where Kerry had a bye in both rounds prior to the final.

Connacht
Semi-final	29/6/1941	**Galway 0-10 Mayo 1-5** Tuam
	6/7/1941	**Roscommon 1-9 Sligo 0-5** Boyle
Final	20/7/1941	**Galway 0-8 Roscommon 1-4** Roscommon

Leinster

First Round
27/4/1941	**Longford 1-5 Westmeath 1-3** Longford
11/5/1941	**Kildare 2-5 Offaly 1-7** Tullamore
11/5/1941	**Wexford 2-3 Wicklow 1-5** Enniscorthy
18/5/1941	**Carlow 3-4 Laois 3-1** Carlow
18/5/1941	**Dublin 2-7 Louth 3-4** Drogheda
25/5/1941	**Dublin 1-9 Louth 1-4** Croke Park
	Meath *bye*

Quarter-final
1/6/1941	**Dublin 1-8 Meath 1-6** Mullingar
8/6/1941	**Kildare 5-7 Longford 0-6** Mullingar
	Carlow *bye*
	Wexford *bye*

Semi-final
8/6/1941	**Carlow 3-10 Wexford 4-7** Carlow
22/6/1941	**Carlow 2-7 Wexford 2-7** Wexford
20/7/1941	**Carlow 1-12 Wexford 3-6** Croke Park
27/7/1941	**Carlow 2-8 Wexford 0-3** Croke Park
13/7/1941	**Dublin 2-11 Kildare 2-10** Croke Park

Final
9/11/1941	**Dublin 4-6 Carlow 1-4** Carlow

Munster

First Round
11/5/1941	**Tipperary 1-4 Waterford 0-5** Dungarvan
25/5/1941	**Clare 1-8 Cork 1-3** Ennis
	Kerry *bye*

Semi-final
	Clare w/o **Tipperary**
	Kerry *bye*

Final
10/8/1941	**Kerry 2-9 Clare 0-6** Limerick

Ulster	*First Round*	8/6/1941	**Armagh 4-8 Tyrone 1-17** Armagh
		6/7/1941	**Armagh 0-1 Tyrone 3-13** Coalisland
		15/6/1941	**Down 5-4 Antrim 0-4** Corrigan Park
		6/7/1941	**Monaghan 3-2 Cavan 3-7** Cavan
			Donegal *bye*
	Semi-final	13/7/1941	**Cavan 0-9 Donegal 0-7** Bundoran
		13/7/1941	**Tyrone 1-10 Down 1-9** Newcastle
	Final	3/8/1941	**Cavan 3-9 Tyrone 0-5** Armagh

All-Ireland	*Semi-final*	10/8/1941	**Kerry 0-4 Dublin 0-4** Croke Park
		17/8/1941	**Kerry 2-9 Dublin 0-3** Tralee
		17/8/1941	**Galway 1-12 Cavan 1-4** Croke Park
	Final	7/9/1941	**Kerry 1-8 Galway 0-7** Croke Park

1942

Derry, Fermanagh, Kilkenny and Limerick did not enter the 1942 Championship.

Connacht	*First Round*	14/6/1942	**Roscommon 1-8 Mayo 0-8** Tuam
	Semi-final	21/6/1942	**Galway 4-9 Leitrim 1-2** Mohill
		28/6/1942	**Roscommon 0-14 Sligo 0-6** Boyle
	Final	19/7/1942	**Galway 2-6 Roscommon 3-2** Ballinasloe
Leinster	*First Round*	26/4/1942	**Longford 0-4 Westmeath 0-3** Longford
		26/4/1942	**Wexford 3-5 Wicklow 2-4** Aughrim
		10/5/1942	**Offaly 1-6 Kildare 0-7** Newbridge
	Quarter-final	3/5/1942	**Meath 2-11 Louth 0-8** Navan
		10/5/1942	**Carlow 0-10 Wexford 0-7** Kilkenny
		10/5/1942	**Dublin 0-7 Longford 0-7** Mullingar
		24/5/1942	**Dublin 2-15 Longford 1-3** Croke Park
		24/5/1942	**Offaly 6-5 Laois 2-7** Portlaoise
	Semi-final	31/5/1942	**Dublin 3-5 Meath 1-3** Drogheda
		14/6/1942	**Offaly 1-10 Carlow 0-13** Athy
		21/6/1942	**Offaly 0-6 Carlow 1-9** Portlaoise
	Final	19/7/1942	**Dublin 0-8 Carlow 0-6** Athy
Munster	*First Round*	14/6/1942	**Kerry 3-8 Clare 1-3** Ennis
	Semi-final	14/6/1942	**Cork 1-8 Waterford 0-2** Dungarvan
		28/6/1942	**Kerry 3-6 Tipperary 1-5** Tipperary
	Final	19/7/1942	**Kerry 3-7 Cork 0-8** Tralee
Ulster	*First Round*	31/5/1942	**Armagh 3-4 Tyrone 0-0** Armagh
		14/6/1942	**Cavan 1-4 Monaghan 0-6** Castleblayney
		14/6/1942	**Down 4-4 Antrim 3-7** Newcastle
		21/6/1942	**Down 2-11 Antrim 1-5** Corrigan Park
			Donegal *bye*
	Semi-final	28/6/1942	**Cavan 7-10 Donegal 4-4** Cavan
		5/7/1942	**Down 0-7 Armagh 0-6** Newcastle
		12/7/1942	**Down 1-12 Armagh 2-5** Newcastle
	Final	19/7/1942	**Cavan 5-11 Down 1-3** Dundalk
All-Ireland	*Semi-final*	2/8/1942	**Dublin 1-6 Cavan 1-3** Croke Park
		19/8/1942	**Galway 1-3 Kerry 0-3** Croke Park
	Final	20/9/1942	**Dublin 1-10 Galway 1-8** Croke Park

Derry and Fermanagh did not enter the 1943 Championship.

Connacht

First Round	27/6/1943	Leitrim 4-9 Sligo 2-8 Boyle
Semi-final	20/6/1943	Galway 3-6 Mayo 1-5 Kiltimagh
	4/7/1943	Roscommon 2-12 Leitrim 1-3 Ck-on-Shn
Final	18/7/1943	Roscommon 2-8 Galway 0-8 Roscommon

Leinster

First Round	18/4/1943	Carlow 1-11 Wicklow 1-10 Enniscorthy
	2/5/1943	Louth 2-10 Meath 1-8 Drogheda
	9/5/1943	Wexford 3-6 Kilkenny 0-0 New Ross
	9/5/1943	Westmeath 1-5 Longford 2-2 Mullingar
	23/5/1943	Longford 2-6 Westmeath 1-8 Longford
Quarter-final	16/5/1943	Kildare 1-10 Laois 4-8 Athy
	23/5/1943	Carlow 2-6 Wexford 2-6 Carlow
	6/6/1943	Carlow 1-7 Wexford 1-1 Wexford
	30/5/1943	Louth 4-5 Dublin 1-6 Drogheda
	6/6/1943	Offaly 2-11 Longford 2-9 Tullamore
Semi-final	27/6/1943	Laois 3-8 Carlow 3-6 Athy
	20/6/1943	Louth 1-9 Offaly 2-3 Croke Park
Final	25/7/1943	Louth 3-16 Laois 2-4 Croke Park

Munster

First Round	16/5/1943	Tipperary 2-7 Waterford 0-9 Clonmel
	23/5/1943	Clare 2-10 Limerick 2-4 Foynes
Semi-final	6/6/1943	Cork 0-9 Kerry 0-9 Cork
	11/7/1943	Cork 1-5 Kerry 1-4 Cork
	20/6/1943	Tipperary 3-5 Clare 2-6 Limerick
Final	25/7/1943	Cork 1-7 Tipperary 1-4 Fermoy

Ulster

First Round	20/6/1943	Donegal 0-7 Tyrone 1-8 Omagh
	27/6/1943	Antrim 0-13 Down 1-8 Corrigan Park
	27/6/1943	Monaghan 3-8 Armagh 3-4 Armagh
		Cavan bye
Semi-final	4/7/1943	Cavan 4-10 Tyrone 1-3 Enniskillen
	11/7/1943	Monaghan 1-10 Antrim 1-5 Armagh
Final	1/8/1943	Cavan 2-3 Monaghan 0-5 Cavan

All-Ireland

Semi-final	8/8/1943	Roscommon 3-10 Louth 3-6 Croke Park
	15/8/1943	Cavan 1-8 Cork 1-7 Croke Park
Final	26/9/1943	Roscommon 1-6 Cavan 1-6 Croke Park
	10/10/1943	Roscommon 2-7 Cavan 2-2 Croke Park

1944

Derry and Fermanagh did not enter the 1944 Championship.

Connacht

First Round	25/6/1944	**Leitrim 4-5 Sligo 4-10** Boyle
	18/6/1944	**Galway 1-3 Mayo 1-11** Castlebar
Semi-final	2/7/1944	**Roscommon 1-5 Sligo 0-8** Boyle
	9/7/1944	**Roscommon 0-13 Sligo 1-6** Boyle
Final	6/8/1944	**Roscommon 2-11 Mayo 1-6** Tuam

Leinster

	14/5/1944	**Carlow 1-10 Kildare 2-7** Athy
First Round	28/5/1944	**Carlow 3-11 Kildare 2-5** Carlow
	14/5/1944	**Wexford 4-12 Kilkenny 0-2** New Ross
	21/5/1944	**Offaly 3-9 Westmeath 2-8** Tullamore
	28/5/1944	**Dublin 1-8 Meath 1-6** Drogheda
	4/6/1944	**Longford 4-3 Offaly 1-4** Longford
Quarter-final	11/6/1944	**Wexford 2-7 Wicklow 1-4** Aughrim
	18/6/1944	**Carlow 2-8 Laois 2-3** Athy
	18/6/1944	**Dublin 2-10 Louth 3-6** Croke Park
Semi-final	9/7/1944	**Dublin 2-2 Longford 1-4** Mullingar
	16/7/1944	**Carlow 5-7 Wexford 3-6** Kilkenny
Final	30/7/1944	**Carlow 2-6 Dublin 1-6** Athy

Munster

First Round	14/5/1944	**Kerry 4-8 Clare 1-4** Tralee
	14/5/1944	**Tipperary 1-10 Waterford 0-5** Waterford
Semi-final	18/6/1944	**Kerry 3-9 Limerick 1-4** Listowel
	18/6/1944	**Tipperary 1-9 Cork 1-3** Clonmel
Final	9/7/1944	**Kerry 1-6 Tipperary 0-5** Limerick

Ulster

	2/7/1944	**Cavan 1-4 Antrim 0-2** Corrigan Park
First Round	2/7/1944	**Down 3-4 Tyrone 0-4** Corrigan Park
	2/7/1944	**Monaghan 3-7 Armagh 3-3** Armagh
		Donegal *bye*
Semi-final	9/7/1944	**Monaghan 1-5 Down 1-4** Corrigan Park
	16/7/1944	**Cavan 5-9 Donegal 2-3** Omagh
Final	30/7/1944	**Cavan 1-9 Monaghan 1-6** Clones

All-Ireland

Semi-final	20/8/1944	**Roscommon 5-8 Cavan 1-3** Croke Park
	27/8/1944	**Kerry 3-3 Carlow 0-10** Croke Park
Final	24/9/1944	**Roscommon 1-9 Kerry 2-4** Croke Park

164

1945

All counties participated in the 1945 Championship for the first time since 1919 and for only the second time ever.

Connacht

First Round	10/6/1945	**Mayo 3-12 Leitrim 0-6** Castlerea
Semi-final	24/6/1945	**Galway 2-7 Sligo 1-5** Roscommon
	8/7/1945	**Mayo 2-8 Roscommon 1-6** Sligo
Final	22/7/1945	**Galway 2-6 Mayo 1-7** Roscommon

Leinster

First Round	29/4/1945	**Wicklow 3-10 Kilkenny 0-2** Enniscorthy
	29/4/1945	**Longford 1-5 Westmeath 1-5** Mullingar
	6/5/1945	**Longford 1-10 Westmeath 2-6** Mullingar
	6/5/1945	**Kildare 2-13 Carlow 2-10** Carlow
	6/5/1945	**Meath 2-9 Louth 2-7** Navan
Quarter-final	27/5/1945	**Wexford 5-5 Kildare 0-6** Carlow
	10/6/1945	**Longford 1-6 Offaly 3-4** Mullingar
	10/6/1945	**Meath 3-6 Dublin 4-3** Drogheda
	17/6/1945	**Meath 2-16 Dublin 1-10** Croke Park
	17/6/1945	**Laois 2-10 Wicklow 2-8** Carlow
Semi-final	24/6/1945	**Meath 0-5 Offaly 1-8** Portlaoise
	1/7/1945	**Wexford 4-5 Laois 1-11** Kilkenny
Final	22/7/1945	**Wexford 1-9 Offaly 1-4** Portlaoise

Munster

First Round	13/5/1945	**Tipperary 0-7 Waterford 0-3** Carrick on-Suir
	20/5/1945	**Limerick 6-2 Clare 3-3** Ennis
Semi-final	10/6/1945	**Kerry 5-8 Limerick 2-7** Limerick
	24/6/1945	**Cork 1-7 Tipperary 1-6** Dungarvan
Final	8/7/1945	**Cork 1-11 Kerry 1-6** Killarney

Ulster

First Round	17/6/1945	**Cavan 2-11 Antrim 2-3** Cavan
Quarter-final	10/6/1945	**Donegal 3-7 Derry 2-3** Letterkenny
	24/6/1945	**Armagh 3-13 Tyrone 0-2** Armagh
	24/6/1945	**Fermanagh 4-13 Monaghan 0-5** Enniskillen
	1/7/1945	**Cavan 0-14 Down 1-3** Armagh
Semi-final	8/7/1945	**Fermanagh 2-4 Armagh 1-6** Clones
	15/7/1945	**Cavan 6-12 Donegal 2-4** Clones
Final	29/7/1945	**Cavan 4-10 Fermanagh 1-4** Clones

All-Ireland

Semi-final	12/8/1945	**Cork 2-12 Galway 2-8** Croke Park
	19/8/1945	**Cavan 1-14 Wexford 0-5** Croke Park
Final	23/9/1945	**Cork 2-5 Cavan 0-7** Croke Park

Kilkenny did not enter the 1946 Championship.

Connacht	*First Round*	26/5/1946	**Sligo 6-10 Leitrim 0-6** Carrick-on-Shannon	
	Semi-final	23/6/1946	**Mayo 2-9 Sligo 2-6** Ballina	
		16/6/1946	**Roscommon 0-7 Galway 0-4** Roscommon	
	Final	21/7/1946	**Roscommon 1-4 Mayo 0-6** Ballinasloe	

Leinster	*First Round*	12/5/1946	**Meath 2-11 Longford 0-8** Mullingar
		19/5/1946	**Offaly 2-6 Westmeath 0-4** Mullingar
		19/5/1946	**Dublin 0-5 Laois 1-3** Athy
		19/5/1946	**Louth 2-7 Wicklow 0-7** Croke Park
	Quarter-final	5/5/1946	**Kildare 2-3 Carlow 2-3** Athy
		12/5/1946	**Kildare 3-5 Carlow 0-7** Carlow
		2/6/1946	**Laois 1-7 Offaly 1-5** Tullamore
		9/6/1946	**Louth 1-6 Meath 0-6** Drogheda
			Wexford *bye*
	Semi-final	16/6/1946	**Kildare 3-3 Wexford 0-10** Carlow
		30/6/1946	**Laois 1-9 Louth 0-10** Croke Park
	Final	14/7/1946	**Laois 0-11 Kildare 1-6** Croke Park

Munster	*First Round*	26/5/1946	**Limerick 4-3 Clare 3-6** Milltown Malbay
		9/6/1946	**Limerick 1-0 Clare 2-12** Limerick
		2/6/1946	**Kerry 1-8 Cork 1-4** Killarney
	Semi-final	7/7/1946	**Kerry 1-6 Clare 0-7** Ennis
		9/6/1946	**Waterford 2-4 Tipperary 1-5** Dungarvan
	Final	21/7/1946	**Kerry 2-16 Waterford 2-1** Tralee

Ulster	*First Round*	9/6/1946	**Derry 4-6 Fermanagh 0-4** Magherafelt
	Quarter-final	23/6/1946	**Armagh 0-13 Down 0-4** Newcastle
		23/6/1946	**Cavan 8-13 Tyrone 2-3** Omagh
		23/6/1946	**Donegal 4-5 Monaghan 1-9** Clones
		30/6/1946	**Antrim 1-11 Derry 0-10** Corrigan Park
	Semi-final	7/7/1946	**Cavan 5-8 Donegal 0-3** Omagh
		15/7/1946	**Antrim 1-12 Armagh 0-6** Omagh
	Final	21/7/1946	**Antrim 2-8 Cavan 1-7** Clones

All-Ireland	*Semi-final*	18/8/1946	**Kerry 2-7 Antrim 0-10** Croke Park
		25/8/1946	**Roscommon 3-5 Laois 2-6** Croke Park
	Final	6/10/1946	**Kerry 2-4 Roscommon 1-7** Croke Park
		27/10/1946	**Kerry 2-8 Roscommon 0-10** Croke Park

Kilkenny did not enter the 1947 Championship.

Connacht

First Round	25/5/1947	Roscommon 1-10 Mayo 0-4 Ballina
Semi-final	1/6/1947	Sligo 2-6 Galway 1-6 Roscommon
	29/6/1947	Roscommon 1-9 Leitrim 0-3 Ck-on-Shannon
Final	20/7/1947	Roscommon 2-12 Sligo 1-8 Ballina

Leinster

First Round	11/5/1947	Meath 5-7 Wicklow 2-3 Newbridge
	18/5/1947	Dublin 1-11 Longford 0-5 Mullingar
	18/5/1947	Kildare 2-8 Wexford 1-9 Carlow
Quarter-final	11/5/1947	Offaly 2-6 Carlow 1-3 Portlaoise
	1/6/1947	Louth 3-11 Dublin 1-9 Navan
	15/6/1947	Meath 1-8 Westmeath 0-5 Mullingar
	22/6/1947	Laois 2-7 Kildare 1-8 Tullamore
Semi-final	6/7/1947	Meath 0-9 Louth 1-4 Croke Park
	6/7/1947	Offaly 0-4 Laois 5-11 Portlaoise
Final	20/7/1947	Meath 3-7 Laois 1-7 Croke Park

Munster

First Round	1/6/1947	Tipperary 4-13 Waterford 0-4 Carrick-on-Suir
	8/6/1947	Clare 4-9 Limerick 2-4 Ennis
Semi-final	6/7/1947	Cork 2-3 Tipperary 1-2 Fermoy
	6/7/1947	Kerry 9-10 Clare 0-4 Limerick
Final	27/7/1947	Kerry 3-8 Cork 2-6 Cork

Ulster

First Round	8/6/1947	Tyrone 0-7 Fermanagh 1-4 Irvinestown
	15/6/1947	Tyrone 3-5 Fermanagh 2-6 Coalisland
Quarter-final	8/6/1947	Antrim 2-8 Donegal 0-3 Letterkenny
	15/6/1947	Down 2-11 Derry 2-5 Lurgan
	15/6/1947	Cavan 0-9 Monaghan 1-6 Cavan
	22/6/1947	Cavan 1-11 Monaghan 1-9 Clones
	22/6/1947	Armagh 1-6 Tyrone 1-6 Armagh
	29/6/1947	Armagh 1-4 Tyrone 2-5 Dungannon
Semi-final	6/7/1947	Antrim 3-13 Down 1-7 Lurgan
	6/7/1947	Cavan 4-5 Tyrone 0-2 Dungannon
Final	20/7/1947	Cavan 3-4 Antrim 1-6 Clones

All-Ireland

Semi-final	3/8/1947	Cavan 2-4 Roscommon 0-6 Croke Park
	10/8/1947	Kerry 1-11 Meath 0-5 Croke Park
Final	14/9/1947	Cavan 2-11 Kerry 2-7 New York

1948

Kilkenny did not enter the 1948 Championship.

Connacht	*First Round*	13/6/1948	**Mayo 4-9 Leitrim 1-2** Sligo
	Semi-final	20/6/1948	**Galway 3-4 Roscommon 1-4** Ballinasloe
		27/6/1948	**Mayo 4-2 Sligo 1-5** Sligo
	Final	18/7/1948	**Mayo 2-4 Galway 1-7** Roscommon
		25/7/1948	**Mayo 2-10 Galway 2-7** Roscommon

Leinster	*First Round*	2/5/1948	**Carlow 3-11 Wicklow 1-5** Enniscorthy
		9/5/1948	**Louth 2-14 Longford 1-2** Navan
		9/5/1948	**Offaly 5-5 Kildare 1-8** Portlaoise
	Quarter-final	2/5/1948	**Meath 0-14 Westmeath 1-6** Mullingar
		16/5/1948	**Carlow 4-4 Laois 1-7** Athy
		6/6/1948	**Offaly 3-8 Wexford 4-6** Carlow
		13/6/1948	**Louth 1-8 Dublin 0-6** Croke Park
	Semi-final	4/7/1948	**Wexford 3-9 Carlow 4-5** Croke Park
		11/7/1948	**Meath 2-5 Louth 2-6** Croke Park
	Final	25/7/1948	**Louth 2-10 Wexford 2-5** Croke Park

Munster	*First Round*	30/5/1948	**Clare 4-10 Limerick 0-2** Ennis
		20/6/1948	**Tipperary 3-13 Waterford 1-7** Fermoy
	Semi-final	4/7/1948	**Cork 0-12 Tipperary 1-8** Dungarvan
		4/7/1948	**Kerry 6-6 Clare 1-8** Ballylongford
	Final	25/7/1948	**Kerry 2-9 Cork 2-6** Killarney

Ulster	*First Round*	13/6/1948	**Down 5-7 Armagh 2-3** Newcastle
	Quarter-final	6/6/1948	**Derry 2-6 Monaghan 2-9** Clones
		6/6/1948	**Antrim 1-3 Donegal 0-1** Corrigan Park
		20/6/1948	**Antrim 4-5 Donegal 1-4** Corrigan Park
		13/6/1948	**Tyrone 5-8 Fermanagh 0-4** Dungannon
		20/6/1948	**Cavan 2-9 Down 2-4** Lurgan
	Semi-final	3/7/1948	**Antrim 0-12 Tyrone 1-3** Lurgan
		10/7/1948	**Cavan 1-9 Monaghan 0-7** Cavan
	Final	24/7/1948	**Cavan 2-12 Antrim 2-4** Clones

All-Ireland	*Semi-final*	22/8/1948	**Cavan 1-14 Louth 4-2** Croke Park
		29/8/1948	**Mayo 0-13 Kerry 0-3** Croke Park
	Final	26/9/1948	**Cavan 4-5 Mayo 4-4** Croke Park

1949

Fermanagh, Kilkenny and Limerick did not enter the 1949 Championship.

Connacht

First Round	5/6/1949	**Mayo 2-10 Roscommon 1-9** Ballymote
Semi-final	12/6/1949	**Leitrim 3-3 Galway 1-7** Carrick-on-Shannon
	19/6/1949	**Mayo 7-10 Sligo 0-2** Ballina
Final	30/7/1949	**Mayo 4-6 Leitrim 0-3** Roscommon

Leinster

First Round	1/5/1949	**Dublin 2-9 Longford 2-5** Mullingar
	8/5/1949	**Westmeath 3-7 Carlow 1-5** Portlaoise
	15/5/1949	**Meath 0-11 Kildare 1-5** Croke Park
Quarter-final	22/5/1949	**Louth 0-7 Wicklow 0-5** Croke Park
	29/5/1949	**Westmeath 2-5 Laois 0-7** Tullamore
	5/6/1949	**Offaly 4-7 Dublin 3-7** Portlaoise
	12/6/1949	**Meath 0-14 Wexford 4-0** Croke Park
Semi final	3/7/1949	**Meath 1-5 Louth 1-5** Croke Park
	10/7/1949	**Meath 2-9 Louth 3-6** Croke Park
	24/7/1949	**Meath 2-5 Louth 1-7** Croke Park
	10/7/1949	**Offaly 1-9 Westmeath 2-6** Tullamore
	17/7/1949	**Offaly 1-2 Westmeath 0-8** Mullingar
Final	31/7/1949	**Meath 4-5 Westmeath 0-6** Croke Park

Munster

First Round	22/5/1949	**Tipperary 3-8 Waterford 3-4** Dungarvan
Semi-final	19/6/1949	**Clare 3-7 Kerry 1-8** Ennis
	10/7/1949	**Cork 4-2 Tipperary 2-4** Dungarvan
Final	31/7/1949	**Cork 3-6 Clare 0-7** Limerick

Ulster

First Round	4/6/1949	**Antrim 5-9 Derry 1-6** Magherafelt
	4/6/1949	**Armagh 3-6 Monaghan 1-8** Lurgan
	12/6/1949	**Cavan 7-10 Tyrone 1-7** Cavan
	12/6/1949	**Down 0-8 Donegal 2-6** Letterkenny
Semi-final	26/6/1949	**Antrim 1-6 Cavan 3-7** Corrigan Park
	3/7/1949	**Armagh 0-14 Donegal 1-4** Dungannon
Final	31/7/1949	**Cavan 1-7 Armagh 1-6** Clones

All-Ireland

Semi-final	14/8/1949	**Meath 3-10 Mayo 1-10** Croke Park
	21/8/1949	**Cavan 1-9 Cork 2-3** Croke Park
Final	25/9/1949	**Meath 1-10 Cavan 1-6** Croke Park

1950

Fermanagh, Kilkenny and Limerick did not enter the 1950 Championship.

Connacht

First Round	4/6/1950	**Sligo 4-5 Leitrim 2-3** Bocage
Semi-final	11/6/1950	**Roscommon 0-10 Galway 1-4** Roscommon
	25/6/1950	**Mayo 0-10 Sligo 1-5** Ballina
Final	16/7/1950	**Mayo 1-7 Roscommon 0-4** Tuam

Leinster

First Round	7/5/1950	**Kildare 2-11 Dublin 1-9** Mullingar
	14/5/1950	**Wicklow 2-4 Longford 0-6** Newbridge
	14/5/1950	**Laois 0-12 Westmeath 0-5** Tullamore
Quarter-final	21/5/1950	**Louth 1-7 Carlow 1-6** Croke Park
	28/5/1950	**Kildare 2-5 Offaly 1-6** Portlaoise
	4/6/1950	**Wexford 4-3 Laois 1-5** Carlow
	18/6/1950	**Meath 6-8 Wicklow 0-4** Croke Park
Semi-final	25/6/1950	**Louth 1-10 Kildare 1-8** Croke Park
	2/7/1950	**Meath 1-5 Wexford 0-6** Croke Park
Final	23/7/1950	**Louth 1-3 Meath 1-3** Croke Park
	6/8/1950	**Louth 3-5 Meath 0-13** Croke Park

Munster

First Round	2/7/1950	**Cork 3-8 Waterford 2-2** Fermoy
Semi-final	18/6/1950	**Kerry 1-6 Clare 1-6** Tralee
	16/7/1950	**Kerry 6-6 Clare 2-4** Limerick
	16/7/1950	**Cork 3-5 Tipperary 0-3** Cork
Final	30/7/1950	**Kerry 2-5 Cork 1-5** Cork

Ulster

First Round	4/6/1950	**Antrim 5-10 Derry 0-5** Corrigan Park
	11/6/1950	**Cavan 8-7 Tyrone 0-3** Coalisland
	18/6/1950	**Down 2-8 Donegal 3-5** Newcastle
	25/6/1950	**Down 4-3 Donegal 1-7** Letterkenny
	25/6/1950	**Armagh 0-14 Monaghan 1-5** Clones
Semi-final	2/7/1950	**Antrim 2-6 Cavan 1-12** Clones
	9/7/1950	**Armagh 1-8 Down 1-7** Dungannon
Final	23/7/1950	**Armagh 1-11 Cavan 1-7** Clones

All-Ireland

Semi-final	13/8/1950	**Mayo 3-9 Armagh 0-6** Croke Park
	20/8/1950	**Louth 1-7 Kerry 0-8** Croke Park
Final	24/9/1950	**Mayo 2-5 Louth 1-6** Croke Park

Fermanagh, Kilkenny and Leitrim did not enter the 1951 Championship.

Connacht	Semi-final	1/7/1951	**Galway 2-10 Roscommon 1-4** Tuam
		24/6/1951	**Mayo 3-7 Sligo 1-5** Ballymote
	Final	15/7/1951	**Mayo 4-13 Galway 2-3** Tuam

Leinster	First Round	13/5/1951	**Kildare 2-9 Wicklow 1-3** Carlow
		20/5/1951	**Longford 2-5 Carlow 1-8** Portlaoise
		27/5/1951	**Longford 1-7 Carlow 1-1** Mullingar
		20/5/1951	**Offaly 1-3 Dublin 1-8** Newbridge
		27/5/1951	**Louth 2-9 Kildare 2-6** Croke Park
	Quarter-final	27/5/1951	**Wexford 2-5 Westmeath 2-5** Portlaoise
		10/6/1951	**Wexford 1-10 Westmeath 2-5** Croke Park
		3/6/1951	**Laois 1-12 Longford 2-2** Tullamore
		3/6/1951	**Meath 0-11 Dublin 1-5** Drogheda
	Semi-final	1/7/1951	**Laois 1-9 Wexford 2-4** Carlow
		8/7/1951	**Meath 0-6 Louth 0-6** Croke Park
		22/7/1951	**Meath 0-7 Louth 0-6** Croke Park
	Final	5/8/1951	**Meath 4-9 Laois 0-3** Croke Park

Munster	First Round	3/6/1951	**Clare 1-7 Tipperary 1-5** Tralee
		3/6/1951	**Cork 2-13 Limerick 2-4** Buttevant
	Semi-final	24/6/1951	**Cork 4-9 Clare 1-1** Cork
		1/7/1951	**Kerry 5-6 Waterford 1-1** Waterford
	Final	15/7/1951	**Kerry 1-6 Cork 0-4** Killarney

Ulster	First Round	3/6/1951	**Antrim 2-7 Donegal 2-7** Letterkenny
		17/6/1951	**Antrim 1-6 Donegal 1-5** Corrigan Park
		17/6/1951	**Armagh 7-13 Tyrone 2-3** Armagh
		17/6/1951	**Cavan 2-9 Down 0-7** Kingscourt
		24/6/1951	**Derry 1-3 Monaghan 0-5** Magherafelt
	Semi-final	1/7/1951	**Antrim 1-8 Armagh 0-5** Coalisland
		8/7/1951	**Cavan 1-6 Derry 1-4** Lurgan
	Final	29/7/1951	**Antrim 1-7 Cavan 2-3** Clones

All-Ireland	Semi-final	12/8/1951	**Mayo 1-5 Kerry 1-5** Croke Park
		9/9/1951	**Mayo 2-4 Kerry 1-5** Croke Park
		19/8/1951	**Meath 2-6 Antrim 1-7** Croke Park
	Final	23/9/1951	**Mayo 2-8 Meath 0-9** Croke Park

1952

Fermanagh, Kilkenny and Leitrim did not enter the 1952 Championship.

Connacht

Semi-final	22/6/1952	**Mayo 0-9 Sligo 0-6** Charlestown
	29/6/1952	**Roscommon 1-6 Galway 1-5** Roscommon
Final	13/7/1952	**Roscommon 3-4 Mayo 0-6** Castlebar

Leinster

First Round	4/5/1952	**Longford 3-8 Kildare 0-5** Mullingar
	11/5/1952	**Carlow 2-8 Wicklow 1-7** Athy
	11/5/1952	**Offaly 0-8 Westmeath 1-1** Mullingar
Quarter-final	25/5/1952	**Meath 2-7 Dublin 2-5** Drogheda
	1/6/1952	**Carlow 2-7 Laois 2-5** Athy
	1/6/1952	**Louth 0-9 Wexford 1-2** Croke Park
	8/6/1952	**Offaly 0-7 Longford 0-9** Mullingar
Semi-final	22/6/1952	**Louth 3-11 Carlow 0-4** Croke Park
	29/6/1952	**Meath 1-9 Longford 0-9** Mullingar
Final	13/7/1952	**Meath 1-6 Louth 0-8** Croke Park

Munster

First Round	18/5/1952	**Waterford 1-3 Clare 0-5** Ennis
	25/5/1952	**Tipperary 0-9 Limerick 1-4** Kilmallock
Semi-final	6/7/1952	**Cork 1-7 Tipperary 0-5** Clonmel
	6/7/1952	**Kerry 0-14 Waterford 1-7** Tralee
Final	20/7/1952	**Cork 0-11 Kerry 0-2** Cork

Ulster

First Round	15/6/1952	**Armagh 1-8 Tyrone 1-6** Dungannon
	15/6/1952	**Cavan 2-10 Down 1-3** Newcastle
	22/6/1952	**Monaghan 2-12 Derry 0-12** Clones
	29/6/1952	**Antrim 1-7 Donegal 2-3** Corrigan Park
Semi-final	6/7/1952	**Monaghan 1-8 Armagh 1-5** Dungannon
	13/7/1952	**Cavan 3-6 Antrim 2-6** Clones
Final	27/7/1952	**Cavan 1-8 Monaghan 0-8** Cavan

All-Ireland

Semi-final	3/8/1952	**Meath 1-6 Roscommon 0-7** Croke Park
	17/8/1952	**Cavan 0-10 Cork 0-3** Croke Park
Final	28/9/1952	**Cavan 2-4 Meath 1-7** Croke Park
	12/10/1952	**Cavan 0-9 Meath 0-5** Croke Park

1953

Fermanagh, Kilkenny and Limerick did not enter the 1953 Championship.

Connacht

First Round	21/6/1953	**Galway 1-8 Leitrim 0-2** Roscommon
Semi-final	28/6/1953	**Sligo 1-6 Mayo 2-6** Ballymote
	5/7/1953	**Roscommon 4-4 Galway 0-3** Tuam
Final	19/7/1953	**Roscommon 1-6 Mayo 0-6** Roscommon

Leinster

First Round	10/5/1953	**Carlow 1-9 Kildare 2-1** Athy
	10/5/1953	**Louth 2-11 Westmeath 0-5** Navan
	10/5/1953	**Wicklow 4-7 Longford 2-10** Tullamore
Quarter-final	24/5/1953	**Meath 2-6 Dublin 2-5** Navan
	24/5/1953	**Wexford 1-9 Laois 0-11** Carlow
	31/5/1953	**Offaly 1-7 Carlow 0-9** Portlaoise
	7/6/1953	**Louth 1-10 Wicklow 0-4** Croke Park
Semi-final	28/6/1953	**Offaly 0-7 Wexford 1-7** Carlow
	5/7/1953	**Louth 1-7 Meath 1-6** Croke Park
Final	26/7/1953	**Louth 1-7 Wexford 0-7** Croke Park

Munster

First Round	31/5/1953	**Waterford 2-4 Tipperary 0-4** Waterford
Semi-final	5/7/1953	**Cork 1-7 Waterford 1-5** Waterford
	5/7/1953	**Kerry 6-10 Clare 0-2** Ennis
Final	19/7/1953	**Kerry 2-7 Cork 2-3** Killarney

Ulster

First Round	30/5/1953	**Derry 1-11 Down 2-5** Magherafelt
	14/6/1953	**Tyrone 8-7 Donegal 0-3** Ballybofey
	21/6/1953	**Armagh 1-8 Antrim 1-4** Lurgan
	21/6/1953	**Cavan 2-7 Monaghan 0-2** Cavan
Semi-final	5/7/1953	**Cavan 2-10 Tyrone 2-4** Clones
	12/7/1953	**Armagh 4-11 Derry 1-5** Casement Park
Final	26/7/1953	**Armagh 1-6 Cavan 0-5** Casement Park

All-Ireland

Semi-final	9/8/1953	**Armagh 0-8 Roscommon 0-7** Croke Park
	23/8/1953	**Kerry 3-6 Louth 0-10** Croke Park
Final	27/9/1953	**Kerry 0-13 Armagh 1-6** Croke Park

1954

Clare, Fermanagh, Kilkenny and Limerick did not enter the 1954 Championship.

Connacht

First Round	13/6/1954	**Mayo 4-9 Roscommon 1-7** Castlebar
Semi-final	27/6/1954	**Sligo 1-8 Leitrim 1-7** Carrick-on-Shannon
	4/7/1954	**Galway 2-4 Mayo 1-5** Tuam
Final	18/7/1954	**Galway 2-10 Sligo 3-4** Tuam

Leinster

First Round	9/5/1954	**Longford 1-6 Laois 0-7** Tullamore
	23/5/1954	**Kildare 1-5 Carlow 0-8** Carlow
	30/5/1954	**Kildare 1-9 Carlow 2-6** Carlow
	13/6/1954	**Kildare 1-7 Carlow 1-6** Athy
	13/6/1954	**Meath 1-9 Wicklow 1-8** Croke Park
Quarter-final	23/5/1954	**Dublin 0-11 Louth 0-2** Drogheda
	30/5/1954	**Longford 1-7 Westmeath 1-4** Longford
	30/5/1954	**Wexford 0-7 Offaly 1-5** Carlow
	27/6/1954	**Meath 3-2 Kildare 0-5** Croke Park
Semi-final	4/7/1954	**Dublin 2-4 Offaly 2-5** Portlaoise
	11/7/1954	**Meath 2-9 Longford 1-5** Longford
Final	25/7/1954	**Meath 4-7 Offaly 2-10** Croke Park

Munster

Semi-final	4/7/1954	**Cork 3-11 Tipperary 2-7** Clonmel
	4/7/1954	**Kerry 3-10 Waterford 1-2** Waterford
Final	25/7/1954	**Kerry 4-9 Cork 2-3** Cork

Ulster

First Round	13/6/1954	**Derry 4-11 Down 3-4** Newcastle
	13/6/1954	**Tyrone 1-7 Donegal 1-5** Dungannon
	27/6/1954	**Cavan 3-8 Monaghan 2-5** Clones
	10/7/1954	**Armagh 1-8 Antrim 1-6** Casement Park
Semi-final	4/7/1954	**Armagh 1-12 Derry 2-6** Casement Park
	11/7/1954	**Cavan 3-10 Tyrone 2-10** Castleblayney
Final	25/7/1954	**Cavan 2-10 Armagh 2-5** Clones

All-Ireland

Semi-final	1/8/1954	**Meath 1-5 Cavan 0-7** Croke Park
	15/8/1954	**Kerry 2-6 Galway 1-6** Croke Park
Final	26/9/1954	**Meath 1-13 Kerry 1-7** Croke Park

1955

Fermanagh, Kilkenny and Limerick did not enter the 1955 Championship.

Connacht

First Round	19/6/1955	Galway 0-3 Roscommon 1-6 Castlebar
Semi-final	26/6/1955	Mayo 3-11 Leitrim 0-9 Sligo
	3/7/1955	Sligo 0-4 Roscommon 1-8 Castlebar
Final	17/7/1955	Mayo 3-11 Roscommon 1-3 Tuam

Leinster

First Round	8/5/1955	Carlow 3-5 Laois 3-4 Athy
	15/5/1955	Kildare 1-6 Wexford 1-5 Carlow
	15/5/1955	Louth 1-3 Longford 0-5 Croke Park
Quarter-final	1/5/1955	Westmeath 0-7 Wicklow 0-6 Newbridge
	22/5/1955	Dublin 3-9 Carlow 0-6 Newbridge
	29/5/1955	Meath 3-4 Kildare 2-7 Croke Park
	12/6/1955	Meath 1-9 Kildare 0-11 Croke Park
	5/6/1955	Offaly 5-12 Louth 0-7 Croke Park
Semi-final	3/7/1955	Meath 0-10 Westmeath 1-6 Croke Park
	10/7/1955	Dublin 1-9 Offaly 2-3 Portlaoise
Final	24/7/1955	Dublin 5-12 Meath 0-7 Croke Park

Munster

First Round	12/6/1955	Clare 1-10 Tipperary 0-7 Limerick
Semi-final	26/6/1955	Cork 2-8 Tipperary 0-7 Clonmel
	3/7/1955	Kerry 3-7 Waterford 0-4 Listowel
Final	24/7/1955	Kerry 0-14 Cork 2-6 Killarney

Ulster

First Round	5/6/1955	Derry 0-13 Tyrone 1-5 Magherafelt
	5/6/1955	Donegal 3-8 Monaghan 2-8 Bundoran
	12/6/1955	Armagh 1-8 Down 0-5 Lurgan
	19/6/1955	Cavan 1-10 Antrim 2-1 Breffni Park
Semi-final	3/7/1955	Armagh 0-2 Derry 3-4 Casement Park
	10/7/1955	Cavan 2-5 Donegal 1-6 Clones
Final	31/7/1955	Cavan 0-11 Derry 0-8 Clones

All-Ireland

Semi-final	14/8/1955	Kerry 2-10 Cavan 1-13 Croke Park
	11/9/1955	Kerry 4-7 Cavan 0-5 Croke Park
	21/8/1955	Dublin 0-7 Mayo 1-4 Croke Park
	11/9/1955	Dublin 1-8 Mayo 1-7 Croke Park
Final	25/9/1955	Kerry 0-12 Dublin 1-6 Croke Park

Fermanagh, Kilkenny and Limerick did not enter the 1956 Championship.

Connacht	*First Round*	17/6/1956	**Galway 5-13 Mayo 2-5** Castlebar
	Semi-final	24/6/1956	**Sligo 3-5 Leitrim 0-11** Sligo
		8/7/1956	**Galway 1-9 Roscommon 0-2** Tuam
	Final	15/7/1956	**Galway 3-12 Sligo 1-5** Sligo

Leinster	*First Round*	6/5/1956	**Longford 3-7 Laois 1-6** Tullamore
		6/5/1956	**Wicklow 4-12 Carlow 1-4** Athy
		20/5/1956	**Kildare 1-9 Louth 0-9** Navan
	Quarter-final	13/5/1956	**Wexford 2-11 Westmeath 1-5** Carlow
		27/5/1956	**Dublin 0-11 Wicklow 0-5** Enniscorthy
		27/5/1956	**Offaly 1-14 Meath 1-5** Newbridge
		10/6/1956	**Kildare 1-12 Longford 2-6** Mullingar
	Semi-final	24/6/1956	**Wexford 2-7 Dublin 0-7** Carlow
		1/7/1956	**Kildare 1-8 Offaly 0-7** Portlaoise
	Final	22/7/1956	**Kildare 2-11 Wexford 1-8** Croke Park

Munster	*First Round*	3/6/1956	**Tipperary 2-4 Clare 0-7** Limerick
	Semi-final	24/6/1956	**Cork 0-12 Waterford 0-1** Lismore
		24/6/1956	**Kerry 3-7 Tipperary 3-2** Tralee
	Final	15/7/1956	**Cork 2-2 Kerry 2-2** Cork
		29/7/1956	**Cork 1-8 Kerry 1-7** Killarney

Ulster	*First Round*	3/6/1956	**Tyrone 3-7 Derry 2-4** Dungannon
		10/6/1956	**Donegal 1-8 Monaghan 2-8** Bundoran
		17/6/1956	**Cavan 3-15 Antrim 2-4** Casement Park
		24/6/1956	**Armagh 2-5 Down 0-6** Newry
	Semi-final	8/7/1956	**Tyrone 2-9 Monaghan 0-7** Lurgan
		15/7/1956	**Cavan 1-9 Armagh 1-5** Castleblayney
	Final	29/7/1956	**Tyrone 3-5 Cavan 0-4** Clones

All-Ireland	*Semi-final*	5/8/1956	**Cork 0-9 Kildare 0-5** Croke Park
		12/8/1956	**Galway 0-8 Tyrone 0-6** Croke Park
	Final	7/10/1956	**Galway 2-13 Cork 3-7** Croke Park

1957

Fermanagh, Kilkenny and Limerick did not enter the 1957 Championship.

Connacht

First Round	9/6/1957	**Roscommon 0-7 Mayo 0-6** Roscommon
Semi-final	23/6/1957	**Sligo 2-1 Leitrim 1-8** Carrick-on-Shannon
	30/6/1957	**Galway 0-13 Roscommon 0-7** Roscommon
Final	14/7/1957	**Galway 4-8 Leitrim 0-4** Pearse Stadium

Leinster

First Round	5/5/1957	**Longford 1-10 Westmeath 0-6** Mullingar
	5/5/1957	**Louth 3-6 Carlow 0-4** Navan
	12/5/1957	**Wicklow 3-6 Laois 1-6** Athy
Quarter-final	19/5/1957	**Kildare 2-10 Offaly 1-3** Portlaoise
	26/5/1957	**Louth 1-12 Wexford 0-9** Croke Park
	26/5/1957	**Wicklow 3-7 Meath 1-11** Athy
	2/6/1957	**Dublin 2-10 Longford 1-4** Mullingar
Semi-final	16/6/1957	**Louth 5-8 Kildare 1-9** Croke Park
	23/6/1957	**Dublin 3-9 Wicklow 0-9** Newbridge
Final	14/7/1957	**Louth 2-9 Dublin 1-7** Croke Park

Munster

First Round	19/5/1957	**Tipperary 2-9 Clare 4-5** Limerick
Semi-final	2/6/1957	**Waterford 2-5 Kerry 0-10** Waterford
	9/6/1957	**Cork 1-7 Clare 0-3** Charleville
Final	21/7/1957	**Cork 0-16 Waterford 1-2** Semple Stadium

Ulster

First Round	9/6/1957	**Derry 4-14 Antrim 0-8** Ballinascreen
	16/6/1957	**Cavan 1-12 Monaghan 1-5** Cavan
	16/6/1957	**Donegal 3-2 Down 0-6** Ballyshannon
	30/6/1957	**Tyrone 2-9 Armagh 3-5** Lurgan
Semi-final	7/7/1957	**Derry 1-10 Cavan 1-9** Dungannon
	14/7/1957	**Tyrone 3-5 Donegal 2-3** Cavan
Final	28/7/1957	**Tyrone 1-9 Derry 0-10** Clones

All-Ireland

Semi-final	11/8/1957	**Cork 2-4 Galway 0-9** Croke Park
	18/8/1957	**Louth 0-13 Tyrone 0-7** Croke Park
Final	22/9/1957	**Louth 1-9 Cork 1-7** Croke Park

Fermanagh, Kilkenny and Limerick did not enter the 1958 Championship.

Connacht

First Round	15/6/1958	**Mayo 3-10 Sligo 1-6** Charlestown
Semi-final	22/6/1958	**Leitrim 0-11 Roscommon 0-9** Roscommon
	29/6/1958	**Galway 2-9 Mayo 0-6** Tuam
Final	13/7/1958	**Galway 2-10 Leitrim 1-11** Roscommon

Leinster

First Round	27/4/1958	**Meath 3-9 Longford 0-7** Mullingar
	4/5/1948	**Carlow 1-10 Wicklow 1-9** Athy
	11/5/1958	**Offaly 4-3 Laois 1-5** Newbridge
Quarter-final	11/5/1958	**Louth 2-9 Westmeath 3-4** Navan
	18/5/1958	**Carlow 2-6 Wexford 1-6** Carlow
	1/6/1958	**Dublin 1-12 Meath 2-7** Drogheda
	1/6/1958	**Offaly 1-11 Kildare 1-6** Portlaoise
Semi-final	22/6/1958	**Dublin 3-9 Carlow 2-7** Portlaoise
	29/6/1958	**Louth 4-3 Offaly 1-5** Croke Park
Final	20/7/1958	**Dublin 1-11 Louth 1-6** Croke Park

Munster

First Round	15/6/1958	**Waterford 3-9 Clare 1-7** Dungarvan
Semi-final	29/6/1958	**Cork 1-11 Waterford 1-4** Fermoy
	29/6/1958	**Kerry 1-6 Tipperary 0-7** Semple Stadium
Final	13/7/1958	**Kerry 2-7 Cork 0-3** Cork

Ulster

First Round	1/6/1958	**Derry 0-8 Antrim 0-5** Casement Park
	15/6/1958	**Cavan 0-7 Monaghan 0-7** Clones
	29/6/1958	**Cavan 1-9 Monaghan 1-5** Cavan
	6/7/1958	**Cavan 0-14 Monaghan 1-6** Casement Park
	15/6/1958	**Down 3-11 Donegal 3-5** Newry
	22/6/1958	**Tyrone 1-9 Armagh 0-10** Dungannon
Semi-final	6/7/1958	**Down 1-9 Tyrone 0-2** Lurgan
	13/7/1958	**Derry 4-7 Cavan 3-6** Clones
Final	27/7/1958	**Derry 1-11 Down 2-4** Clones

All-Ireland

Semi-final	17/8/1958	**Dublin 2-7 Galway 1-9** Croke Park
	24/8/1958	**Derry 2-6 Kerry 2-5** Croke Park
Final	28/9/1958	**Dublin 2-12 Derry 1-9** Croke Park

Fermanagh, Kilkenny and Limerick did not enter the 1959 Championship.

Connacht	First Round	21/6/1959	Mayo 3-8 Sligo 1-8 Sligo
	Semi-final	21/6/1959	Galway 0-12 Roscommon 0-4 Pearse Stadium
		28/6/1959	Mayo 2-4 Leitrim 0-10 Castlebar
		12/7/1959	Mayo 2-5 Leitrim 2-7 Roscommon
	Final	9/8/1959	Galway 5-8 Leitrim 0-12 Sligo
Leinster	First Round	3/5/1959	Carlow 1-12 Wexford 0-3 Enniscorthy
		3/5/1959	Laois 0-11 Wicklow 0-5 Athy
		3/5/1959	Longford 4-3 Westmeath 0-10 Athy
	Quarter-final	17/5/1959	Offaly 1-9 Laois 2-6 Portlaoise
		7/6/1959	Offaly 0-10 Laois 3-8 Tullamore
		24/5/1959	Dublin 1-11 Carlow 2-4 Portlaoise
		31/5/1959	Longford 2-7 Meath 1-5 Mullingar
		21/6/1959	Louth 1-13 Kildare 3-6 Croke Park
	Semi-final	28/6/1959	Longford 0-8 Laois 2-9 Tullamore
		5/7/1959	Dublin 1-8 Louth 0-11 Navan
		26/7/1959	Dublin 3-14 Louth 1-9 Navan
	Final	2/8/1959	Dublin 1-18 Laois 2-8 Tullamore
Munster	First Round	31/5/1959	Tipperary 2-6 Waterford 1-7 Clonmel
	Semi-final	17/5/1959	Cork 4-9 Clare 1-7 Ennis
		5/7/1959	Kerry 1-15 Tipperary 1-2 Killarney
	Final	2/8/1959	Kerry 2-15 Cork 2-8 Killarney
Ulster	First Round	31/5/1959	Derry 0-5 Armagh 1-6 Lurgan
		7/6/1959	Cavan 2-9 Donegal 0-4 Ballybofey
		14/6/1959	Down 4-9 Antrim 1-3 Newcastle
		21/6/1959	Tyrone 1-9 Monaghan 0-7 Castleblayney
	Semi-final	5/7/1959	Cavan 0-13 Armagh 2-7 Castleblayney
		21/7/1959	Cavan 1-9 Armagh 1-7 Clones
		12/7/1959	Down 1-6 Tyrone 1-6 Casement Park
		28/7/1959	Down 1-12 Tyrone 0-4 Casement Park
	Final	9/8/1959	Down 2-16 Cavan 0-7 Clones
All-Ireland	Semi-final	16/8/1959	Kerry 1-10 Dublin 2-5 Croke Park
		23/8/1959	Galway 1-11 Down 1-4 Croke Park
	Final	27/9/1959	Kerry 3-7 Galway 1-4 Croke Park

1960

Kilkenny and Limerick did not enter the 1960 Championship.

Connacht

First Round	12/6/1960	Mayo 1-6 Galway 2-5 Castlebar
Semi-final	19/6/1960	Leitrim 2-8 Roscommon 1-6 Sligo
	26/6/1960	Galway 1-8 Sligo 1-3 Tuam
Final	10/7/1960	Galway 2-5 Leitrim 0-5 Sligo

Leinster

First Round	1/5/1960	Kildare 1-9 Wexford 2-3 Carlow
	1/5/1960	Longford 0-9 Meath 0-8 Mullingar
	8/5/1960	Westmeath 2-10 Laois 1-11 Tullamore
Quarter-final	15/5/1960	Offaly 2-12 Carlow 2-9 Newbridge
	22/5/1960	Louth 1-10 Wicklow 1-5 Croke Park
	29/5/1960	Dublin 10-13 Longford 3-8 Mullingar
	5/6/1960	Kildare 2-8 Westmeath 2-9 Tullamore
Semi-final	26/6/1960	Offaly 3-9 Dublin 0-9 Portlaoise
	3/7/1960	Louth 1-8 Westmeath 1-1 Navan
Final	31/7/1960	Offaly 0-10 Louth 1-6 Croke Park

Munster

First Round	29/5/1960	Clare 1-6 Tipperary 1-8 Limerick
Semi-final	10/7/1960	Tipperary 0-3 Kerry 0-11 Clonmel
	10/7/1960	Waterford 1-9 Cork 0-11 Lismore
Final	24/7/1960	Kerry 3-15 Waterford 0-8 Cork

Ulster

First Round	5/6/1960	Cavan 1-10 Donegal 1-0 Cavan
Quarter-finals	5/6/1960	Derry 3-10 Armagh 1-9 Magherafelt
	12/6/1960	Antrim 1-4 Down 0-14 Casement Park
	19/6/1960	Fermanagh 2-7 Cavan 3-4 Irvinestown
	26/6/1960	Cavan 3-9 Fermanagh 2-2 Cavan
	26/6/1960	Tyrone 3-6 Monaghan 3-11 Dungannon
Semi-final	10/7/1960	Down 2-11 Monaghan 0-7 Dungannon
	17/7/1960	Cavan 3-6 Derry 0-5 Casement Park
Final	31/7/1960	Down 3-7 Cavan 1-8 Clones

All-Ireland

Semi-final	14/8/1960	Down 1-10 Offaly 2-7 Croke Park
	11/9/1960	Down 1-7 Offaly 1-5 Croke Park
	7/8/1960	Kerry 1-8 Galway 0-8 Croke Park
Final	25/9/1960	Down 2-10 Kerry 0-8 Croke Park

1961

Limerick did not enter the 1961 Championship.

Connacht

First Round	11/6/1961	**Galway 0-10 Mayo 0-6** Tuam
Semi-final	18/6/1961	**Roscommon 2-9 Sligo 2-6** Charlestown
	25/6/1961	**Leitrim 2-9 Galway 4-11** Ballinamore
Final	9/7/1961	**Roscommon 1-11 Galway 2-7** Castlebar

Leinster

	30/4/1961	**Wexford 2-11 Wicklow 0-11** Carlow
First Round	7/5/1961	**Kildare 3-8 Kilkenny 3-4** Newbridge
	7/5/1961	**Longford 3-10 Westmeath 0-8** Tullamore
	14/5/1961	**Carlow 3-11 Laois 3-9** Athy
	21/5/1961	**Longford 0-8 Meath 1-6** Croke Park
Quarter final	28/5/1961	**Kildare 4-7 Louth 2-5** Croke Park
	4/6/1961	**Dublin 4-7 Wexford 0-7** Carlow
	11/6/1961	**Offaly 0-17 Carlow 2-6** Newbridge
Semi-final	2/7/1961	**Offaly 3-9 Kildare 0-6** Portlaoise
	9/7/1961	**Dublin 4-14 Meath 1-7** Navan
Final	23/7/1961	**Offaly 1-13 Dublin 1-8** Portlaoise

Munster

First Round	14/5/1961	**Waterford 1-7 Tipperary 3-13** Dungarvan
Semi-final	18/6/1961	**Cork 2-9 Tipperary 2-4** Fermoy
	25/6/1961	**Kerry 1-13 Clare 1-0** Newcastlewest
Final	16/7/1961	**Kerry 0-10 Cork 1-7** Cork
	23/7/1961	**Kerry 2-13 Cork 1-4** Killarney

Ulster

First Round	28/5/1961	**Derry 2-10 Donegal 0-4** Ballybofey
Quarter-finals	4/6/1961	**Armagh 2-7 Cavan 0-8** Lurgan
	4/6/1961	**Monaghan 1-10 Antrim 0-6** Castleblayney
	11/6/1961	**Derry 1-9 Tyrone 0-10** Ballinascreen
	11/6/1961	**Down 0-12 Fermanagh 0-7** Newry
Semi-final	25/6/1961	**Armagh 5-9 Monaghan 0-5** Dungannon
	2/7/1961	**Down 2-12 Derry 1-10** Casement Park
Final	23/7/1961	**Down 2-10 Armagh 1-10** Casement Park

All-Ireland

Semi-final	6/8/1961	**Down 1-12 Kerry 0-9** Croke Park
	20/8/1961	**Offaly 3-6 Roscommon 0-6** Croke Park
Final	24/9/1961	**Down 3-6 Offaly 2-8** Croke Park

1962

Limerick did not enter the 1962 Championship.

Connacht

First Round	10/6/1962	**Mayo 1-13 Sligo 3-7** Charlestown
	24/6/1962	**Sligo 1-7 Mayo 1-6** Sligo
Semi-final	17/6/1962	**Galway 3-7 Leitrim 1-10** Ballinasloe
	8/7/1962	**Roscommon 3-6 Sligo 1-11** Charlestown
Final	22/7/1962	**Roscommon 3-7 Galway 2-9** Castlebar

Leinster

	29/4/1962	**Carlow 3-12 Kilkenny 2-12** Kilkenny
First Round	6/5/1962	**Laois 2-11 Longford 1-9** Tullamore
	13/5/1962	**Kildare 5-12 Wexford 1-6** Carlow
	20/5/1962	**Louth 1-11 Wicklow 0-6** Croke Park
	20/5/1962	**Carlow 2-4 Offaly 2-9** Portlaoise
Quarter-final	27/5/1962	**Laois 2-8 Westmeath 1-9** Tullamore
	3/6/1962	**Dublin 1-8 Louth 0-10** Navan
	10/6/1962	**Kildare 0-8 Meath 0-6** Croke Park
Semi-final	17/6/1962	**Dublin 0-13 Laois 1-8** Carlow
	1/7/1962	**Kildare 2-6 Offaly 3-5** Croke Park
Final	15/7/1962	**Dublin 2-8 Offaly 1-7** Croke Park

Munster

First Round	27/5/1962	**Tipperary 0-6 Waterford 3-5** Clonmel
Semi-final	17/6/1962	**Cork 2-8 Clare 0-4** Buttevant
	24/6/1962	**Kerry 2-18 Waterford 2-6** Listowel
Final	15/7/1962	**Cork 0-4 Kerry 4-8** Cork

Ulster

First Round	3/6/1962	**Derry 2-10 Donegal 2-7** Magherafelt
	10/6/1962	**Antrim 2-7 Monaghan 0-2** Casement Park
Quarter-finals	17/6/1962	**Tyrone 1-9 Derry 2-2** Dungannon
	24/6/1962	**Cavan 3-8 Armagh 2-2** Cavan
	1/7/1962	**Fermanagh 1-8 Down 4-10** Irvinestown
Semi-final	8/7/1962	**Antrim 0-5 Cavan 1-6** Casement Park
	15/7/1962	**Down 1-12 Tyrone 1-6** Casement Park
Final	29/7/1962	**Cavan 3-6 Down 0-5** Casement Park

All-Ireland

Semi-final	5/8/1962	**Kerry 2-12 Dublin 0-10** Croke Park
	19/8/1962	**Roscommon 1-8 Cavan 1-6** Croke Park
Final	23/9/1962	**Kerry 1-12 Roscommon 1-6** Croke Park

1963

Limerick did not enter the 1963 Championship.

Connacht

First Round	9/6/1963	**Sligo 1-9 Leitrim 1-10** Sligo
Semi-final	16/6/1963	**Mayo 1-6 Galway 2-8** Castlebar
	23/6/1963	**Leitrim 1-8 Roscommon 1-3** Sligo
Final	14/7/1963	**Galway 4-11 Leitrim 1-6** Castlebar

Leinster

	5/5/1963	**Carlow 4-10 Kilkenny 1-4** Carlow
First Round	5/5/1963	**Westmeath 1-6 Longford 3-8** Mullingar
	19/5/1963	**Meath 1-10 Wexford 1-3** Croke Park
	26/5/1963	**Louth 2-15 Wicklow 1-6** Croke Park
	19/5/1963	**Offaly 2-5 Longford 1-2** Mullingar
Quarter-final	26/5/1963	**Laois 3-9 Carlow 0-10** Athy
	2/6/1963	**Dublin 2-6 Meath 2-5** Croke Park
	9/6/1963	**Kildare 2-11 Louth 1-12** Croke Park
Semi-final	23/6/1963	**Dublin 2-7 Kildare 1-5** Croke Park
	30/6/1963	**Laois 2-7 Offaly 0-9** Portlaoise
Final	14/7/1963	**Dublin 2-11 Laois 2-9** Croke Park

Munster

First Round	2/6/1963	**Tipperary 1-12 Clare 0-6** Limerick
Semi-final	9/6/1963	**Cork 2-14 Waterford 2-1** Fermoy
	23/6/1963	**Kerry 5-10 Tipperary 1-6** Listowel
Final	14/7/1963	**Kerry 1-18 Cork 3-7** Killarney

Ulster

First Round	2/6/1963	**Antrim 2-9 Tyrone 0-3** Casement Park
	9/6/1963	**Down 6-11 Monaghan 1-3** Newry
Quarter-finals	16/6/1963	**Armagh 1-8 Antrim 2-3** Lurgan
	16/6/1963	**Donegal 2-12 Fermanagh 1-6** Ballybofey
	23/6/1963	**Derry 2-8 Cavan 3-9** Ballinascreen
Semi-final	7/7/1963	**Down 0-9 Armagh 0-5** Casement Park
	14/7/1963	**Donegal 4-5 Cavan 0-6** Clones
Final	28/7/1963	**Down 2-11 Donegal 1-4** Cavan

All-Ireland

Semi-final	4/8/1963	**Galway 1-7 Kerry 0-8** Croke Park
	18/8/1963	**Dublin 2-11 Down 0-7** Croke Park
Final	22/9/1963	**Dublin 1-9 Galway 0-10** Croke Park

1964

Kilkenny and Limerick did not enter the 1964 Championship.

Connacht

First Round	7/6/1964	**Leitrim 2-5 Roscommon 1-8** Ck-on-Shn.
	21/6/1964	**Roscommon 1-10 Leitrim 1-10** Roscomn.
	28/6/1964	**Leitrim 1-10 Roscommon 5-9** Ck-on-Shn.
Semi-final	21/6/1964	**Sligo 1-12 Galway 2-12** Sligo
	5/7/1964	**Mayo 3-9 Roscommon 1-7** Castlebar
Final	19/7/1964	**Galway 2-12 Mayo 1-5** Tuam

Leinster

First Round	26/4/1964	**Longford 0-8 Westmeath 0-12** Longford
	3/5/1964	**Carlow 3-7 Wicklow 2-9** Athy
	31/5/1964	**Louth 1-10 Wexford 1-6** Croke Park
Quarter-final	24/5/1964	**Dublin 1-14 Carlow 1-5** Newbridge
	31/5/1964	**Laois 2-8 Westmeath 0-13** Tullamore
	7/6/1964	**Meath 2-12 Kildare 0-8** Croke Park
	14/6/1964	**Louth 1-9 Offaly 1-4** Croke Park
Semi-final	21/6/1964	**Dublin 0-8 Laois 1-2** Croke Park
	28/6/1964	**Meath 1-12 Louth 2-7** Croke Park
Final	26/7/1964	**Meath 2-12 Dublin 1-7** Croke Park

Munster

First Round	14/6/1964	**Tipperary 2-5 Clare 1-7** Limerick
Semi-final	14/6/1964	**Waterford 1-2 Cork 2-8** Dungarvan
	28/6/1964	**Tipperary 1-7 Kerry 1-14** Semple Stadium
Final	19/7/1964	**Cork 1-8 Kerry 2-11** Cork

Ulster

First Round	31/5/1964	**Tyrone 0-8 Antrim 1-9** Dungannon
Quarter-finals	7/6/1964	**Fermanagh 0-7 Donegal 1-10** Irvinestown
	14/6/1964	**Antrim 2-6 Armagh 1-8** Casement Park
	14/6/1964	**Cavan 3-9 Derry 2-3** Cavan
	21/6/1964	**Down 2-9 Monaghan 1-6** Ballybofey
Semi-final	28/6/1964	**Cavan 1-9 Donegal 0-7** Irvinestown
	5/7/1964	**Down 2-8 Antrim 1-9** Clones
Final	19/7/1964	**Cavan 2-10 Down 1-10** Casement Park

All-Ireland

Semi-final	9/8/1964	**Galway 1-8 Meath 0-9** Croke Park
	23/8/1964	**Kerry 2-12 Cavan 0-6** Croke Park
Final	27/9/1964	**Galway 0-15 Kerry 0-10** Croke Park

Kilkenny did not enter the 1965 Championship.

Connacht

First Round	6/6/1965	Mayo 2-15 Roscommon 1-6 Roscommon
	27/6/1965	Sligo 4-12 Leitrim 0-6 Carrick-on-Shannon
Semi-final	4/7/1965	Sligo 2-11 Mayo 2-8 Charlestown
		Galway *bye*
Final	1/8/1965	Galway 1-12 Sligo 2-6 Tuam

Leinster

First Round	2/5/1965	Kildare 3-14 Wicklow 1-4 Carlow
	2/5/1965	Offaly 0-5 Longford 1-5 Mullingar
	9/5/1965	Westmeath 2-11 Louth 0-9 Navan
Quarter-final	23/5/1965	Kildare 4-10 Carlow 2-9 Carlow
	30/5/1965	Dublin 2-11 Wexford 1-7 Carlow
	6/6/1965	Longford 1-9 Laois 0-8 Mullingar
	13/6/1965	Meath 1-12 Westmeath 1-9 Croke Park
Semi-final	20/6/1965	Dublin 1-11 Kildare 0-5 Tullamore
	4/7/1965	Longford 2-8 Meath 1-7 Croke Park
Final	25/7/1965	Dublin 3-6 Longford 1-9 Croke Park

Munster

First Round	2/5/1965	Tipperary 0-4 Clare 2-7 Limerick
	16/5/1965	Limerick 4-10 Waterford 0-6 Tipperary
Semi-final	13/6/1965	Kerry 2-10 Clare 1-6 Limerick
	20/6/1965	Limerick 2-5 Cork 0-6 Killarney
Final	18/7/1965	Kerry 2-16 Limerick 2-7 Limerick

Ulster

First Round	6/6/1965	Monaghan 2-12 Fermanagh 1-5 Irvinestown
Quarter-finals	30/5/1965	Antrim 2-9 Derry 1-6 Ballinascreen
	13/6/1965	Down 3-13 Tyrone 1-6 Newry
	20/6/1965	Armagh 3-7 Monaghan 1-9 Lurgan
	20/6/1965	Cavan 1-8 Donegal 1-8 Ballybofey
	4/7/1965	Cavan 0-14 Donegal 2-8 Cavan
	11/7/1965	Cavan 0-9 Donegal 0-8 Cavan
Semi-final	4/7/1965	Down 0-10 Antrim 1-5 Newry
	18/7/1965	Cavan 1-10 Armagh 0-4 Clones
Final	1/8/1965	Down 1-10 Cavan 1-8 Clones

All-Ireland

Semi-final	8/8/1965	Kerry 4-8 Dublin 2-6 Croke Park
	22/8/1965	Galway 0-10 Down 0-7 Croke Park
Final	26/9/1965	Galway 0-12 Kerry 0-9 Croke Park

1966

Kilkenny did not enter the 1966 Championship.

Connacht

First Round	12/6/1966	Leitrim 0-4 Roscommon 3-7	Ck-on-Shn.
Semi-final	19/6/1966	Sligo 1-12 Mayo 1-12	Sligo
	3/7/1966	Mayo 4-7 Sligo 3-7	Castlebar
	26/6/1966	Galway 1-11 Roscommon 0-5	Castlebar
Final	17/7/1966	Mayo 1-8 Galway 0-12	Castlebar

Leinster

First Round	1/5/1966	Westmeath 2-10 Carlow 2-6	Newbridge
	1/5/1966	Wexford 0-12 Wicklow 0-6	Gorey
	8/5/1966	Louth 0-13 Longford 0-7	Navan
Quarter-final	15/5/1966	Kildare 1-9 Offaly 2-6	Croke Park
	19/6/1966	Offaly 1-7 Kildare 1-12	Croke Park
	15/5/1966	Meath 4-15 Wexford 0-3	Croke Park
	5/6/1966	Westmeath 2-12 Laois 1-5	Tullamore
	12/6/1966	Louth 0-8 Dublin 2-10	Drogheda
Semi-final	26/6/1966	Meath 2-14 Westmeath 1-8	Croke Park
	10/7/1966	Kildare 3-9 Dublin 2-5	Navan
Final	24/7/1966	Meath 1-9 Kildare 1-8	Croke Park

Munster

First Round	8/5/1966	Clare 0-4 Cork 3-11	Ennis
	29/5/1966	Waterford 2-3 Tipperary 3-8	Dungarvan
Semi-final	26/6/1966	Cork 5-10 Limerick 1-8	Killarney
	26/6/1966	Kerry 3-16 Tipperary 2-6	Killarney
Final	17/7/1966	Kerry 1-7 Cork 2-7	Killarney

Ulster

First Round	5/6/1966	Monaghan 0-12 Fermanagh 3-8	Clones
Quarter-finals	5/6/1966	Antrim 2-7 Derry 0-6	Casement Park
	12/6/1966	Tyrone 0-4 Down 2-9	Dungannon
	19/6/1966	Cavan 1-11 Donegal 5-6	Cavan
	26/6/1966	Fermanagh 3-8 Armagh 0-8	Irvinestown
Semi-final	10/7/1966	Antrim 0-5 Down 0-9	Casement Park
	17/7/1966	Fermanagh 1-8 Donegal 4-17	Dungannon
Final	31/7/1966	Down 1-7 Donegal 0-8	Casement Park

All-Ireland

Semi-final	7/8/1966	Galway 1-11 Cork 1-9	Croke Park
	21/8/1966	Meath 2-16 Down 1-9	Croke Park
Final	25/9/1966	Galway 1-10 Meath 0-7	Croke Park

1967

Kilkenny and Limerick did not enter the 1967 Championship.

Connacht

First Round	28/5/1967	**Sligo 1-7 Mayo 3-6** Sligo
Semi-final	11/6/1967	**Roscommon 2-6 Leitrim 2-8** Roscommon
	25/6/1967	**Galway 1-8 Mayo 3-13** Pearse Stadium
Final	16/7/1967	**Mayo 4-15 Leitrim 0-7** Tuam

Leinster

First Round	23/4/1967	**Wicklow 0-10 Wexford 0-8** Aughrim
	14/5/1967	**Laois 3-8 Carlow 3-6** Athy
Second Round	28/5/1967	**Wicklow 0-11 Laois 0-8** Carlow
Quarter-final	21/5/1967	**Longford 1-7 Kildare 0-10** Croke Park
	18/6/1967	**Longford 3-12 Kildare 2-10** Croke Park
	21/5/1967	**Meath 2-9 Louth 0-3** Croke Park
	11/6/1967	**Westmeath 1-6 Dublin 0-8** Tullamore
	18/6/1967	**Offaly 0-13 Wicklow 0-7** Croke Park
Semi-final	2/7/1967	**Longford 1-7 Offaly 0-13** Croke Park
	9/7/1967	**Meath 0-12 Westmeath 0-6** Tullamore
Final	23/7/1967	**Meath 0-8 Offaly 0-6** Croke Park

Munster

First Round	21/5/1967	**Clare 0-9 Waterford 0-2** Milltown Malbay
	21/5/1967	**Limerick 4-10 Tipperary 2-5** Limerick
Semi-final	18/6/1967	**Cork 1-13 Clare 1-6** Cork
	18/6/1967	**Kerry 1-17 Limerick 1-8** Tralee
Final	16/7/1967	**Cork 0-8 Kerry 0-7** Cork

Ulster

First Round	11/6/1967	**Tyrone 0-13 Fermanagh 3-2** Irvinestown
Quarter-finals	4/6/1967	**Armagh 1-8 Donegal 2-13** Armagh
	11/6/1967	**Down 3-9 Derry 1-10** Newry
	18/6/1967	**Antrim 2-8 Cavan 2-12** Casement Park
	25/6/1967	**Tyrone 1-13 Monaghan 1-7** Dungannon
Semi-final	2/7/1967	**Down 2-8 Donegal 2-5** Clones
	9/7/1967	**Tyrone 3-3 Cavan 1-13** Irvinestown
Final	23/7/1967	**Cavan 2-12 Down 0-8** Clones

All-Ireland

Semi-final	6/8/1967	**Cork 2-7 Cavan 0-12** Croke Park
	20/8/1967	**Meath 3-14 Mayo 1-14** Croke Park
Final	24/9/1967	**Meath 1-9 Cork 0-9** Croke Park

1968

Kilkenny did not enter the 1968 Championship.

Connacht

First Round	2/6/1968	**Sligo 2-17 Leitrim 0-12** Sligo
Semi-final	16/6/1968	**Galway 2-10 Roscommon 3-7** Castlebar
	14/7/1968	**Roscommon 1-9 Galway 2-8** Roscomn.
	23/6/1968	**Mayo 1-9 Sligo 0-7** Castlebar
Final	21/7/1968	**Mayo 2-9 Galway 2-10** Castlebar

Leinster

First Round	21/4/1968	**Carlow 2-9 Wicklow 0-10** Athy
	28/4/1968	**Laois 2-12 Wexford 1-9** Carlow
Second Round	12/5/1968	**Laois 1-12 Carlow 0-7** Athy
Quarter-final	2/6/1968	**Longford 1-12 Dublin 0-12** Tullamore
	9/6/1968	**Laois 3-9 Kildare 0-9** Carlow
	9/6/1968	**Offaly 0-11 Louth 0-6** Croke Park
	23/6/1968	**Meath 1-11 Westmeath 1-7** Croke Park
Semi-final	30/6/1968	**Offaly 0-6 Laois 0-11** Tullamore
	7/7/1968	**Longford 0-12 Meath 0-7** Mullingar
Final	21/7/1968	**Longford 3-9 Laois 1-4** Croke Park

Munster

First Round	12/5/1968	**Waterford 3-5 Clare 1-15** Dungarvan
	19/5/1968	**Tipperary 0-9 Limerick 0-7** Tipperary
Semi-final	16/6/1968	**Clare 1-7 Cork 1-8** Ennis
	23/6/1968	**Tipperary 2-7 Kerry 0-17** Clonmel
Final	14/7/1968	**Kerry 1-21 Cork 3-8** Killarney

Ulster

First Round	2/6/1968	**Fermanagh 2-8 Tyrone 0-8** Irvinestown
Quarter-finals	9/6/1968	**Derry 1-6 Down 1-8** Ballinascreen
	16/6/1968	**Cavan 5-9 Antrim 1-11** Cavan
	16/6/1968	**Donegal 2-10 Armagh 1-3** Ballybofey
	23/6/1968	**Monaghan 1-12 Fermanagh 2-9** Clones
	30/6/1968	**Fermanagh 2-5 Monaghan 2-12** Irvinestn.
Semi-final	30/6/1968	**Down 2-14 Donegal 0-8** Cavan
	7/7/1968	**Cavan 1-11 Monaghan 0-5** Clones
Final	28/7/1968	**Down 0-16 Cavan 1-8** Casement Park

All-Ireland

Semi-final	4/8/1968	**Kerry 2-13 Longford 2-11** Croke Park
	18/8/1968	**Down 2-10 Galway 2-8** Croke Park
Final	22/9/1968	**Down 2-12 Kerry 1-13** Croke Park

1969

Kilkenny did not enter the 1969 Championship.

Connacht	*First Round*	15/6/1969	**Sligo 1-6 Roscommon 2-12** Sligo
	Semi-final	22/6/1969	**Leitrim 1-8 Mayo 6-13** Carrick-on-Shannon
		6/7/1969	**Galway 0-8 Roscommon 0-1** Ballinasloe
	Final	20/7/1969	**Galway 1-8 Mayo 0-11** Pearse Stadium
		3/8/1969	**Mayo 1-11 Galway 1-8** Castlebar
Leinster	*First Round*	27/4/1969	**Carlow 1-13 Wicklow 2-7** Gorey
	Second Round	11/5/1969	**Wexford 2-7 Carlow 1-10** Kilkenny
		1/6/1969	**Wexford 2-9 Carlow 2-7** Croke Park
		1/6/1969	**Westmeath 1-7 Louth 1-6** Croke Park
	Quarter-final	4/5/1969	**Dublin 3-7 Laois 1-5** Carlow
		25/5/1969	**Kildare 2-16 Meath 1-11** Croke Park
		8/6/1969	**Wexford 3-5 Longford 1-8** Croke Park
		29/6/1969	**Offaly 3-14 Westmeath 1-8** Croke Park
	Semi-final	15/6/1969	**Kildare 0-18 Dublin 0-7** Carlow
		13/7/1969	**Offaly 3-9 Wexford 1-10** Croke Park
	Final	27/7/1969	**Offaly 3-7 Kildare 1-8** Croke Park
Munster	*First Round*	4/5/1969	**Limerick 1-6 Clare 1-10** Limerick
		18/5/1969	**Tipperary 0-10 Waterford 1-7** Clonmel
		8/6/1969	**Waterford 0-15 Tipperary 0-10** Dungarvan
	Semi-final	25/5/1969	**Cork 2-4 Clare 0-5** Cork
		15/6/1969	**Waterford 2-7 Kerry 1-18** Dungarvan
	Final	20/7/1969	**Cork 1-4 Kerry 0-16** Cork
Ulster	*First Round*	8/6/1969	**Antrim 2-10 Donegal 0-14** Casement Park
	Quarter-finals	1/6/1969	**Tyrone 0-8 Derry 2-8** Dungannon
		15/6/1969	**Armagh 0-8 Monaghan 1-9** Armagh
		15/6/1969	**Fermanagh 2-4 Cavan 1-9** Irvinestown
		22/6/1969	**Down 0-8 Antrim 0-4** Newry
	Semi-final	29/6/1969	**Cavan 2-3 Derry 0-9** Clones
		13/7/1969	**Cavan 1-8 Derry 0-6** Clones
		6/7/1969	**Down 2-15 Monaghan 1-7** Armagh
	Final	27/7/1969	**Cavan 2-13 Down 2-6** Casement Park
All-Ireland	*Semi-final*	10/8/1969	**Kerry 0-14 Mayo 1-10** Croke Park
		24/8/1969	**Offaly 0-12 Cavan 1-9** Croke Park
		14/9/1969	**Offaly 3-8 Cavan 1-10** Croke Park
	Final	28/9/1969	**Kerry 0-10 Offaly 0-7** Croke Park

1970

Kilkenny did not enter the 1970 Championship. From 1970 provincial finals and All-Ireland semi-finals and finals had a duration of eighty minutes (all other games were sixty minutes).

Connacht

First Round	7/6/1970	**Leitrim 1-7 Roscommon 4-14** Ck-on-Shn.
Semi-final	21/6/1970	**Roscommon 2-10 Mayo 1-9** Tuam
	28/6/1970	**Galway 1-8 Sligo 0-7** Charlestown
Final	12/7/1970	**Galway 2-15 Roscommon 1-8** Pearse Stdm.

Leinster

First Round	17/5/1970	**Longford 2-14 Dublin 3-8** Mullingar
	10/5/1970	**Westmeath 1-12 Laois 1-9** Tullamore
	17/5/1970	**Kildare 5-8 Wicklow 1-8** Carlow
Quarter-final	7/6/1970	**Kildare 3-10 Wexford 1-11** Croke Park
	7/6/1970	**Longford 1-12 Louth 1-9** Croke Park
	14/6/1970	**Offaly 2-12 Westmeath 1-10** Navan
	21/6/1970	**Meath 1-17 Carlow 1-4** Newbridge
Semi-final	28/6/1970	**Longford 1-9 Offaly 0-12** Croke Park
	5/7/1970	**Offaly 1-13 Longford 1-8** Croke Park
	5/7/1970	**Kildare 1-8 Meath 0-13** Croke Park
Final	19/7/1970	**Meath 2-22 Offaly 5-12** Croke Park

Munster

First Round	10/5/1970	**Tipperary 2-12 Clare 1-7** Limerick
	10/5/1970	**Waterford 0-5 Limerick 1-3** Dungarvan
Semi-final	5/7/1970	**Limerick 2-5 Kerry 2-19** Askeaton
	5/7/1970	**Tipperary 3-9 Cork 2-15** Clonmel
Final	26/7/1970	**Kerry 2-22 Cork 2-9** Killarney

Ulster

First Round	7/6/1970	**Donegal 2-6 Antrim 3-8** Ballybofey
Quarter-finals	7/6/1970	**Cavan 3-13 Fermanagh 1-3** Cavan
	7/6/1970	**Derry 3-12 Tyrone 0-7** Ballinascreen
	14/6/1970	**Monaghan 3-7 Armagh 1-7** Castleblayney
	21/6/1970	**Antrim 2-9 Down 1-6** Casement Park
Semi-final	28/6/1970	**Cavan 1-5 Derry 1-8** Irvinestown
	5/7/1970	**Antrim 2-10 Monaghan 1-8** Newry
Final	26/7/1970	**Derry 2-13 Antrim 1-12** Clones

All-Ireland

Semi-final	9/8/1970	**Galway 0-11 Meath 0-15** Croke Park
	23/8/1970	**Kerry 0-23 Derry 0-10** Croke Park
Final	27/9/1970	**Kerry 2-19 Meath 0-18** Croke Park

1971

Kilkenny did not enter the 1971 Championship.

Connacht

First Round	13/6/1971	**Mayo 5-7 Leitrim 2-4** Charlestown
Semi-final	20/6/1971	**Roscommon 1-5 Sligo 0-10** Roscommon
	27/6/1971	**Galway 1-7 Mayo 0-7** Tuam
Final	11/7/1971	**Galway 2-15 Sligo 2-15** Castlebar
	25/7/1971	**Galway 1-17 Sligo 3-10** Castlebar

Leinster

First Round	25/4/1971	**Wicklow 2-8 Wexford 0-6** Carlow
	2/5/1971	**Laois 4-12 Carlow 2-7** Newbridge
Second Round	23/5/1971	**Laois 2-9 Wicklow 2-5** Carlow
Quarter-final	2/5/1971	**Meath 1-14 Westmeath 0-9** Tullamore
	9/5/1971	**Offaly 1-7 Longford 0-3** Mullingar
	30/5/1971	**Louth 1-7 Kildare 1-7** Croke Park
	13/6/1971	**Kildare 0-11 Louth 1-5** Croke Park
	6/6/1971	**Laois 3-8 Dublin 0-13** Carlow
Semi-final	27/6/1971	**Kildare 4-8 Meath 2-12** Croke Park
	4/7/1971	**Laois 0-10 Offaly 2-12** Portlaoise
Final	18/7/1971	**Offaly 2-14 Kildare 0-6** Croke Park

Munster

First Round	6/6/1971	**Clare 1-9 Limerick 3-2** Milltown Malbay
	6/6/1971	**Tipperary 1-14 Waterford 1-9** Clonmel
Semi-final	13/6/1971	**Clare 0-5 Cork 2-10** Doonbeg
	13/6/1971	**Kerry 1-14 Tipperary 1-7** Killarney
Final	18/7/1971	**Cork 0-25 Kerry 0-14** Cork

Ulster

First Round	6/6/1971	**Derry 4-10 Fermanagh 1-10** Ballinascreen
Quarter-finals	6/6/1971	**Armagh 4-9 Tyrone 2-10** Lurgan
	13/6/1971	**Antrim 0-4 Derry 0-8** Casement Park
	13/6/1971	**Monaghan 1-12 Cavan 2-10** Ballybay
	20/6/1971	**Down 3-14 Donegal 3-6** Newry
Semi-final	4/7/1971	**Derry 3-12 Armagh 1-10** Casement Park
	11/7/1971	**Down 0-11 Cavan 2-3** Castleblayney
Final	25/7/1971	**Down 4-15 Derry 4-11** Casement Park

All-Ireland

Semi-final	8/8/1971	**Galway 3-11 Down 2-7** Croke Park
	22/8/1971	**Offaly 1-16 Cork 1-11** Croke Park
Final	26/9/1971	**Offaly 1-14 Galway 2-8** Croke Park

Kilkenny did not enter the 1972 Championship.

Connacht

First Round	11/6/1972	**Roscommon 1-11 Leitrim 0-5** Roscommon	
Semi-final	18/6/1972	**Sligo 2-7 Mayo 1-10** Sligo	
	2/7/1972	**Mayo 1-18 Sligo 0-17** Castlebar	
	25/6/1972	**Roscommon 3-9 Galway 2-12** Roscommon	
	9/7/1972	**Galway 0-7 Roscommon 1-8** Tuam	
Final	16/7/1972	**Mayo 3-10 Roscommon 5-8** Castlebar	

Leinster

First Round	7/5/1972	**Carlow 0-16 Wexford 0-9** Kilkenny
	7/5/1972	**Longford 4-9 Wicklow 0-5** Portlaoise
Second Round	28/5/1972	**Laois 1-7 Carlow 1-5** Athy
	28/5/1972	**Longford 5-5 Louth 3-7** Croke Park
Quarter-final	11/6/1972	**Dublin 2-8 Westmeath 0-8** Croke Park
	11/6/1972	**Kildare 1-11 Laois 0-7** Navan
	11/6/1972	**Longford 1-9 Meath 0-16** Croke Park
Semi-final	25/6/1972	**Offaly 2-17 Meath 3-5** Croke Park
	2/7/1972	**Kildare 0-16 Dublin 3-5** Navan
Final	23/7/1972	**Offaly 1-18 Kildare 2-8** Croke Park

Munster

First Round	14/5/1972	**Clare 1-6 Tipperary 2-10** Limerick
	14/5/1972	**Limerick 0-8 Waterford 0-10** Kilmallock
Semi-final	11/6/1972	**Cork 2-8 Waterford 0-9** Fermoy
	11/6/1972	**Tipperary 0-9 Kerry 1-12** Clonmel
Final	16/7/1972	**Kerry 2-21 Cork 2-15** Killarney

Ulster

First Round	4/6/1972	**Fermanagh 0-7 Derry 5-7** Irvinestown
Quarter-finals	4/6/1972	**Tyrone 0-13 Armagh 1-7** Dungannon
	11/6/1972	**Cavan 3-9 Monaghan 0-6** Casement Park
	18/6/1972	**Donegal 1-8 Down 0-8** Ballybofey
	25/6/1972	**Derry 2-9 Antrim 2-5** Ballinascreen
Semi-final	2/7/1972	**Donegal 0-12 Cavan 2-6** Irvinestown
	16/7/1972	**Donegal 2-11 Cavan 1-9** Clones
	9/7/1972	**Tyrone 1-8 Derry 0-9** Dungannon
Final	30/7/1972	**Donegal 2-13 Tyrone 1-11** Clones

All-Ireland

Semi-final	13/8/1972	**Kerry 1-22 Roscommon 1-12** Croke Park
	20/8/1972	**Offaly 1-17 Donegal 2-10** Croke Park
Final	24/9/1972	**Offaly 1-13 Kerry 1-13** Croke Park
	15/10/1972	**Offaly 1-19 Kerry 0-13** Croke Park

1973

Kilkenny did not enter the 1973 Championship.

Connacht

First Round	10/6/1973	**Galway 3-6 Sligo 1-9** Tuam	
Semi-final	17/6/1973	**Leitrim 0-3 Mayo 7-6** Carrick-on-Shannon	
	24/6/1973	**Roscommon 1-8 Galway 1-13** Roscommon	
Final	8/7/1973	**Mayo 2-12 Galway 1-17** Castlebar	

Leinster

First Round	13/5/1973	**Louth 0-14 Carlow 1-3** Drogheda	
	20/5/1973	**Dublin 3-11 Wexford 0-5** Wexford	
Second Round	27/5/1973	**Louth 1-9 Dublin 2-6** Navan	
	10/6/1973	**Louth 1-8 Dublin 0-9** Navan	
Quarter-final	3/6/1973	**Westmeath 0-8 Meath 1-6** Mullingar	
	3/6/1973	**Wicklow 0-14 Laois 3-15** Aughrim	
	10/6/1973	**Kildare 0-13 Longford 0-8** Athy	
	17/6/1973	**Offaly 1-8 Louth 0-8** Croke Park	
Semi-final	17/6/1973	**Meath 2-17 Laois 2-11** Croke Park	
	1/7/1973	**Offaly 1-15 Kildare 2-6** Croke Park	
Final	22/7/1973	**Offaly 3-21 Meath 2-12** Croke Park	

Munster

First Round	3/6/1973	**Clare 0-18 Waterford 1-5** Limerick	
	3/6/1973	**Limerick 1-7 Tipperary 4-13** Limerick	
Semi-final	17/6/1973	**Cork 2-14 Clare 0-3** Cork	
	17/6/1973	**Kerry 3-11 Tipperary 0-5** Tralee	
Final	15/7/1973	**Cork 5-12 Kerry 1-15** Cork	

Ulster

First Round	10/6/1973	**Down 2-10 Armagh 2-9** Newry	
Quarter-finals	3/6/1973	**Monaghan 0-5 Derry 1-7** Castleblayney	
	17/6/1973	**Fermanagh 3-9 Antrim 4-4** Irvinestown	
	24/6/1973	**Donegal 1-7 Tyrone 0-12** Ballybofey	
	24/6/1973	**Down 1-7 Cavan 0-8** Newry	
Semi-final	8/7/1973	**Tyrone 1-15 Fermanagh 0-11** Clones	
	15/7/1973	**Down 1-12 Derry 0-9** Lurgan	
Final	29/7/1973	**Tyrone 3-13 Down 1-11** Clones	

All-Ireland

Semi-final	12/8/1973	**Galway 0-16 Offaly 2-8** Croke Park	
	19/8/1973	**Cork 5-10 Tyrone 2-4** Croke Park	
Final	23/9/1973	**Cork 3-17 Galway 2-13** Croke Park	

1974

Kilkenny did not enter the 1974 Championship.

Connacht

First Round	9/6/1974	**Leitrim 1-6 Sligo 3-12** Carrick-on-Shn.
	16/6/1974	**Galway 3-11 Mayo 0-13** Tuam
Semi-final	23/6/1974	**Sligo 1-11 Roscommon 2-8** Sligo
	7/7/1974	**Roscommon 0-13 Sligo 0-8** Roscommon
Final	14/7/1974	**Galway 2-14 Roscommon 0-8** Pearse Stdm

Leinster

First Round	19/5/1974	**Carlow 3-7 Louth 3-14** Carlow
	26/5/1974	**Dublin 3-9 Wexford 0-6** Croke Park
Second Round	2/6/1974	**Dublin 2-11 Louth 1-9** Navan
Quarter-final	9/6/1974	**Laois 3-6 Wicklow 0-2** Portlaoise
	9/6/1974	**Meath 3-8 Westmeath 0-7** Croke Park
	16/6/1974	**Dublin 1-11 Offaly 0-13** Croke Park
	16/6/1974	**Kildare 2-10 Longford 0-11** Longford
Semi-final	30/6/1974	**Meath 1-14 Laois 0-7** Croke Park
	14/7/1974	**Dublin 1-13 Kildare 0-10** Croke Park
Final	28/7/1974	**Dublin 1-14 Meath 1-9** Croke Park

Munster

First Round	26/5/1974	**Clare 1-4 Tipperary 1-9** Limerick
	2/6/1974	**Waterford 1-11 Limerick 0-5** Dungarvan
Semi-final	9/6/1974	**Cork 3-14 Tipperary 2-2** Fermoy
	16/6/1974	**Kerry 7-16 Waterford 0-8** Killarney
Final	14/7/1974	**Kerry 0-7 Cork 1-11** Killarney

Ulster

First Round	9/6/1974	**Down 1-10 Armagh 0-6** Newry
Quarter-finals	2/6/1974	**Antrim 2-7 Fermanagh 1-8** Casement Park
	9/6/1974	**Derry 3-6 Monaghan 0-8** Ballinascreen
	16/6/1974	**Tyrone 0-8 Donegal 1-9** Ballybofey
	23/6/1974	**Down 2-8 Cavan 0-12** Cavan
Semi-final	7/7/1974	**Donegal 5-9 Antrim 1-7** Clones
	14/7/1974	**Down 1-12 Derry 0-7** Lurgan
Final	28/7/1974	**Donegal 1-14 Down 2-11** Clones
	4/8/1974	**Donegal 3-9 Down 1-12** Clones

All-Ireland

Semi-final	11/8/1974	**Dublin 2-11 Cork 1-8** Croke Park
	18/8/1974	**Galway 3-13 Donegal 1-14** Croke Park
Final	22/9/1974	**Dublin 0-14 Galway 1-6** Croke Park

All counties, including London, participated in the 1975 Championship. All games were now seventy minutes in duration.

Connacht	*First Round*	25/5/1975	**Mayo 4-12 London 1-12** Castlebar
		1/6/1975	**Leitrim 0-4 Roscommon 0-12** Ck-on-Shannon
	Semi-final	8/6/1975	**Sligo 1-13 Galway 0-6** Sligo
		15/6/1975	**Roscommon 1-9 Mayo 1-12** Roscommon
	Final	6/7/1975	**Sligo 2-10 Mayo 1-13** Sligo
		20/7/1975	**Mayo 0-15 Sligo 2-10** Castlebar
Leinster	*First Round*	11/5/1975	**Wexford 2-8 Carlow 1-10** Kilkenny
		25/5/1975	**Laois 3-13 Longford 1-8** Tullamore
		1/6/1975	**Westmeath 2-14 Kilkenny 2-2** Athy
		8/6/1975	**Louth 2-22 Wicklow 2-6** Croke Park
	Quarter-final	8/6/1975	**Dublin 4-17 Wexford 3-10** Carlow
		15/6/1975	**Offaly 0-13 Laois 0-13** Tullamore
		29/6/1975	**Laois 3-7 Offaly 3-14** Portlaoise
		22/6/1975	**Louth 0-15 Meath 1-9** Croke Park
		29/6/1975	**Kildare 1-15 Westmeath 1-8** Navan
	Semi-final	6/7/1975	**Dublin 3-14 Louth 4-7** Navan
		13/7/1975	**Offaly 0-11 Kildare 2-11** Croke Park
	Final	27/7/1975	**Dublin 3-13 Kildare 0-8** Croke Park
Munster	*First Round*	1/6/1975	**Clare 1-15 Waterford 1-10** Kilrush
		1/6/1975	**Tipperary 7-18 Limerick 1-5** Emly
	Semi-final	15/6/1975	**Clare 0-7 Cork 1-16** Doonbeg
		15/6/1975	**Tipperary 0-9 Kerry 3-13** Clonmel
	Final	13/7/1975	**Kerry 1-14 Cork 0-7** Killarney
Ulster	*First Round*	1/6/1975	**Fermanagh 0-10 Armagh 4-6** Irvinestown
	Quarter-finals	1/6/1975	**Monaghan 0-13 Tyrone 1-5** Castleblayney
		8/6/1975	**Cavan 0-15 Donegal 0-13** Ballybofey
		15/6/1975	**Down 3-12 Antrim 0-7** Newcastle
		22/6/1975	**Derry 2-15 Armagh 1-7** Omagh
	Semi-final	29/6/1975	**Down 1-13 Cavan 1-10** Castleblayney
		6/7/1975	**Monaghan 1-11 Derry 1-11** Dungannon
		13/7/1975	**Monaghan 1-6 Derry 0-14** Dungannon
	Final	27/7/1975	**Derry 1-16 Down 2-6** Clones
All-Ireland	*Semi-final*	10/8/1975	**Kerry 3-13 Sligo 0-5** Croke Park
		24/8/1975	**Dublin 3-13 Derry 3-8** Croke Park
	Final	28/9/1975	**Kerry 2-12 Dublin 0-11** Croke Park

1976

Kilkenny did not enter the 1976 Championship.

Connacht

First Round
23/5/1976	**Mayo 0-11 Leitrim 0-11** Charlestown
30/5/1976	**Leitrim 2-8 Mayo 0-10** Carrick-on-Shannon
30/5/1976	**Roscommon 2-18 London 1-7** Roscommon

Semi-final
6/6/1976	**Leitrim 0-8 Galway 3-21** Carrick-on-Shn.
13/6/1976	**Sligo 0-7 Roscommon 2-10** Sligo

Final
4/7/1976	**Roscommon 1-8 Galway 1-8** Castlebar
18/7/1976	**Galway 1-14 Roscommon 0-9** Tuam

Leinster

First Round
9/5/1976	**Meath 2-13 Wicklow 1-10** Croke Park
9/5/1976	**Wexford 2-11 Westmeath 0-14** Athy
23/5/1976	**Laois 2-12 Carlow 0-8** Athy

Quarter-final
6/6/1976	**Offaly 0-8 Meath 3-8** Croke Park
20/6/1976	**Laois 1-13 Kildare 0-12** Carlow
20/6/1976	**Wexford 0-15 Louth 1-8** Croke Park
27/6/1976	**Dublin 5-16 Longford 0-7** Mullingar

Semi-final
4/7/1976	**Wexford 1-9 Meath 2-14** Croke Park
11/7/1976	**Dublin 3-12 Laois 0-11** Tullamore

Final
25/7/1976	**Dublin 2-8 Meath 1-9** Croke Park

Munster

First Round
9/5/1976	**Waterford 5-11 Tipperary 1-11** Dungarvan
16/5/1976	**Limerick 1-6 Clare 2-4** Limerick

Semi-final
20/6/1976	**Cork 2-15 Clare 1-10** Semple Stadium
20/6/1976	**Waterford 0-6 Kerry 3-17** Dungarvan

Final
11/7/1976	**Cork 0-10 Kerry 0-10** Páirc Uí Chaoimh
25/7/1976	**Cork 2-19 Kerry 3-20** Páirc Uí Chaoimh

Ulster

First Round
23/5/1976	**Armagh 1-13 Fermanagh 1-12** Armagh

Quarter-finals
30/5/1976	**Cavan 1-9 Donegal 0-8** Cavan
6/6/1976	**Antrim 2-6 Down 0-14** Casement Park
6/6/1976	**Tyrone 2-10 Monaghan 1-10** Dungannon
13/6/1976	**Derry 1-19 Armagh 2-1** Omagh

Semi-final
20/6/1976	**Down 0-10 Cavan 1-18** Castleblayney
27/6/1976	**Tyrone 0-8 Derry 0-12** Clones

Final
18/7/1976	**Derry 1-8 Cavan 1-8** Clones
25/7/1976	**Derry 0-22 Cavan 1-16** Clones

All-Ireland

Semi-final
8/8/1976	**Kerry 5-14 Derry 1-10** Croke Park
29/8/1976	**Dublin 1-8 Galway 0-8** Croke Park

Final
26/9/1976	**Dublin 3-8 Kerry 0-10** Croke Park

1977

All counties participated in the 1977 Championship.

Connacht

First Round	15/5/1977	**Leitrim 0-6 London 0-9** Carrick-on-Shannon
	22/5/1977	**Mayo 0-13 Roscommon 0-16** Castlebar
Semi-final	12/6/1977	**Galway 5-13 London 1-9** Ballinasloe
	19/6/1977	**Roscommon 2-9 Sligo 1-6** Roscommon
Final	10/7/1977	**Roscommon 1-12 Galway 2-8** Roscommon

Leinster

	8/5/1977	**Kildare 4-13 Kilkenny 2-4** Athy
	8/5/1977	**Offaly 0-19 Wicklow 0-7** Croke Park
First Round	15/5/1977	**Louth 2-9 Westmeath 0-12** Navan
	22/5/1977	**Carlow 1-9 Longford 1-9** Tullamore
	5/6/1977	**Carlow 1-10 Longford 1-8** Portlaoise
	29/5/1977	**Dublin 1-14 Kildare 2-8** Navan
Quarter-final	5/6/1977	**Wexford 4-6 Offaly 2-10** Croke Park
	12/6/1977	**Laois 4-15 Louth 1-16** Croke Park
	19/6/1977	**Meath 1-18 Carlow 0-7** Croke Park
Semi-final	3/7/1977	**Dublin 3-11 Wexford 0-6** Carlow
	10/7/1977	**Meath 3-20 Laois 1-13** Croke Park
Final	31/7/1977	**Dublin 1-9 Meath 0-8** Croke Park

Munster

First Round	15/5/1977	**Waterford 3-6 Clare 1-18** Dungarvan
	22/5/1977	**Limerick 1-5 Tipperary 4-10** Limerick
Semi-final	12/6/1977	**Clare 1-5 Cork 3-12** Ennis
	3/7/1977	**Kerry 3-14 Tipperary 0-9** Tralee
Final	24/7/1977	**Kerry 3-15 Cork 0-9** Killarney

Ulster

First Round	29/5/1977	**Donegal 0-12 Derry 1-12** Ballybofey
	29/5/1977	**Monaghan 0-10 Antrim 0-6** Castleblayney
Quarter-finals	5/6/1977	**Armagh 2-14 Cavan 1-12** Armagh
	12/6/1977	**Down 3-9 Fermanagh 0-7** Newry
	19/6/1977	**Derry 3-10 Tyrone 1-11** Lurgan
Semi-final	26/6/1977	**Armagh 2-12 Monaghan 3-5** Dungannon
	3/7/1977	**Down 0-8 Derry 0-10** Clones
Final	24/7/1977	**Armagh 3-10 Derry 1-5** Clones

All-Ireland

Semi-final	14/8/1977	**Armagh 3-9 Roscommon 2-12** Croke Park
	28/8/1977	**Armagh 0-15 Roscommon 0-14** Croke Park
	21/8/1977	**Dublin 3-12 Kerry 1-13** Croke Park
Final	25/9/1977	**Dublin 5-12 Armagh 3-6** Croke Park

All counties participated in the 1978 Championship.

Connacht	*First Round*	21/5/1978	**Sligo 4-13 London 2-10** Sligo
		28/5/1978	**Mayo 2-18 Leitrim 1-8** Ballina
	Semi-final	11/6/1978	**Galway 1-11 Sligo 1-8** Tuam
		18/6/1978	**Roscommon 1-12 Mayo 1-9** Roscommon
	Final	9/7/1978	**Galway 0-9 Roscommon 2-7** Pearse Stdm
Leinster	*First Round*	7/5/1978	**Carlow 5-8 Westmeath 3-9** Portlaoise
		7/5/1978	**Wicklow 2-16 Kilkenny 0-3** Athy
		4/6/1978	**Kildare 4-15 Louth 1-8** Navan
		4/6/1978	**Offaly 2-12 Longford 0-8** Mullingar
	Quarter-final	28/5/1978	**Wicklow 4-15 Wexford 1-8** Carlow
		18/6/1978	**Dublin 6-15 Carlow 2-9** Croke Park
		18/6/1978	**Kildare 3-14 Meath 1-12** Croke Park
		25/6/1978	**Laois 2-8 Offaly 0-16** Portlaoise
	Semi-final	2/7/1978	**Kildare 4-14 Wicklow 2-6** Croke Park
		9/7/1978	**Dublin 2-9 Offaly 0-12** Portlaoise
	Final	30/7/1978	**Dublin 1-17 Kildare 1-6** Croke Park
Munster	*First Round*	28/5/1978	**Clare 0-19 Limerick 1-4** Dunbeg
		28/5/1978	**Tipperary 1-16 Waterford 2-13** Clonmel
		4/6/1978	**Waterford 2-19 Tipperary 2-17** Dungarvan
	Semi-final	11/6/1978	**Cork 3-16 Clare 0-11** Páirc Uí Chaoimh
		18/6/1978	**Kerry 4-27 Waterford 2-8** Killarney
	Final	16/7/1978	**Cork 3-7 Kerry 3-14** Páirc Uí Chaoimh
Ulster	*First Round*	28/5/1978	**Derry 3-12 Donegal 0-7** Ballinascreen
	Quarter-finals	21/5/1978	**Antrim 4-6 Monaghan 2-4** Casement Park
		11/6/1978	**Cavan 0-16 Armagh 0-9** Cavan
		11/6/1978	**Fermanagh 2-7 Down 0-14** Irvinestown
		18/6/1978	**Derry 3-11 Tyrone 0-9** Lurgan
	Semi-final	2/7/1978	**Down 1-14 Derry 2-8** Casement Park
		9/7/1978	**Cavan 2-13 Antrim 1-10** Castleblayney
	Final	23/7/1978	**Down 2-19 Cavan 2-12** Clones
All-Ireland	*Semi-final*	13/8/1978	**Kerry 3-11 Roscommon 0-8** Croke Park
		20/8/1978	**Dublin 1-16 Down 0-8** Croke Park
	Final	24/9/1978	**Kerry 5-11 Dublin 0-9** Croke Park

All counties participated in the 1979 Championship.

Connacht	*First Round*	27/5/1979	**Galway 2-20 London 3-5** Pearse Stadium
		3/6/1979	**Sligo 0-12 Leitrim 1-13** Sligo
	Semi-final	17/6/1979	**Leitrim 1-10 Mayo 3-12** Carrick-on-Shannon
		24/6/1979	**Roscommon 3-11 Galway 1-11** Roscommon
	Final	15/7/1979	**Mayo 2-10 Roscommon 3-15** Castlebar
Leinster	*First Round*	13/5/1979	**Carlow 1-16 Wexford 4-7** Kilkenny
		27/5/1979	**Wexford 2-6 Carlow 0-12** Kilkenny
		3/6/1979	**Wexford 1-12 Carlow 0-7** Kilkenny
		13/5/1979	**Meath 6-19 Kilkenny 0-3** Navan
		20/5/1979	**Laois 4-13 Westmeath 2-8** Tullamore
		20/5/1979	**Louth 1-14 Longford 1-6** Croke Park
	Quarter-final	3/6/1979	**Dublin 4-16 Louth 0-4** Navan
		10/6/1979	**Meath 0-12 Kildare 1-9** Croke Park
		17/6/1979	**Meath 1-20 Kildare 3-9** Croke Park
		10/6/1979	**Wicklow 3-11 Wexford 0-13** Carlow
		17/6/1979	**Offaly 1-12 Laois 0-13** Tullamore
	Semi-final	1/7/1979	**Dublin 3-13 Wicklow 2-7** Newbridge
		8/7/1979	**Meath 2-6 Offaly 0-16** Croke Park
	Final	29/7/1979	**Dublin 1-8 Offaly 0-9** Croke Park
Munster	*First Round*	20/5/1979	**Limerick 1-9 Clare 1-15** Limerick
		20/5/1979	**Tipperary 1-14 Waterford 0-7** Clonmel
	Semi-final	24/6/1979	**Cork 2-18 Tipperary 0-5** Páirc Uí Chaoimh
		1/7/1979	**Clare 1-9 Kerry 9-21** Milltown Malbay
	Final	22/7/1979	**Kerry 2-14 Cork 2-4** Killarney
Ulster	*First Round*	20/5/1979	**Tyrone 2-9 Antrim 2-5** Dungannon
	Quarter-finals	27/5/1979	**Monaghan 0-14 Down 0-10** Castleblayney
		3/6/1979	**Armagh 5-3 Fermanagh 1-7** Lurgan
		10/6/1979	**Cavan 1-13 Derry 2-12** Cavan
		17/6/1979	**Donegal 1-11 Tyrone 1-9** Ballinascreen
	Semi-final	24/6/1979	**Monaghan 2-10 Armagh 2-8** Cavan
		1/7/1979	**Donegal 2-9 Derry 0-14** Omagh
	Final	22/7/1979	**Monaghan 1-15 Donegal 0-11** Clones
All-Ireland	*Semi-final*	12/8/1979	**Kerry 5-14 Monaghan 0-7** Croke Park
		19/8/1979	**Dublin 0-14 Roscommon 1-10** Croke Park
	Final	16/9/1979	**Kerry 3-13 Dublin 1-8** Croke Park

1980

All counties participated in the 1980 Championship. In Munster, Kerry had a bye directly into the final.

Connacht	*First Round*	1/6/1980	**Roscommon 9-19 London 1-10** Roscomn.
		8/6/1980	**Sligo 1-7 Mayo 2-11** Sligo
	Semi-final	15/6/1980	**Galway 0-10 Roscommon 1-14** Tuam
		22/6/1980	**Mayo 1-17 Leitrim 1-8** Crossmolina
	Final	13/7/1980	**Roscommon 3-13 Mayo 0-8** Roscommon
Leinster	*First Round*	11/5/1980	**Carlow 2-11 Kildare 2-17** Carlow
		11/5/1980	**Westmeath 2-15 Kilkenny 0-4** Portlaoise
		18/5/1980	**Laois 5-12 Longford 1-10** Portlaoise
		18/5/1980	**Wexford 1-13 Louth 3-10** Croke Park
	Quarter-final	1/6/1980	**Kildare 1-13 Wicklow 0-4** Croke Park
		1/6/1980	**Offaly 0-13 Louth 0-7** Croke Park
		8/6/1980	**Dublin 2-14 Laois 2-8** Tullamore
		15/6/1980	**Meath 4-12 Westmeath 1-5** Tullamore
	Semi-final	29/6/1980	**Offaly 2-14 Kildare 1-10** Croke Park
		6/7/1980	**Meath 2-7 Dublin 3-13** Navan
	Final	27/7/1980	**Offaly 1-10 Dublin 1-8** Croke Park
Munster	*First Round*	11/5/1980	**Clare 1-11 Limerick 1-11** Doonbeg
		25/5/1980	**Limerick 0-10 Clare 0-9** Limerick
		11/5/1980	**Waterford 2-10 Tipperary 1-15** Dungarvan
	Second Round	1/6/1980	**Tipperary 2-7 Limerick 1-11** Semple Stdm
	Semi-final	8/6/1980	**Cork 5-19 Limerick 1-6** Páirc Uí Chaoimh
	Final	6/7/1980	**Cork 0-12 Kerry 3-13** Páirc Uí Chaoimh
Ulster	*First Round*	18/5/1980	**Antrim 1-7 Tyrone 1-8** Casement Park
	Quarter-finals	25/5/1980	**Down 1-4 Monaghan 0-13** Newry
		1/6/1980	**Fermanagh 1-4 Armagh 3-8** Irvinestown
		8/6/1980	**Derry 2-7 Cavan 2-9** Ballinascreen
		15/6/1980	**Donegal 0-8 Tyrone 1-17** Irvinestown
	Semi-final	22/6/1980	**Monaghan 0-5 Armagh 0-12** Cavan
		29/6/1980	**Tyrone 2-12 Cavan 1-9** Clones
	Final	20/7/1980	**Tyrone 4-7 Armagh 4-10** Clones
All-Ireland	*Semi-final*	24/8/1980	**Kerry 4-15 Offaly 4-10** Croke Park
		10/8/1980	**Roscommon 2-20 Armagh 3-11** Croke Pk
	Final	21/9/1980	**Kerry 1-9 Roscommon 1-6** Croke Park

All counties participated in the 1981 Championship.

Connacht

First Round	30/5/1981	**London 1-4 Mayo 3-11** Ruislip
	7/6/1981	**Galway 2-16 Leitrim 0-6** Tuam
Semi-final	14/6/1981	**Sligo 2-9 Roscommon 1-8** Sligo
	21/6/1981	**Mayo 2-8 Galway 1-9** Castlebar
Final	12/7/1981	**Mayo 0-12 Sligo 0-4** Castlebar

Leinster

First Round	10/5/1981	**Kilkenny 2-4 Wexford 2-11** Kilkenny
	10/5/1981	**Longford 1-10 Westmeath 3-10** Longford
	10/5/1981	**Wicklow 3-11 Carlow 1-8** Athy
	17/5/1981	**Laois 5-8 Louth 3-8** Croke Park
Quarter-final	31/5/1981	**Dublin 0-10 Wicklow 0-8** Newbridge
	31/5/1981	**Westmeath 1-9 Offaly 1-14** Mullingar
	7/6/1981	**Wexford 2-9 Meath 1-11** Croke Park
	14/6/1981	**Laois 3-13 Kildare 1-9** Tullamore
Semi-final	28/6/1981	**Offaly 1-16 Wexford 0-14** Croke Park
	5/7/1981	**Dublin 0-11 Laois 2-9** Tullamore
Final	26/7/1981	**Offaly 1-18 Laois 3-9** Croke Park

Munster

First Round	31/5/1981	**Limerick 0-10 Waterford 0-10** Limerick
	14/6/1981	**Waterford 0-10 Limerick 1-4** Dungarvan
	31/5/1981	**Tipperary 0-9 Clare 3-14** Limerick
Semi-final	28/6/1981	**Kerry 4-17 Clare 0-6** Listowel
	28/6/1981	**Waterford 0-7 Cork 2-18** Dungarvan
Final	19/7/1981	**Kerry 1-11 Cork 0-3** Killarney

Ulster

First Round	17/5/1981	**Monaghan 2-9 Tyrone 0-6** Castleblayney
Quarter-finals	24/5/1981	**Antrim 2-13 Cavan 2-12** Casement Park
	31/5/1981	**Armagh 2-16 Donegal 0-13** Armagh
	7/6/1981	**Derry 0-12 Fermanagh 0-10** Ballinascreen
	14/6/1981	**Down 0-10 Monaghan 0-10** Newry
	28/6/1981	**Monaghan 1-9 Down 3-4** Castleblayney
Semi-final	21/6/1981	**Armagh 4-7 Antrim 1-3** Castleblayney
	5/7/1981	**Down 0-12 Derry 0-9** Clones
Final	19/7/1981	**Down 3-12 Armagh 1-10** Clones

All-Ireland

Semi-final	9/8/1981	**Mayo 1-6 Kerry 2-19** Croke Park
	23/8/1981	**Down 0-6 Offaly 0-12** Croke Park
Final	20/9/1981	**Kerry 1-12 Offaly 0-8** Croke Park

1982

All counties participated in the 1982 Championship.

Connacht

First Round	23/5/1982	**London 0-5 Leitrim 1-13** Ruislip
	6/6/1982	**Roscommon 3-8 Sligo 0-13** Roscommon
Semi-final	13/6/1982	**Leitrim 1-7 Mayo 2-7** Carrick-on-Shannon
	20/6/1982	**Roscommon 0-9 Galway 1-9** Roscommon
Final	11/7/1982	**Galway 3-17 Mayo 0-10** Tuam

Leinster

First Round	9/5/1982	**Kildare 4-10 Kilkenny 1-2** Kilkenny
	16/5/1982	**Louth 2-13 Carlow 0-8** Croke Park
	16/5/1982	**Meath 0-11 Longford 0-12** Tullamore
	23/5/1982	**Westmeath 1-8 Wicklow 0-11** Newbridge
	6/6/1982	**Westmeath 3-7 Wicklow 2-5** Croke Park
Quarter-final	6/6/1982	**Dublin 1-15 Longford 2-6** Tullamore
	6/6/1982	**Kildare 1-17 Wexford 1-9** Croke Park
	13/6/1982	**Laois 2-9 Westmeath 1-7** Croke Park
	13/6/1982	**Offaly 0-17 Louth 0-8** Croke Park
Semi-final	27/6/1982	**Offaly 3-13 Laois 1-15** Tullamore
	4/7/1982	**Dublin 1-13 Kildare 0-12** Navan
Final	1/8/1982	**Offaly 1-16 Dublin 1-7** Croke Park

Munster

First Round	9/5/1982	**Tipperary 0-11 Waterford 0-9** Clonmel
	16/5/1982	**Clare 4-12 Limerick 0-8** Ennis
Semi-final	6/6/1982	**Clare 0-7 Kerry 1-15** Ennis
	6/6/1982	**Cork 1-19 Tipperary 1-5** Fermoy
Final	4/7/1982	**Kerry 0-9 Cork 0-9** Páirc Uí Chaoimh
	1/8/1982	**Kerry 2-18 Cork 0-12** Killarney

Ulster

First Round	16/5/1982	**Monaghan 0-9 Tyrone 1-9** Dungannon
Quarter-finals	23/5/1982	**Antrim 1-7 Cavan 0-8** Cavan
	30/5/1982	**Donegal 0-13 Armagh 1-11** Ballybofey
	6/6/1982	**Derry 1-8 Fermanagh 1-9** Irvinestown
	13/6/1982	**Down 0-11 Tyrone 1-12** Newry
Semi-final	20/6/1982	**Armagh 1-20 Antrim 1-6** Clones
	27/6/1982	**Fermanagh 1-8 Tyrone 0-10** Cavan
Final	18/7/1982	**Armagh 0-10 Fermanagh 1-4** Clones

All-Ireland

Semi-final	15/8/1982	**Armagh 1-11 Kerry 3-15** Croke Park
	22/8/1982	**Galway 1-11 Offaly 1-12** Croke Park
Final	19/9/1982	**Offaly 1-15 Kerry 0-17** Croke Park

1983

Kilkenny did not enter the 1983 Championship.

Connacht	*First Round*	5/6/1983	**London 0-7 Sligo 2-8** Ruislip
		12/6/1983	**Mayo 0-9 Roscommon 0-7** Castlebar
	Semi-final	26/6/1983	**Leitrim 1-6 Galway 1-8** Carrick-on-Shannon
		3/7/1983	**Sligo 0-9 Mayo 0-13** Sligo
	Final	17/7/1983	**Mayo 1-10 Galway 1-13** Castlebar

Leinster	*First Round*	15/5/1983	**Longford 3-15 Carlow 0-13** Tullamore
		15/5/1983	**Louth 2-11 Westmeath 2-5** Croke Park
		22/5/1983	**Wicklow 0-11 Wexford 0-11** Carlow
		5/6/1983	**Wexford 4-20 Wicklow 2-14** Croke Park
	Quarter-final	5/6/1983	**Kildare 3-9 Longford 2-9** Tullamore
		5/6/1983	**Louth 3-11 Laois 0-8** Croke Park
		12/6/1983	**Offaly 2-18 Wexford 1-8** Croke Park
		12/6/1983	**Dublin 2-8 Meath 2-8** Croke Park
		3/7/1983	**Dublin 3-9 Meath 0-16** Croke Park
	Semi-final	26/6/1983	**Offaly 2-15 Kildare 0-6** Navan
		17/7/1983	**Dublin 1-12 Louth 0-3** Croke Park
	Final	31/7/1983	**Dublin 2-13 Offaly 1-11** Croke Park

Munster	*First Round*	29/5/1983	**Limerick 1-9 Tipperary 2-16** Limerick
		12/6/1983	**Clare 4-16 Waterford 0-5** Ennis
	Semi-final	26/6/1983	**Tipperary 2-5 Kerry 5-16** Clonmel
		3/7/1983	**Clare 1-5 Cork 1-11** Ennis
	Final	17/7/1983	**Cork 3-10 Kerry 3-9** Páirc Uí Chaoimh

Ulster	*First Round*	22/5/1983	**Derry 0-11 Cavan 1-12** Ballinascreen
	Quarter-finals	29/5/1983	**Fermanagh 0-10 Down 0-8** Irvinestown
		5/6/1983	**Monaghan 2-18 Antrim 0-4** Castleblayney
		13/6/1983	**Donegal 1-10 Armagh 0-7** Ballybofey
		19/6/1983	**Cavan 0-11 Tyrone 0-10** Cavan
	Semi-final	26/6/1983	**Donegal 1-14 Monaghan 1-9** Irvinestown
		3/7/1983	**Cavan 2-12 Fermanagh 1-7** Clones
	Final	24/7/1983	**Donegal 1-14 Cavan 1-11** Clones

All-Ireland	*Semi-final*	14/8/1983	**Galway 1-12 Donegal 1-11** Croke Park
		21/8/1983	**Dublin 2-11 Cork 2-11** Croke Park
		28/8/1983	**Cork 2-10 Dublin 4-15** Páirc Uí Chaoimh
	Final	18/9/1983	**Dublin 1-10 Galway 1-8** Croke Park

1984

Kilkenny did not enter the 1984 Championship.

Connacht

First Round	3/6/1984	**London 0-10 Galway 3-16** Ruislip
	10/6/1984	**Leitrim 1-14 Sligo 0-9** Carrick-on-Shannon
Semi-final	17/6/1984	**Galway 1-17 Roscommon 0-7** Tuam
	24/6/1984	**Mayo 3-16 Leitrim 1-8** Castlebar
Final	8/7/1984	**Galway 2-13 Mayo 2-9** Pearse Stadium

Leinster

First Round	13/5/1984	**Carlow 1-6 Laois 1-12** Carlow
	20/5/1984	**Wicklow 1-9 Longford 4-4** Aughrim
	27/5/1984	**Westmeath 1-5 Meath 2-15** Mullingar
	3/6/1984	**Kildare 0-7 Laois 1-10** Newbridge
Quarter-final	3/6/1984	**Meath 1-12 Louth 0-10** Navan
	10/6/1984	**Dublin 4-12 Wexford 0-9** Croke Park
	10/6/1984	**Longford 0-15 Offaly 1-12** Longford
	17/6/1984	**Offaly 3-15 Longford 3-10** Croke Park
Semi-final	24/6/1984	**Dublin 0-13 Offaly 0-5** Croke Park
	24/6/1984	**Meath 3-15 Laois 3-10** Croke Park
Final	22/7/1984	**Dublin 2-10 Meath 1-9** Croke Park

Munster

First Round	20/5/1984	**Waterford 1-6 Tipperary 0-9** Dungarvan
	27/5/1984	**Tipperary 4-13 Waterford 0-10** Semple Stdm
	27/5/1984	**Clare 0-10 Limerick 1-7** Semple Stadium
	3/6/1984	**Limerick 0-10 Clare 2-5** Limerick
Semi-final	10/6/1984	**Kerry 0-23 Tipperary 0-6** Tralee
	17/6/1984	**Cork 3-11 Clare 1-5** Semple Stadium
Final	1/7/1984	**Kerry 3-14 Cork 2-10** Killarney

Ulster

First Round	27/5/1984	**Cavan 0-13 Derry 1-13** Cavan
Quarter-finals	20/5/1984	**Down 3-6 Fermanagh 0-8** Newry
	27/5/1984	**Antrim 1-6 Monaghan 2-17** Casement Park
	3/6/1984	**Armagh 1-10 Donegal 0-12** Armagh
	10/6/1984	**Derry 3-4 Tyrone 1-13** Ballinascreen
Semi-final	17/6/1984	**Armagh 2-8 Monaghan 0-9** Cavan
	24/6/1984	**Tyrone 0-10 Down 0-5** Casement Park
Final	15/7/1984	**Tyrone 0-15 Armagh 1-7** Clones

All-Ireland

Semi-final	12/8/1984	**Kerry 2-17 Galway 0-11** Croke Park
	22/8/1984	**Dublin 2-11 Tyrone 0-8** Croke Park
Final	23/9/1984	**Kerry 0-14 Dublin 1-6** Croke Park

Kilkenny did not enter the 1985 Championship.

Connacht

First Round	2/6/1985	London 0-10 Roscommon 1-15	Ruislip
	2/6/1985	Sligo 2-3 Leitrim 1-6	Sligo
	16/6/1985	Leitrim 3-7 Sligo 0-11	Carrick-on-Shannon
Semi-final	16/6/1985	Roscommon 0-11 Galway 0-11	Roscommon
	30/6/1985	Galway 1-12 Roscommon 1-14	Tuam
	23/6/1985	Leitrim 0-5 Mayo 2-11	Carrick-on-Shannon
Final	14/7/1985	Roscommon 0-8 Mayo 2-11	Roscommon

Leinster

First Round	5/5/1985	Kildare 1-11 Wicklow 0-9	Newbridge
	19/5/1985	Carlow 3-11 Westmeath 1-4	Carlow
	26/5/1985	Longford 0-14 Wexford 3-8	Longford
Quarter-final	2/6/1985	Meath 0-13 Kildare 0-7	Navan
	9/6/1985	Carlow 1-7 Laois 2-8	Carlow
	16/6/1985	Offaly 3-16 Louth 1-8	Tullamore
	16/6/1985	Wexford 0-6 Dublin 4-13	Wexford
Semi-final	30/6/1985	Laois 2-11 Meath 0-7	Tullamore
	7/7/1985	Offaly 0-10 Dublin 2-13	Tullamore
Final	28/7/1985	Dublin 0-10 Laois 0-4	Croke Park

Munster

First Round	26/5/1985	Waterford 0-7 Limerick 2-10	Dungarvan
	9/6/1985	Clare 1-7 Tipperary 0-10	Ennis
	16/6/1985	Tipperary 2-12 Clare 2-9	Páirc Uí Chaoimh
Semi-final	23/6/1985	Kerry 2-18 Limerick 0-9	Listowel
	23/6/1985	Tipperary 1-10 Cork 4-19	Semple Stadium
Final	21/7/1985	Cork 0-11 Kerry 2-11	Páirc Uí Chaoimh

Ulster

First Round	19/5/1985	Donegal 2-12 Down 2-8	Ballybofey
Quarter-finals	26/5/1985	Cavan 0-9 Antrim 0-5	Cavan
	2/6/1985	Derry 1-9 Tyrone 1-8	Ballinascreen
	9/6/1985	Armagh 2-13 Fermanagh 0-5	Armagh
	16/6/1985	Monaghan 1-14 Donegal 0-7	Castleblayney
Semi-final	23/6/1985	Cavan 0-7 Derry 0-11	Armagh
	30/6/1985	Monaghan 0-10 Armagh 0-10	Cavan
	7/7/1985	Monaghan 1-11 Armagh 2-7	Cavan
Final	21/7/1985	Monaghan 2-9 Derry 0-8	Clones

All-Ireland	*Semi-final*	11/8/1985	**Kerry 1-12 Monaghan 2-9** Croke Park
		25/8/1985	**Kerry 2-9 Monaghan 0-9** Croke Park
		18/8/1985	**Dublin 1-13 Mayo 1-13** Croke Park
		8/9/1985	**Dublin 2-12 Mayo 1-7** Croke Park
	Final	22/9/1985	**Kerry 2-12 Dublin 2-8** Croke Park

Kilkenny did not enter the 1986 Championship.

Connacht	*First Round*	1/6/1986	**London 0-4 Mayo 3-14** Ruislip
		1/6/1986	**Sligo 3-5 Galway 2-13** Sligo
	Semi-final	15/6/1986	**Mayo 0-12 Roscommon 1-11** Castlebar
		22/6/1986	**Galway 2-15 Leitrim 2-8** Pearse Stadium
	Final	13/7/1986	**Roscommon 1-5 Galway 1-8** Roscommon

Leinster	*First Round*	18/5/1986	**Louth 2-11 Longford 1-5** Drogheda
		18/5/1986	**Wexford 1-11 Kildare 1-8** Wexford
		25/5/1986	**Wicklow 0-15 Westmeath 1-5** Aughrim
	Quarter-final	8/6/1986	**Dublin 0-17 Wexford 3-3** Croke Park
		8/6/1986	**Louth 2-8 Offaly 1-13** Drogheda
		15/6/1986	**Carlow 1-12 Meath 1-15** Carlow
		15/6/1986	**Wicklow 2-10 Laois 1-9** Aughrim
	Semi-final	29/6/1986	**Dublin 1-10 Offaly 0-7** Portlaoise
		6/7/1986	**Meath 1-17 Wicklow 0-11** Newbridge
	Final	27/7/1986	**Meath 0-9 Dublin 0-7** Croke Park

Munster	*First Round*	18/5/1986	**Clare 1-10 Waterford 0-9** Ennis
		18/5/1986	**Tipperary 2-14 Limerick 1-4** Clonmel
	Semi-final	15/6/1986	**Cork 1-12 Clare 0-9** Fermoy
		15/6/1986	**Tipperary 0-12 Kerry 5-9** Clonmel
	Final	6/7/1986	**Kerry 0-12 Cork 0-8** Killarney

Ulster	*First Round*	18/5/1986	**Down 2-8 Donegal 1-10** Newcastle
	Quarter-finals	25/5/1986	**Antrim 0-7 Cavan 1-8** Casement Park
		1/6/1986	**Tyrone 2-6 Derry 1-7** Omagh
		8/6/1986	**Fermanagh 0-7 Armagh 1-11** Irvinestown
		15/6/1986	**Monaghan 0-13 Down 1-10** Castleblayney
		22/6/1986	**Monaghan 0-11 Down 2-11** Castleblayney
	Semi-final	22/6/1986	**Tyrone 2-16 Cavan 1-12** Irvinestown
		29/6/1986	**Down 3-7 Armagh 0-12** Castleblayney
	Final	20/7/1986	**Tyrone 1-11 Down 0-10** Clones

All-Ireland	*Semi-final*	17/8/1986	**Tyrone 1-12 Galway 1-9** Croke Park
		24/8/1986	**Meath 0-12 Kerry 2-13** Croke Park
	Final	21/9/1986	**Kerry 2-15 Tyrone 1-10** Croke Park

1987

Kilkenny did not enter the 1987 Championship.

Connacht

First Round	31/5/1987	**London 1-8 Leitrim 1-12** Ruislip
	31/5/1987	**Sligo 2-8 Roscommon 0-12** Sligo
Semi-final	14/6/1987	**Leitrim 0-10 Galway 1-10** Carrick-on-Shannon
	21/6/1987	**Mayo 3-17 Sligo 0-6** Castlebar
Final	12/7/1987	**Mayo 0-7 Galway 0-8** Castlebar

Leinster

First Round	24/5/1987	**Kildare 0-14 Wexford 2-6** Newbridge
	24/5/1987	**Laois 1-12 Carlow 2-7** Portlaoise
	24/5/1987	**Longford 0-8 Louth 0-13** Longford
Quarter-final	7/6/1987	**Dublin 0-14 Westmeath 0-5** Croke Park
	7/6/1987	**Offaly 1-8 Kildare 1-8** Tullamore
	14/6/1987	**Kildare 1-12 Offaly 0-10** Newbridge
	14/6/1987	**Laois 2-5 Meath 1-11** Portlaoise
	14/6/1987	**Wicklow 1-7 Louth 0-8** Aughrim
Semi-final	28/6/1987	**Meath 0-15 Kildare 0-9** Tullamore
	5/7/1987	**Dublin 2-18 Wicklow 0-6** Newbridge
Final	26/7/1987	**Meath 1-13 Dublin 0-12** Croke Park

Munster

First Round	17/5/1987	**Waterford 2-9 Clare 2-9** Dungarvan
	17/5/1987	**Limerick 0-12 Tipperary 0-11** Askeaton
	31/5/1987	**Clare 0-16 Waterford 2-12** Ennis
Semi-final	21/6/1987	**Cork 1-14 Limerick 0-11** Páirc Uí Chaoimh
	21/6/1987	**Waterford 2-8 Kerry 3-15** Dungarvan
Final	26/7/1987	**Cork 1-10 Kerry 2-7** Páirc Uí Chaoimh
	2/8/1987	**Kerry 1-5 Cork 0-13** Killarney

Ulster

First Round	17/5/1987	**Armagh 2-9 Fermanagh 0-9** Armagh
Quarter-finals	24/5/1987	**Cavan 0-12 Monaghan 0-10** Cavan
	31/5/1987	**Down 2-7 Derry 1-12** Newry
	7/6/1987	**Antrim 0-9 Tyrone 0-9** Casement Park
	14/6/1987	**Tyrone 2-6 Antrim 2-5** Omagh
	14/6/1987	**Donegal 0-6 Armagh 1-8** Ballybofey
Semi-final	21/6/1987	**Derry 2-7 Cavan 1-10** Omagh
	5/7/1987	**Derry 2-11 Cavan 2-8** Omagh
	28/6/1987	**Armagh 5-9 Tyrone 1-9** Irvinestown
Final	19/7/1987	**Derry 0-11 Armagh 0-9** Clones

All-Ireland

Semi-final	16/8/1987	**Cork 1-11 Galway 1-11** Croke Park
	30/8/1987	**Cork 0-18 Galway 1-4** Croke Park
	23/8/1987	**Meath 0-15 Derry 0-8** Croke Park
Final	20/9/1987	**Meath 1-14 Cork 0-11** Croke Park

1988

Kilkenny did not enter the 1988 Championship.

Connacht

Quarter-final	5/6/1988	**London 2-10 Sligo 2-13** Ruislip
	19/6/1988	**Mayo 1-13 Leitrim 0-4** Charlestown
Semi-final	26/6/1988	**Roscommon 2-10 Galway 1-10** Pearse Stdm
	3/7/1988	**Sligo 0-6 Mayo 2-19** Sligo
Final	24/7/1988	**Roscommon 0-8 Mayo 1-12** Roscommon

Leinster

First Round	22/5/1988	**Carlow 3-5 Laois 2-7** Carlow
	22/5/1988	**Longford 1-11 Westmeath 0-7** Longford
	22/5/1988	**Offaly 1-18 Wexford 1-7** Tullamore
Quarter-final	5/6/1988	**Kildare 1-10 Offaly 0-13** Newbridge
	18/6/1988	**Offaly 0-16 Kildare 0-10** Tullamore
	5/6/1988	**Longford 1-15 Wicklow 2-4** Longford
	5/6/1988	**Louth 0-9 Meath 3-13** Drogheda
	6/6/1988	**Carlow 0-8 Dublin 1-14** Carlow
Semi-final	26/6/1988	**Dublin 4-15 Longford 0-9** Mullingar
	3/7/1988	**Meath 0-19 Offaly 0-10** Croke Park
Final	31/7/1988	**Meath 2-5 Dublin 0-9** Croke Park

Munster

First Round	8/5/1988	**Limerick 2-4 Clare 0-5** Limerick
	8/5/1988	**Waterford 3-9 Tipperary 1-11** Dungarvan
Semi-final	29/5/1988	**Kerry 3-19 Waterford 1-7** Tralee
	29/5/1988	**Limerick 1-3 Cork 0-9** Askeaton
Final	3/7/1988	**Cork 1-14 Kerry 0-16** Páirc Uí Chaoimh

Ulster

First Round	15/5/1988	**Fermanagh 1-13 Armagh 2-12** Irvinestown
Quarter-finals	22/5/1988	**Monaghan 0-16 Cavan 0-14** Clones
	29/5/1988	**Derry 0-7 Down 1-11** Ballinascreen
	5/6/1988	**Tyrone 3-13 Antrim 2-4** Omagh
	12/6/1988	**Armagh 2-10 Donegal 0-8** Armagh
Semi-final	19/6/1988	**Monaghan 1-11 Down 0-9** Cavan
	26/6/1988	**Tyrone 0-15 Armagh 1-8** Irvinestown
Final	17/7/1988	**Monaghan 1-10 Tyrone 0-11** Clones

All-Ireland

Semi-final	14/8/1988	**Cork 1-14 Monaghan 0-6** Croke Park
	21/8/1988	**Meath 0-16 Mayo 2-5** Croke Park
Final	18/9/1988	**Meath 0-12 Cork 1-9** Croke Park
	9/10/1988	**Meath 0-13 Cork 0-12** Croke Park

Kilkenny did not enter the 1989 Championship.

Connacht

First Round	4/6/1989	**London 1-7 Galway 3-12** Ruislip
	11/6/1989	**Sligo 1-11 Leitrim 1-6** Ballymote
Quarter-final	5/6/1988	**London 2-10 Sligo 2-13** Ruislip
	19/6/1988	**Mayo 1-13 Leitrim 0-4** Charlestown
	25/6/1989	**Galway 1-8 Mayo 1-8** Tuam
Semi-final	9/7/1989	**Mayo 2-13 Galway 1-8** Castlebar
	2/7/1989	**Roscommon 4-11 Sligo 1-8** Roscommon
Final	23/7/1989	**Mayo 0-12 Roscommon 1-9** Castlebar
	30/7/1989	**Roscommon 2-13 Mayo 3-14** Roscommon

Leinster

First Round	14/5/1989	**Carlow 1-7 Wicklow 2-14** Carlow
	14/5/1989	**Louth 3-7 Laois 2-9** Drogheda
	21/5/1989	**Westmeath 3-9 Wexford 1-7** Mullingar
	4/6/1989	**Wicklow 1-15 Longford 2-9** Aughrim
Quarter-final	5/6/1989	**Dublin 1-13 Kildare 1-9** Newbridge
	11/6/1989	**Meath 1-15 Louth 0-13** Croke Park
	11/6/1989	**Offaly 1-8 Westmeath 1-6** Tullamore
Semi-final	25/6/1989	**Dublin 1-12 Wicklow 1-6** Newbridge
	2/7/1989	**Meath 3-11 Offaly 0-9** Croke Park
Final	30/7/1989	**Dublin 2-12 Meath 1-10** Croke Park

Munster

First Round	14/5/1989	**Limerick 5-9 Waterford 1-9** Askeaton
	14/5/1989	**Tipperary 1-18 Clare 2-5** Clonmel
Semi-final	18/6/1989	**Limerick 1-10 Kerry 6-7** Askeaton
	25/6/1989	**Cork 0-22 Tipperary 0-6** Páirc Uí Chaoimh
Final	23/7/1989	**Kerry 1-9 Cork 1-12** Killarney

Ulster

First Round	14/5/1989	**Antrim 0-5 Monaghan 0-8** Casement Park
Quarter-finals	21/5/1989	**Cavan 0-14 Donegal 3-11** Cavan
	28/5/1989	**Fermanagh 1-7 Derry 4-15** Irvinestown
	4/6/1989	**Tyrone 1-11 Armagh 2-7** Omagh
	11/6/1989	**Monaghan 0-9 Down 1-14** Castleblayney
Semi-final	18/6/1989	**Donegal 2-8 Derry 1-9** Clones
	25/6/1989	**Tyrone 1-12 Down 1-7** Castleblayney
Final	16/7/1989	**Donegal 0-11 Tyrone 0-11** Clones
	23/7/1989	**Donegal 0-7 Tyrone 2-13** Clones

All-Ireland

Semi-final	13/8/1989	**Mayo 0-12 Tyrone 1-6** Croke Park
	20/8/1989	**Cork 2-10 Dublin 1-9** Croke Park
Final	17/9/1989	**Cork 0-17 Mayo 1-11** Croke Park

1990

Kilkenny did not enter the 1990 Championship.

Connacht

First Round	3/6/1990	London 1-5 Roscommon 5-16	Ruislip
	10/6/1990	Galway 6-18 Sligo 0-4	Pearse Stadium
Semi-final	24/6/1990	Roscommon 2-11 Leitrim 1-10	Roscommon
	1/7/1990	Galway 2-11 Mayo 1-12	Tuam
Final	22/7/1990	Roscommon 0-16 Galway 1-11	Roscommon

Leinster

First Round	13/5/1990	Carlow 2-7 Louth 3-8	Carlow
	20/5/1990	Westmeath 0-7 Longford 0-15	Mullingar
	20/5/1990	Wexford 0-9 Kildare 3-8	Wexford
Quarter-final	3/6/1990	Louth 1-8 Dublin 1-13	Drogheda
	3/6/1990	Wicklow 1-7 Kildare 0-6	Aughrim
	10/6/1990	Laois 3-15 Offaly 3-5	Portlaoise
	10/6/1990	Meath 3-15 Longford 0-12	Navan
Semi-final	24/6/1990	Dublin 2-14 Wicklow 0-12	Newbridge
	1/7/1990	Meath 4-14 Laois 0-6	Croke Park
Final	29/7/1990	Meath 1-14 Dublin 0-14	Croke Park

Munster

First Round	6/5/1990	Tipperary 1-6 Limerick 1-12	Clonmel
	6/5/1990	Waterford 0-9 Clare 0-13	Dungarvan
Semi-final	27/5/1990	Cork 4-15 Limerick 1-3	Páirc Uí Chaoimh
	27/5/1990	Kerry 1-23 Clare 0-13	Listowel
Final	1/7/1990	Cork 2-23 Kerry 1-11	Páirc Uí Chaoimh

Ulster

First Round	13/5/1990	Monaghan 3-17 Antrim 0-8	Castleblayney
Quarter-finals	20/5/1990	Donegal 0-13 Cavan 0-9	Ballybofey
	27/5/1990	Derry 4-14 Fermanagh 1-7	Celtic Park
	3/6/1990	Armagh 0-12 Tyrone 0-11	Armagh
	10/6/1990	Down 3-11 Monaghan 1-12	Newry
	17/6/1990	Donegal 1-15 Derry 0-8	Clones
Semi final	24/6/1990	Down 2-10 Armagh 1-13	Casement Park
	1/7/1990	Armagh 2-7 Down 0-12	Casement Park
Final	15/7/1990	Donegal 0-15 Armagh 0-14	Clones

All-Ireland

Semi-final	12/8/1990	Cork 0-17 Roscommon 0-10	Croke Park
	19/8/1990	Meath 3-9 Donegal 1-7	Croke Park
Final	16/9/1990	Cork 0-11 Meath 0-9	Croke Park

Kilkenny did not enter the 1991 Championship.

Connacht	First Round	2/6/1991	**London 2-9 Mayo 6-14** Ruislip
		9/6/1991	**Leitrim 1-16 Sligo 0-5** Carrick-on-Shannon
	Semi-final	23/6/1991	**Mayo 3-11 Galway 0-6** Castlebar
		30/6/1991	**Leitrim 0-8 Roscommon 0-12** Ck-on-Shannon
	Final	14/7/1991	**Mayo 0-14 Roscommon 0-14** Castlebar
		28/7/1991	**Roscommon 0-13 Mayo 1-9** Roscommon

Leinster	First Round	19/5/1991	**Carlow 2-7 Wexford 3-14** Carlow
		26/5/1991	**Louth 2-13 Longford 2-12** Drogheda
		2/6/1991	**Dublin 1-12 Meath 1-12** Croke Park
		9/6/1991	**Dublin 1-11 Meath 1-11** Croke Park
		23/6/1991	**Dublin 1-14 Meath 2-11** Croke Park
		6/7/1991	**Dublin 0-15 Meath 2-10** Croke Park
	Quarter-final	9/6/1991	**Laois 1-17 Westmeath 0-6** Portlaoise
		16/6/1991	**Louth 2-11 Kildare 2-10** Drogheda
		16/6/1991	**Wexford 0-7 Offaly 1-7** Wexford
		14/7/1991	**Meath 1-9 Wicklow 0-12** Croke Park
		21/7/1991	**Meath 1-12 Wicklow 1-9** Croke Park
	Semi-final	7/7/1991	**Laois 1-10 Louth 2-7** Croke Park
		14/7/1991	**Laois 2-14 Louth 0-12** Croke Park
		28/7/1991	**Meath 2-13 Offaly 0-7** Croke Park
	Final	10/8/1991	**Meath 1-11 Laois 0-8** Croke Park

Munster	First Round	26/5/1991	**Clare 2-12 Kerry 5-16** Ennis
		26/5/1991	**Limerick 0-14 Tipperary 2-7** Askeaton
	Semi-final	16/6/1991	**Kerry 1-10 Cork 0-11** Killarney
		23/6/1991	**Waterford 0-11 Limerick 0-13** Dungarvan
	Final	21/7/1991	**Kerry 0-23 Limerick 3-12** Killarney

Ulster	*First Round*	19/5/1991	**Tyrone 1-8 Derry 1-9** Omagh
	Quarter-finals	26/5/1991	**Antrim 1-8 Fermanagh 3-12** Casement Park
		2/6/1991	**Donegal 2-14 Cavan 0-12** Ballybofey
		9/6/1991	**Down 1-7 Armagh 0-8** Newry
		16/6/1991	**Derry 0-13 Monaghan 0-8** Celtic Park, Derry
		23/6/1991	**Donegal 1-18 Fermanagh 0-13** Omagh
	Semi-final	30/6/1991	**Down 0-13 Derry 1-10** Armagh
		14/7/1991	**Down 0-14 Derry 0-9** Armagh
	Final	28/7/1991	**Down 1-15 Donegal 0-10** Clones
All-Ireland	*Semi-final*	11/8/1991	**Down 2-9 Kerry 0-8** Croke Park
		18/8/1991	**Meath 0-15 Roscommon 1-11** Croke Park
	Final	15/9/1991	**Down 1-16 Meath 1-14** Croke Park

Kilkenny did not enter the 1992 Championship.

Connacht

First Round	31/5/1992	**London 2-10 Leitrim 3-17** Ruislip
	14/6/1992	**Galway 1-11 Mayo 1-11** Tuam
	21/6/1992	**Mayo 0-15 Galway 1-6** Castlebar
Semi-final	28/6/1992	**Roscommon 2-11 Leitrim 1-9** Roscommon
	5/7/1992	**Mayo 1-11 Sligo 0-10** Castlebar
Final	26/7/1992	**Mayo 1-14 Roscommon 0-10** Castlebar

Leinster

First Round	24/5/1992	**Longford 2-8 Wicklow 2-18** Longford
	24/5/1992	**Meath 1-11 Laois 2-11** Navan
	31/5/1992	**Offaly 1-9 Dublin 2-17** Tullamore
Quarter-final	7/6/1992	**Westmeath 1-9 Carlow 0-8** Mullingar
	14/6/1992	**Kildare 1-20 Wicklow 1-6** Croke Park
	14/6/1992	**Louth 0-13 Laois 1-9** Croke Park
	28/6/1992	**Dublin 1-18 Wexford 0-11** Portlaoise
Semi-final	5/7/1992	**Kildare 4-11 Westmeath 2-5** Tullamore
	12/7/1992	**Dublin 0-15 Louth 1-9** Croke Park
Final	26/7/1992	**Dublin 1-13 Kildare 0-10** Croke Park

Munster

First Round	17/5/1992	**Tipperary 2-13 Waterford 0-13** Clonmel
	24/5/1992	**Cork 0-10 Kerry 2-14** Páirc Uí Chaoimh
Semi-final	21/6/1992	**Clare 2-11 Tipperary 2-7** Limerick
	21/6/1992	**Limerick 1-11 Kerry 1-14** Limerick
Final	19/7/1992	**Clare 2-10 Kerry 0-12** Limerick

Ulster

First Round	17/5/1992	**Derry 1-10 Tyrone 1-7** Celtic Park, Derry
Quarter-finals	24/5/1992	**Cavan 1-15 Donegal 1-15** Cavan
	31/5/1992	**Donegal 0-20 Cavan 1-6** Ballybofey
	31/5/1992	**Fermanagh 1-9 Antrim 1-8** Irvinestown
	7/6/1992	**Armagh 0-9 Down 1-12** Armagh
	14/6/1992	**Monaghan 3-8 Derry 1-14** Castleblayney
	21/6/1992	**Monaghan 0-7 Derry 2-9** Castleblayney
Semi-final	21/6/1992	**Donegal 2-17 Fermanagh 0-7** Omagh
	28/6/1992	**Derry 0-15 Down 0-12** Casement Park
Final	19/7/1992	**Donegal 0-14 Derry 1-9** Clones

All-Ireland

Semi-final	16/8/1992	**Donegal 0-13 Mayo 0-9** Croke Park
	23/8/1992	**Dublin 3-14 Clare 2-12** Croke Park
Final	20/9/1992	**Donegal 0-18 Dublin 0-14** Croke Park

1993

Kilkenny did not enter the 1993 Championship.

Connacht	*First Round*	30/5/1993	**Galway 1-11 Leitrim 1-12** Tuam
		6/6/1993	**London 0-9 Sligo 0-12** Ruislip
	Semi-final	20/6/1993	**Sligo 1-6 Mayo 1-13** Sligo
		27/6/1993	**Leitrim 1-10 Roscommon 1-12** Ck-on-Shn
	Final	25/7/1993	**Roscommon 0-7 Mayo 1-5** Roscommon
Leinster	*First Round*	16/5/1993	**Longford 0-10 Offaly 0-22** Longford
		23/5/1993	**Laois 3-10 Louth 1-13** Portlaoise
		23/5/1993	**Wexford 0-7 Dublin 0-11** Wexford
	Quarter-final	6/6/1993	**Kildare 2-13 Wicklow 2-11** Croke Park
		7/6/1993	**Dublin 2-11 Westmeath 0-8** Tullamore
		7/6/1993	**Offaly 0-13 Carlow 0-11** Tullamore
		13/6/1993	**Laois 0-7 Meath 1-12** Portlaoise
	Semi-final	27/6/1993	**Kildare 2-14 Offaly 0-9** Portlaoise
		4/7/1993	**Dublin 1-10 Meath 0-12** Croke Park
	Final	25/7/1993	**Dublin 0-11 Kildare 0-7** Croke Park
Munster	*First Round*	16/5/1993	**Tipperary 3-18 Limerick 3-8** Semple Stdm
		30/5/1993	**Clare 1-10 Cork 2-14** Ennis
	Semi-final	20/6/1993	**Kerry 0-10 Cork 1-10** Killarney
		20/6/1993	**Waterford 0-13 Tipperary 3-10** Waterford
	Final	18/7/1993	**Tipperary 1-8 Cork 1-16** Semple Stadium
Ulster	*First Round*	16/5/1993	**Fermanagh 1-9 Armagh 1-9** Irvinestown
		23/5/1993	**Armagh 4-8 Fermanagh 1-16** Armagh
		23/5/1993	**Monaghan 2-9 Cavan 0-15** Castleblayney
		30/5/1993	**Cavan 2-8 Monaghan 3-10** Cavan
	Quarter-finals	30/5/1993	**Down 0-9 Derry 3-11** Newry
		6/6/1993	**Donegal 0-12 Antrim 0-9** Ballybofey
		13/6/1993	**Armagh 0-13 Tyrone 1-10** Armagh
		20/6/1993	**Tyrone 0-12 Armagh 2-8** Omagh
		20/6/1993	**Derry 0-19 Monaghan 0-11** Casement Park
	Semi-final	27/6/1993	**Donegal 0-15 Armagh 1-12** Cavan
		4/7/1993	**Donegal 2-16 Armagh 1-7** Cavan
	Final	18/7/1993	**Derry 0-8 Donegal 0-6** Clones
All-Ireland	*Semi-final*	15/8/1993	**Cork 5-15 Mayo 0-10** Croke Park
		22/8/1993	**Derry 0-15 Dublin 0-14** Croke Park
	Final	19/9/1993	**Derry 1-14 Cork 2-8** Croke Park

Kilkenny did not enter the 1994 Championship.

Connacht	First Round	5/6/1994	**London 0-6 Galway 2-21** Ruislip
		5/6/1994	**Roscommon 0-12 Leitrim 1-10** Roscommon
	Semi-final	26/6/1994	**Mayo 2-18 Sligo 1-5** Castlebar
		3/7/1994	**Leitrim 0-9 Galway 1-6** Carrick-on-Shannon
		10/7/1994	**Galway 0-10 Leitrim 0-11** Tuam
	Final	24/7/1994	**Leitrim 0-12 Mayo 2-4** Roscommon

Leinster	First Round	22/5/1994	**Wicklow 0-12 Offaly 1-9** Aughrim
		28/5/1994	**Offaly 3-11 Wicklow 0-14** Tullamore
		29/5/1994	**Laois 4-15 Longford 2-4** Portlaoise
		29/5/1994	**Westmeath 1-9 Louth 0-13** Athlone
	Quarter-final	12/6/1994	**Meath 0-20 Laois 2-10** Navan
		12/6/1994	**Offaly 0-8 Wexford 0-10** Tullamore
		18/6/1994	**Dublin 0-11 Kildare 0-11** Croke Park
		2/7/1994	**Dublin 1-14 Kildare 1-9** Croke Park
		19/6/1994	**Louth 3-19 Carlow 0-11** Drogheda
	Semi-final	3/7/1994	**Meath 4-14 Wexford 2-6** Croke Park
		10/7/1994	**Dublin 1-15 Louth 1-8** Croke Park
	Final	31/7/1994	**Dublin 1-9 Meath 1-8** Croke Park

Munster	First Round	15/5/1994	**Clare 0-13 Tipperary 2-8** Ennis
		22/5/1994	**Kerry 2-19 Limerick 0-8** Killarney
	Semi-final	26/6/1994	**Cork 1-13 Kerry 2-8** Páirc Uí Chaoimh
		26/6/1994	**Tipperary 5-14 Waterford 0-15** Semple Stdm
	Final	24/7/1994	**Cork 2-19 Tipperary 3-9** Páirc Uí Chaoimh

Ulster	First Round	15/5/1994	**Armagh 1-6 Fermanagh 0-6** Armagh
	Quarter-finals	22/5/1994	**Cavan 1-12 Monaghan 3-10** Cavan
		29/5/1994	**Derry 1-12 Down 1-14** Celtic Park, Derry
		5/6/1994	**Antrim 1-9 Donegal 1-12** Casement Park
		12/6/1994	**Tyrone 3-10 Armagh 1-10** Omagh
	Semi-final	19/6/1994	**Down 0-14 Monaghan 0-8** Armagh
		26/6/1994	**Tyrone 1-15 Donegal 0-10** Cavan
	Final	17/7/1994	**Down 1-17 Tyrone 1-11** Clones

All-Ireland	Semi-final	14/8/1994	**Down 1-13 Cork 0-11** Croke Park
		21/8/1994	**Dublin 3-15 Leitrim 1-9** Croke Park
	Final	18/9/1994	**Down 1-12 Dublin 0-13** Croke Park

Kilkenny did not enter the 1995 Championship.

Connacht

First Round	28/5/1995	**Sligo 0-11 Galway 0-11** Sligo
	4/6/1995	**Galway 1-12 Sligo 0-8** Tuam
	4/6/1995	**London 1-7 Roscommon 0-19** Ruislip
Semi-final	11/6/1995	**Leitrim 0-11 Galway 0-12** Carrick-on-Shn
	25/6/1995	**Mayo 2-11 Roscommon 1-10** Castlebar
Final	23/7/1995	**Galway 0-17 Mayo 1-7** Tuam

Leinster

First Round	21/5/1995	**Wexford 1-3 Westmeath 0-13** Wexford
	28/5/1995	**Kildare 0-11 Louth 0-13** Newbridge
	28/5/1995	**Meath 1-15 Offaly 1-5** Navan
Quarter-final	11/6/1995	**Longford 0-10 Meath 4-15** Longford
	11/6/1995	**Westmeath 0-3 Wicklow 0-9** Athlone
	18/6/1995	**Dublin 0-19 Louth 2-5** Navan
	18/6/1995	**Laois 2-10 Carlow 1-13** Portlaoise
	25/6/1995	**Laois 1-16 Carlow 0-15** Portlaoise
Semi-final	2/7/1995	**Meath 3-14 Wicklow 0-9** Portlaoise
	9/7/1995	**Dublin 1-13 Laois 0-9** Navan
Final	30/7/1995	**Dublin 1-18 Meath 1-8** Croke Park

Munster

First Round	28/5/1995	**Cork 0-23 Waterford 0-9** Páirc Uí Chaoimh
	28/5/1995	**Limerick 0-8 Kerry 3-17** Limerick
Semi-final	25/6/1995	**Cork 0-17 Clare 0-11** Páirc Uí Chaoimh
	25/6/1995	**Kerry 7-12 Tipperary 1-13** Tralee
Final	23/7/1995	**Kerry 1-9 Cork 0-15** Killarney

Ulster

First Round	21/5/1995	**Donegal 1-12 Down 0-9** Clones
Quarter-finals	28/5/1995	**Armagh 0-10 Derry 1-17** Armagh
	4/6/1995	**Fermanagh 1-11 Tyrone 1-15** Irvinestown
	11/6/1995	**Cavan 2-11 Antrim 0-8** Cavan
	18/6/1995	**Donegal 0-8 Monaghan 1-14** Ballybofey
Semi-final	25/6/1995	**Tyrone 0-11 Derry 0-10** Clones
	2/7/1995	**Cavan 1-9 Monaghan 0-10** Cavan
Final	23/7/1995	**Tyrone 2-13 Cavan 0-10** Clones

All-Ireland

Semi-final	13/8/1995	**Tyrone 1-13 Galway 0-13** Croke Park
	20/8/1995	**Dublin 1-12 Cork 0-12** Croke Park
Final	17/9/1995	**Dublin 1-10 Tyrone 0-12** Croke Park

1996

Kilkenny did not enter the 1996 Championship.

Connacht

First Round	26/5/1996	**Sligo 1-11 Galway 1-11** Sligo
	9/6/1996	**Galway 0-19 Sligo 2-7** Tuam
	2/6/1996	**London 1-5 Mayo 1-11** Ruislip
Semi-final	16/6/1996	**Galway 2-13 Leitrim 2-11** Tuam
	23/6/1996	**Roscommon 0-11 Mayo 0-14** Roscommon
Final	21/7/1996	**Mayo 3-9 Galway 1-11** Castlebar

Leinster

First Round	12/5/1996	**Carlow 4-17 Wexford 1-11** Carlow
	12/5/1996	**Longford 2-10 Wicklow 2-11** Longford
Second Round	26/5/1996	**Carlow 4-10 Wicklow 3-10** Newbridge
Quarter-final	9/6/1996	**Louth 3-8 Offaly 0-12** Navan
	9/6/1996	**Westmeath 0-11 Dublin 1-18** Navan
	16/6/1996	**Laois 3-9 Kildare 0-13** Croke Park
	16/6/1996	**Meath 0-24 Carlow 0-6** Croke Park
Semi-final	30/6/1996	**Dublin 1-9 Louth 0-8** Navan
	7/7/1996	**Meath 2-14 Laois 1-9** Croke Park
Final	28/7/1996	**Meath 0-10 Dublin 0-8** Croke Park

Munster

First Round	12/5/1996	**Limerick 1-6 Cork 2-19** Kilmallock
	19/5/1996	**Tipperary 1-7 Kerry 2-15** Clonmel
Semi-final	22/6/1996	**Waterford 0-8 Kerry 3-16** Dungarvan
	23/6/1996	**Clare 0-10 Cork 1-7** Ennis
	30/6/1996	**Cork 2-16 Clare 1-16** Páirc Uí Chaoimh
Final	21/7/1996	**Cork 0-11 Kerry 0-14** Páirc Uí Chaoimh

Ulster

First Round	26/5/1996	**Down 1-9 Donegal 0-11** Clones
Quarter-finals	2/6/1996	**Derry 1-13 Armagh 1-6** Celtic Park, Derry
	9/6/1996	**Tyrone 1-18 Fermanagh 0-9** Omagh
	16/6/1996	**Antrim 1-11 Cavan 1-15** Casement Park
	23/6/1996	**Monaghan 0-9 Down 0-14** Clones
Semi-final	30/6/1996	**Tyrone 1-13 Derry 1-8** Clones
	7/7/1996	**Cavan 0-13 Down 1-13** Clones
Final	28/7/1996	**Tyrone 1-9 Down 0-9** Clones

All-Ireland

Semi-final	11/8/1996	**Mayo 2-13 Kerry 1-10** Croke Park
	18/8/1996	**Meath 2-15 Tyrone 0-12** Croke Park
Final	15/9/1996	**Meath 0-12 Mayo 1-9** Croke Park
	29/9/1996	**Meath 2-9 Mayo 1-11** Croke Park

Kilkenny did not enter the 1997 Championship.

Connacht			
	First Round	25/5/1997	**Galway 0-15 Mayo 1-16** Tuam
		1/6/1997	**London 1-13 Leitrim 2-18** Ruislip
	Semi-final	23/6/1997	**Sligo 1-14 Roscommon 1-11** Sligo
		29/6/1997	**Mayo 0-18 Leitrim 0-11** Castlebar
	Final	3/8/1997	**Mayo 0-11 Sligo 1-7** Roscommon

Leinster			
	First Round	11/5/1997	**Offaly 5-17 Longford 0-13** Tullamore
		11/5/1997	**Wexford 2-5 Westmeath 0-11** New Ross
		17/5/1997	**Westmeath 2-17 Wexford 1-15** Mullingar
	Second Round	25/5/1997	**Offaly 0-8 Westmeath 0-8** Tullamore
		7/6/1997	**Westmeath 0-7 Offaly 1-14** Mullingar
	Quarter-final	1/6/1997	**Louth 1-13 Carlow 1-10** Newbridge
		8/6/1997	**Laois 1-7 Kildare 1-11** Croke Park
		15/6/1997	**Meath 1-13 Dublin 1-10** Croke Park
		15/6/1997	**Offaly 1-17 Wicklow 1-8** Croke Park
		29/6/1997	**Offaly 1-10 Louth 0-11** Navan
	Semi-final	6/7/1997	**Kildare 1-9 Meath 0-12** Croke Park
		20/7/1997	**Kildare 3-17 Meath 2-20** Croke Park
		3/8/1997	**Meath 1-12 Kildare 1-10** Croke Park
	Final	16/8/1997	**Offaly 3-17 Meath 1-15** Croke Park

Munster			
	First Round	11/5/1997	**Limerick 1-13 Tipperary 0-16** Limerick
		18/5/1997	**Tipperary 1-17 Limerick 2-8** Clonmel
	Second Round	1/6/1997	**Waterford 1-5 Tipperary 2-7** Dungarvan
	Semi-final	22/6/1997	**Clare 1-14 Cork 1-13** Ennis
		29/6/1997	**Kerry 2-12 Tipperary 1-10** Tralee
	Final	20/7/1997	**Kerry 1-13 Clare 0-11** Limerick

Ulster	*First Round*	18/5/1997	**Down 2-9 Tyrone 0-15** Clones
		25/5/1997	**Down 1-11 Tyrone 3-8** Clones
	Quarter-finals	25/5/1997	**Donegal 2-12 Antrim 1-13** Ballybofey
		1/6/1997	**Monaghan 2-8 Derry 1-11** Clones
		8/6/1997	**Derry 2-15 Monaghan 0-10** Derry
		8/6/1997	**Cavan 1-12 Fermanagh 1-12** Clones
		15/6/1997	**Cavan 0-14 Fermanagh 0-11** Clones
		15/6/1997	**Tyrone 1-12 Armagh 0-12** Omagh
	Semi-final	22/6/1997	**Cavan 2-16 Donegal 2-10** Clones
		29/6/1997	**Tyrone 2-3 Derry 2-15** Clones
	Final	20/7/1997	**Cavan 1-14 Derry 0-16** Clones
All-Ireland	*Semi-final*	24/8/1997	**Cavan 1-10 Kerry 1-17** Croke Park
		31/8/1997	**Mayo 0-13 Offaly 0-7** Croke Park
	Final	28/9/1997	**Kerry 0-13 Mayo 1-7** Croke Park

1998

Kilkenny did not enter the 1998 Championship.

Connacht

First Round	24/5/1998	**Mayo 2-6 Galway 1-13** Castlebar
	31/5/1998	**London 1-7 Sligo 0-14** Ruislip
	14/6/1998	**Leitrim 0-5 Galway 1-16** Carrick-on-Shn.
Semi-final	28/6/1998	**Roscommon 2-12 Sligo 1-15** Roscommon
	5/7/1998	**Sligo 0-15 Roscommon 1-13** Sligo
Final	19/7/1998	**Galway 0-11 Roscommon 0-11** Tuam
	2/8/1998	**Roscommon 0-17 Galway 1-17** Roscomn.

Leinster

First Round	3/5/1998	**Westmeath 1-18 Carlow 2-5** Mullingar
	3/5/1998	**Wexford 2-13 Longford 1-16** New Ross
	10/5/1998	**Longford 0-16 Wexford 2-7** Longford
Second Round	17/5/1998	**Longford 1-13 Westmeath 3-14** Longford
Quarter-final	24/5/1998	**Meath 3-10 Offaly 0-7** Croke Park
	31/5/1998	**Louth 3-14 Wicklow 1-11** Drogheda
	7/6/1998	**Dublin 0-10 Kildare 0-10** Croke Park
	21/6/1998	**Kildare 0-12 Dublin 1-8** Croke Park
	7/6/1998	**Laois 1-15 Westmeath 0-15** Croke Park
Semi-final	28/6/1998	**Meath 0-15 Louth 1-11** Croke Park
	19/7/1998	**Kildare 2-13 Laois 0-8** Croke Park
Final	2/8/1998	**Kildare 1-12 Meath 0-10** Croke Park

Munster

First Round	10/5/1998	**Limerick 1-12 Tipperary 1-13** Limerick
Second Round	30/5/1998	**Tipperary 1-16 Waterford 0-7** Clonmel
Semi-final	28/6/1998	**Tipperary 1-16 Clare 0-12** Limerick
	5/7/1998	**Kerry 1-14 Cork 1-11** Killarney
Final	2/8/1998	**Tipperary 1-10 Kerry 0-17** Semple Stadium

Ulster

First Round	17/5/1998	**Tyrone 2-7 Down 0-15** Omagh
Quarter-finals	24/5/1998	**Antrim 0-11 Donegal 1-11** Casement Park
	31/5/1998	**Derry 3-13 Monaghan 0-11** Celtic Park
	7/6/1998	**Cavan 0-13 Fermanagh 0-11** Cavan
	14/6/1998	**Down 0-11 Armagh 0-16** Clones
Semi-final	21/6/1998	**Cavan 0-13 Donegal 0-15** Clones
	28/6/1998	**Armagh 0-12 Derry 2-13** Armagh
Final	19/7/1998	**Derry 1-7 Donegal 0-8** Clones

All-Ireland

Semi-final	23/8/1998	**Derry 1-8 Galway 0-16** Croke Park
	30/8/1998	**Kildare 0-13 Kerry 1-9** Croke Park
Final	27/9/1998	**Galway 1-14 Kildarc 1-10** Croke Park

1999

Kilkenny did not enter the 1999 Championship. New York entered a team in the Connacht Championship.

Connacht

First Round	30/5/1999	**Mayo 3-13 New York 0-10** Castlebar
	30/5/1999	**Roscommon 0-15 Leitrim 1-7** Ck-on-Shn
	6/6/1999	**Galway 1-18 London 1-8** Ruislip
	13/6/1999	**Mayo 0-21 Roscommon 0-10** Castlebar
Semi-final	27/6/1999	**Sligo 3-7 Galway 1-13** Sligo
	4/7/1999	**Sligo 1-7 Galway 1-17** Tuam
Final	18/7/1999	**Mayo 1-14 Galway 1-10** Tuam

Leinster

First Round	9/5/1999	**Longford 1-13 Wexford 0-16** New Ross
	16/5/1999	**Longford 2-15 Wexford 0-11** Longford
	9/5/1999	**Westmeath 2-10 Carlow 1-8** Carlow
Second Round	30/5/1999	**Westmeath 3-17 Longford 2-9** Mullingar
Quarter-final	6/6/1999	**Dublin 2-15 Louth 0-14** Croke Park
	6/6/1999	**Meath 2-10 Wicklow 0-6** Croke Park
	13/6/1999	**Laois 1-16 Westmeath 1-8** Croke Park
	13/6/1999	**Offaly 0-11 Kildare 0-7** Croke Park
Semi-final	27/6/1999	**Dublin 1-11 Laois 0-14** Croke Park
	18/7/1999	**Dublin 0-16 Laois 1-11** Croke Park
	4/7/1999	**Meath 1-13 Offaly 0-9** Croke Park
Final	1/8/1999	**Meath 1-14 Dublin 0-12** Croke Park

Munster

First Round	3/5/1999	**Cork 3-23 Waterford 0-4** Dungarvan
	23/5/1999	**Kerry 1-11 Tipperary 0-8** Tralee
Semi-final	20/6/1999	**Cork 4-13 Limerick 1-6** Páirc Uí Rinn, Cork
	20/6/1999	**Kerry 3-17 Clare 0-12** Killarney
Final	18/7/1999	**Cork 2-10 Kerry 2-4** Páirc Uí Chaoimh

Ulster

First Round	30/5/1999	**Fermanagh 2-12 Monaghan 1-10** Clones
Quarter-finals	6/6/1999	**Armagh 1-12 Donegal 2-9** Ballybofey
	13/6/1999	**Armagh 2-11 Donegal 0-12** Clones
	20/6/1999	**Derry 2-14 Cavan 0-5** Cavan
	20/6/1999	**Down 1-15 Antrim 0-14** Newry
	27/6/1999	**Tyrone 0-18 Fermanagh 0-8** Clones
Semi-final	5/7/1999	**Armagh 1-10 Derry 0-12** Clones
	12/7/1999	**Down 2-14 Tyrone 0-15** Casement Park
Final	1/8/1999	**Armagh 3-12 Down 0-10** Clones

All-Ireland

Semi-final	22/8/1999	**Cork 2-12 Mayo 0-12** Croke Park
	29/8/1999	**Meath 0-15 Armagh 2-5** Croke Park
Final	26/9/1999	**Meath 1-11 Cork 1-8** Croke Park

Kilkenny did not enter the 2000 Championship. The Leinster Championship included a preliminary group stage.

Connacht

First Round	4/6/2000	**London 0-10 Roscommon 4-18** Ruislip
	10/6/2000	**Galway 1-15 New York 1-5** Tuam
	11/6/2000	**Sligo 1-13 Mayo 1-10** Sligo
Semi-final	2/7/2000	**Roscommon 3-6 Leitrim 1-13** Roscommon
	9/7/2000	**Sligo 0-4 Galway 0-22** Sligo
Final	30/7/2000	**Galway 1-13 Leitrim 0-8** Roscommon

Leinster

Group Stage, First Round	7/5/2000	**Wexford 3-9 Longford 0-12** New Ross
	7/5/2000	**Wicklow 1-8 Carlow 0-7** Aughrim
Group Stage, Second Round	14/5/2000	**Carlow 0-10 Wexford 2-11** Carlow
	14/5/2000	**Longford 2-12 Wicklow 1-10** Longford
Group Stage, Third Round	20/5/2000	**Carlow 2-8 Longford 0-18** Carlow
	20/5/2000	**Wicklow 0-13 Wexford 1-10** Aughrim

Final Table, Group Stage		Won	Drawn	Lost	Points
	Wexford	2	1	0	5
	Longford	2	0	1	4
	Wicklow	1	1	1	1
	Carlow	0	0	3	0

Quarter-final	4/6/2000	**Offaly 0-13 Meath 0-9** Croke Park
	5/6/2000	**Westmeath 1-12 Laois 0-11** Tullamore
	11/6/2000	**Dublin 2-20 Wexford 1-8** Croke Park
	11/6/2000	**Kildare 1-12 Louth 0-12** Croke Park
Semi-final	25/6/2000	**Kildare 0-11 Offaly 1-8** Croke Park
	16/7/2000	**Kildare 0-17 Offaly 2-8** Croke Park
	2/7/2000	**Dublin 1-14 Westmeath 0-11** Croke Park
Final	30/7/2000	**Dublin 0-14 Kildare 0-14** Croke Park
	12/8/2000	**Kildare 2-11 Dublin 0-12** Croke Park

Munster

First Round	14/5/2000	**Clare 0-15 Waterford 1-7** Ennis
	20/5/2000	**Limerick 2-8 Cork 3-13** Kilmallock
Semi-final	18/6/2000	**Kerry 2-15 Cork 1-13** Killarney
	25/6/2000	**Tipperary 0-10 Clare 0-15** Limerick
Final	16/7/2000	**Kerry 3-15 Clare 0-8** Limerick

Ulster	*First Round*	14/5/2000	**Fermanagh 3-12 Monaghan 1-10** Enniskillen
	Quarter-finals	14/5/2000	**Cavan 1-5 Derry 2-13** Cavan
		28/5/2000	**Antrim 0-13 Down 1-7** Casement Park
		4/6/2000	**Tyrone 0-8 Armagh 0-12** Clones
		11/6/2000	**Donegal 0-13 Fermanagh 1-12** Ballybofey
	Semi-final	18/6/2000	**Antrim 2-8 Derry 0-14** Casement Park
		2/7/2000	**Antrim 2-5 Derry 1-17** Casement Park
		25/6/2000	**Armagh 0-13 Fermanagh 0-12** Clones
	Final	16/7/2000	**Armagh 1-12 Derry 1-11** Clones

All-Ireland	*Semi-final*	27/8/2000	**Galway 0-15 Kildare 2-6** Croke Park
		20/8/2000	**Kerry 2-11 Armagh 2-11** Croke Park
		2/9/2000	**Kerry 2-15 Armagh 1-15** Croke Park
	Final	24/9/2000	**Kerry 0-14 Galway 0-14** Croke Park
		7/10/2000	**Kerry 0-17 Galway 1-10** Croke Park

Kilkenny did not enter the 2001 Championship. The 2001 Championship included an All-Ireland qualifier series. Counties eliminated from their provincial championship were drawn in qualifier rounds to leave four teams to face the provincial champions in the All-Ireland quarter-finals. New York did not participate in the qualifier rounds.

Connacht

First Round	19/5/2001	**Roscommon 3-13 New York 1-9** Roscomn
	20/5/2001	**Galway 3-24 Leitrim 3-5** Tuam
	27/5/2001	**Mayo w/o London** Ruislip, London
Semi-final	3/6/2001	**Galway 0-14 Roscommon 2-12** Tuam
	10/6/2001	**Mayo 1-12 Sligo 1-11** Castlebar
Final	1/7/2001	**Roscommon 2-10 Mayo 1-12** Roscommon

Leinster

First Round	6/5/2001	**Laois 0-18 Wexford 0-14** Carlow
	6/5/2001	**Louth 1-9 Longford 1-11** Navan
	13/5/2001	**Wicklow 2-6 Carlow 1-9** Newbridge
	20/5/2001	**Wicklow 0-8 Carlow 0-9** Newbridge
Quarter-final	27/5/2001	**Dublin 2-19 Longford 1-13** Croke Park
	27/5/2001	**Offaly 1-13 Laois 0-12** Croke Park
	3/6/2001	**Kildare 0-19 Carlow 1-11** Croke Park
	3/6/2001	**Meath 2-12 Westmeath 1-14** Croke Park
Semi-final	17/6/2001	**Dublin 1-12 Offaly 0-13** Croke Park
	24/6/2001	**Meath 1-16 Kildare 1-11** Croke Park
Final	15/7/2001	**Dublin 0-14 Meath 2-11** Croke Park

Munster

First Round	13/5/2001	**Tipperary 1-4 Kerry 3-17** Clonmel
	13/5/2001	**Waterford 1-7 Cork 3-16** Páirc Uí Chaoimh
Semi-final	17/6/2001	**Kerry 1-15 Limerick 0-10** Killarney
	24/6/2001	**Cork 2-11 Clare 1-10** Páirc Uí Chaoimh
Final	15/7/2001	**Kerry 0-19 Cork 1-13** Páirc Uí Chaoimh

Ulster

First Round	13/5/2001	**Donegal 1-16 Fermanagh 2-13** Ballybofey
	19/5/2001	**Fermanagh 1-9 Donegal 0-11** Enniskillen
	20/5/2001	**Tyrone 1-14 Armagh 1-9** Clones
Quarter-finals	27/5/2001	**Down 2-10 Cavan 1-14** Casement Park
	3/6/2001	**Derry 1-11 Antrim 0-9** Celtic Park, Derry
	10/6/2001	**Fermanagh 0-14 Monaghan 2-10** E-killen
Semi-final	17/6/2001	**Tyrone 3-7 Derry 0-14** Clones
	24/6/2001	**Monaghan 0-11 Cavan 0-13** Clones
Final	8/7/2001	**Tyrone 1-13 Cavan 1-11** Clones

Qualifiers	*Qualifiers, Round 1*	9/6/2001	**Antrim 0-13 Leitrim 1-8** Casement Park
		9/6/2001	**Down 2-4 Armagh 1-13** Casement Park
		9/6/2001	**Tipperary 1-8 Louth 0-13** Clonmel
		9/6/2001	**Waterford 1-10 Carlow 3-11** Dungarvan
		9/6/2001	**Wexford 1-19 Westmeath 1-19** Wexford
		9/6/2001	**Wicklow 1-14 Longford 0-11** Aughrim
		16/6/2001	**Fermanagh 1-6 Donegal 0-15** Enniskillen
		16/6/2001	**Westmeath 1-16 Wexford 1-8** Mullingar
	Qualifiers, Round 2	23/6/2001	**Antrim 0-7 Derry 0-10** Casement Park
		23/6/2001	**Carlow 2-7 Sligo 2-14** Carlow
		23/6/2001	**Limerick 0-7 Westmeath 0-17** Limerick
		23/6/2001	**Louth 0-12 Offaly 1-8** Navan
		30/6/2001	**Kildare 1-17 Donegal 1-16** Newbridge
		30/6/2001	**Laois 0-13 Clare 1-8** Portlaoise
		30/6/2001	**Monaghan 0-10 Armagh 2-12** Clones
		30/6/2001	**Wicklow 1-9 Galway 3-12** Aughrim
	Qualifiers, Round 3	7/7/2001	**Derry 1-8 Laois 0-8** Cavan
		7/7/2001	**Galway 0-13 Armagh 0-12** Croke Park
		7/7/2001	**Louth 0-13 Westmeath 1-13** Navan
		7/7/2001	**Sligo 0-16 Kildare 0-15** Croke Park
	Qualifiers, Round 4	22/7/2001	**Cavan 2-7 Derry 1-14** Clones
		22/7/2001	**Dublin 3-17 Sligo 0-12** Croke Park
		22/7/2001	**Galway 1-14 Cork 1-10** Croke Park
		21/7/2001	**Mayo 0-16 Westmeath 1-14** Roscommon
All-Ireland	*Quarter-final*	4/8/2001	**Galway 0-14 Roscommon 1-5** Castlebar
		4/8/2001	**Kerry 1-14 Dublin 2-11** Semple Stadium
		11/8/2001	**Kerry 2-12 Dublin 1-12** Semple Stadium
		5/8/2001	**Derry 1-9 Tyrone 0-7** Clones
		5/8/2001	**Meath 2-12 Westmeath 3-9** Croke Park
		11/8/2001	**Meath 2-10 Westmeath 0-11** Croke Park
	Semi-final	26/8/2001	**Galway 1-14 Derry 1-11** Croke Park
		2/9/2001	**Meath 2-14 Kerry 0-5** Croke Park
	Final	23/9/2001	**Galway 0-17 Meath 0-8** Croke Park

2002

Kilkenny did not enter the 2002 Championship.

Connacht

First Round	5/5/2002	**New York 1-11 Sligo 1-19** New York
	19/5/2002	**Roscommon 1-8 Galway 3-12** Roscommon
	26/5/2002	**London 0-10 Leitrim 0-15** Ruislip
Semi-final	2/6/2002	**Mayo 1-7 Galway 0-12** Castlebar
	9/6/2002	**Sligo 2-13 Leitrim 2-4** Sligo
Final	30/6/2002	**Galway 1-11 Sligo 0-11** Castlebar

Leinster

First Round	5/5/2002	**Louth 1-14 Longford 2-11** Navan
	12/5/2002	**Louth 3-17 Longford 1-12** Navan
	6/5/2002	**Laois 3-6 Wicklow 0-8** Carlow
	12/5/2002	**Westmeath 1-14 Carlow 0-10** Portlaoise
Quarter-final	26/5/2002	**Kildare 0-12 Louth 0-11** Mullingar
	26/5/2002	**Offaly 0-13 Laois 2-6** Tullamore
	1/6/2002	**Dublin 0-15 Wexford 1-10** Carlow
	2/6/2002	**Meath 1-12 Westmeath 0-11** Portlaoise
Semi-final	16/6/2002	**Kildare 1-9 Offaly 1-9** Kilkenny
	22/6/2002	**Kildare 3-9 Offaly 1-14** Kilkenny
	23/6/2002	**Dublin 2-11 Meath 0-10** Croke Park
Final	14/7/2002	**Dublin 2-13 Kildare 2-11** Croke Park

Munster

First Round	12/5/2002	**Limerick 1-7 Kerry 0-14** Limerick
	12/5/2002	**Waterford 2-9 Clare 3-10** Dungarvan
	9/6/2002	**Tipperary 3-7 Clare 1-13** Killarney
Semi-final	16/6/2002	**Tipperary 1-8 Clare 0-8** Limerick
	16/6/2002	**Kerry 0-8 Cork 0-8** Killarney
	23/6/2002	**Cork 0-15 Kerry 1-9** Páirc Uí Chaoimh
Final	14/7/2002	**Tipperary 1-14 Cork 2-11** Semple Stadium
	21/7/2002	**Cork 1-23 Tipperary 0-7** Páirc Uí Chaoimh

Ulster

First Round	12/5/2002	**Cavan 0-15 Donegal 1-17** Cavan
Quarter-finals	12/5/2002	**Monaghan 2-11 Fermanagh 4-13** Clones
	19/5/2002	**Armagh 1-12 Tyrone 1-12** Clones
	26/5/2002	**Armagh 2-13 Tyrone 0-16** Clones
	2/6/2002	**Antrim 0-6 Derry 0-16** Casement Park
	2/6/2002	**Donegal 3-12 Down 1-6** Ballybofey
Semi-final	9/6/2002	**Armagh 0-16 Fermanagh 1-5** Clones
	16/6/2002	**Donegal 1-9 Derry 0-10** Clones
Final	7/7/2002	**Armagh 1-14 Donegal 1-10** Clones

231

Qualifiers

2003

Kilkenny did not enter the 2003 Championship.

Connacht

First Round	4/5/2003	New York 0-12 Leitrim 0-14 New York
	18/5/2003	Galway 0-12 Roscommon 0-8 Pearse Stdm
	25/5/2003	Sligo 3-11 London 0-9 Ruislip
Semi-final	1/6/2003	Leitrim 1-7 Galway 2-13 Carrick-on-Shn
	8/6/2003	Sligo 0-11 Mayo 0-14 Markeivicz Park
Final	6/7/2003	Galway 1-14 Mayo 0-13 Pearse Stadium

Leinster

First Round	11/5/2003	Laois 1-19 Wexford 0-10 Croke Park
	11/5/2003	Westmeath 1-17 Carlow 1-12 Croke Park
	11/5/2003	Wicklow 2-7 Louth 4-12 Croke Park
Quarter-final	25/5/2003	Longford 2-6 Kildare 1-14 Mullingar
	25/5/2003	Offaly 1-12 Laois 1-12 Portlaoise
	2/6/2003	Laois 2-10 Offaly 0-13 Tullamore
	1/6/2003	Dublin 1-19 Louth 0-9 Croke Park
	1/6/2003	Meath 2-13 Westmeath 2-13 Croke Park
	7/6/2003	Meath 1-11 Westmeath 0-5 Portlaoise
Semi-final	15/6/2003	Laois 0-16 Dublin 0-14 Croke Park
	14/6/2003	Meath 1-11 Kildare 0-15 Croke Park
Final	20/7/2003	Laois 2-13 Kildare 1-13 Croke Park

Munster

First Round	11/5/2003	Limerick 0-16 Cork 0-6 Páirc Ui Chaoimh
	25/5/2003	Waterford 1-12 Tipperary 0-18 Waterford
Semi-final	15/6/2003	Clare 0-12 Limerick 2-14 Cusack Park
	15/6/2003	Kerry 0-25 Tipperary 1-10 Tralee
Final	13/7/2003	Kerry 1-11 Limerick 0-9 Fitzgerald Stadium

Ulster

First Round	11/5/2003	Monaghan 0-13 Armagh 0-9 Clones
Quarter-finals	18/5/2003	Tyrone 0-12 Derry 1-9 Clones
	24/5/2003	Tyrone 0-17 Derry 1-5 Casement Park
	25/5/2003	Antrim 2-9 Cavan 1-10 Casement Park
	1/6/2003	Fermanagh 0-10 Donegal 0-6 Enniskillen
	8/6/2003	Down 1-12 Monaghan 0-13 Casement Park
Semi-final	15/6/2003	Tyrone 1-17 Antrim 1-9 Casement Park
	22/6/2003	Down 2-10 Fermanagh 0-11 Clones
Final	13/7/2003	Down 4-8 Tyrone 1-17 Clones
	20/7/2003	Down 1-5 Tyrone 0-23 Clones

Qualifiers	Qualifiers, Round 1	7/6/2003	**Carlow 0-18 Wicklow 0-13** Carlow
		7/6/2003	**Donegal 1-17 Longford 1-11** Ballybofey
		7/6/2003	**Offaly 4-15 London 0-10** Tullamore
		7/6/2003	**Roscommon 0-14 Cork 1-10** Waterford
		7/6/2003	**Waterford 0-8 Armagh 2-21** Waterford
		7/6/2003	**Wexford 0-9 Derry 3-10** Wexford
		8/6/2003	**Cavan 1-12 Louth 2-7** Navan
		14/6/2003	**Monaghan 0-14 Westmeath 1-9** Clones
	Qualifiers, Round 2	21/6/2003	**Armagh 0-15 Antrim 0-12** Casement Park
		21/6/2003	**Meath 2-10 Monaghan 0-12** Clones
		21/6/2003	**Offaly 1-12 Clare 1-8** Cusack Park
		21/6/2003	**Roscommon 2-9 Leitrim 1-11** Ck-on-Shannon
		21/6/2003	**Tipperary 1-14 Carlow 0-13** Thurles
		22/6/2003	**Donegal 0-16 Sligo 0-11** Ballybofey
		28/6/2003	**Dublin 3-9 Derry 1-9** Clones
		29/6/2003	**Fermanagh 0-16 Cavan 1-10** Enniskillen
	Qualifiers, Round 3	5/7/2003	**Donegal 2-19 Tipperary 0-15** Croke Park
		5/7/2003	**Dublin 0-11 Armagh 0-15** Croke Park
		5/7/2003	**Offaly 1-15 Roscommon 1-20** Mullingar
		6/7/2003	**Meath 0-9 Fermanagh 1-12** Clones
	Qualifiers, Round 4	19/7/2003	**Fermanagh 0-12 Mayo 1-8** Sligo
		20/7/2003	**Armagh 4-10 Limerick 0-11** Roscommon
		26/7/2003	**Donegal 3-15 Down 2-10** Clones
		26/7/2003	**Kildare 0-19 Roscommon 1-18** Portlaoise
All-Ireland	Quarter-final	3/8/2003	**Armagh 0-15 Laois 0-13** Croke Park
		3/8/2003	**Tyrone 1-21 Fermanagh 0-5** Croke Park
		4/8/2003	**Galway 1-11 Donegal 0-14** Croke Park
		9/8/2003	**Galway 0-11 Donegal 0-14** Croke Park
		4/8/2003	**Kerry 1-21 Roscommon 3-10** Croke Park
	Semi-final	24/8/2003	**Kerry 0-6 Tyrone 0-13** Croke Park
		31/8/2003	**Armagh 2-10 Donegal 1-9** Croke Park
	Final	28/9/2003	**Armagh 0-9 Tyrone 0-12** Croke Park

2004

Kilkenny did not enter the 2004 Championship.

Connacht

First Round	2/5/2004	**New York 1-8 Mayo 3-28** New York
	23/5/2004	**Roscommon 1-10 Sligo 0-13** Roscommon
	29/5/2004	**Roscommon 2-16 Sligo 1-15** Sligo
	30/5/2004	**London 0-8 Galway 8-14** Ruislip
Semi-final	20/6/2004	**Leitrim 1-10 Roscommon 0-13** Ck-on-Shn
	26/6/2004	**Roscommon 1-9 Leitrim 0-5** Roscommon
	27/6/2004	**Mayo 0-18 Galway 1-9** Castlebar
Final	13/5/2004	**Mayo 2-13 Roscommon 0-9** Castlebar

Leinster

First Round	9/5/2004	**Carlow 4-15 Longford 1-16** Tullamore
	16/5/2004	**Wexford 2-10 Louth 0-8** Parnell Park
	23/5/ 2004	**Offaly 0-10 Westmeath 0-11** Croke Park
Quarter-final	23/5/2004	**Wicklow 1-8 Meath 2-13** Croke Park
	30/5/2004	**Carlow 1-7 Laois 0-15** Carlow
	6/6/2004	**Westmeath 0-14 Dublin 0-12** Croke Park
	6/6/2004	**Wexford 0-12 Kildare 0-10** Croke Park
Semi-final	20/6/2004	**Meath 0-9 Laois 1-13** Croke Park
	27/6/2004	**Wexford 1-14 Westmeath 2-15** Croke Park
Final	18/7/2004	**Laois 0-13 Westmeath 0-13** Croke Park
	24/7/2004	**Laois 0-10 Westmeath 0-12** Croke Park

Munster

First Round	16/5/2004	**Tipperary 3-5 Limerick 0-16** Ui Chaoimh
	23/5/2004	**Clare 0-9 Kerry 2-10** Ennis
Semi-final	13/6/2004	**Cork 0-7 Kerry 0-15** Killarney
	13/6/2004	**Waterford 0-7 Limerick 1-18** Limerick
Final	10/6/2004	**Limerick 1-10 Kerry 1-10** Limerick
	18/7/2004	**Limerick 2-9 Kerry 3-10** Killarney

Ulster

First Round	9/5/2004	**Tyrone 1-17 Derry 1-6** Omagh
Quarter-finals	16/5/2004	**Down 1-13 Cavan 1-13** Casement Park
	30/5/2004	**Cavan 3-13 Down 2-12** Breffni Park
	23/5/2004	**Armagh 2-19 Monaghan 0-10** Clones
	30/5/2004	**Donegal 1-15 Antrim 1-9** Ballybofey
	6/6/2004	**Tyrone 1-13 Fermanagh 0-12** Clones
Semi-final	13/6/ 2004	**Cavan 0-11 Armagh 0-13** Clones
	20/6/2004	**Donegal 1-11 Tyrone 0-9** Clones
Final	11/7/2004	**Armagh 3-15 Donegal 0-11** Croke Park

Qualifiers

Qualifiers	*Qualifiers, Round 1*	12/6/2004	**Carlow 1-13 Down 1-19** Carlow
		12/6/2004	**Clare 1-15 Sligo 1-7** Ennis
		12/6/2004	**Dublin 3-24 London 0-6** Parnell Park
		12/6/2004	**Kildare 1-16 Offaly 2-17** Newbridge
		12/6/2004	**Louth 2-13 Antrim 0-14** Drogheda
		12/6/2004	**Monaghan 1-16 Longford 4-15** Clones
		12/6/2004	**Tipperary Fermanagh w/o** Semple Stadium
		12/6/2004	**Wicklow 1-10 Derry 1-15** Aughrim
	Qualifiers, Round 2	3/7/2004	**Cork 0-15 Clare 0-11** Cusack Park
		3/7/2004	**Galway 2-8 Louth 0-9** Parnell Park
		3/7/2004	**Leitrim 0-4 Dublin 1-13** Carrick-on-Shannon
		3/7/2004	**Meath 2-12 Fermanagh 0-19** Enniskillen
		3/7/2004	**Tyrone 1-15 Down 0-10** Newry
		3/7/2004	**Waterford 1-5 Longford 1-14** Pearse Park
		4/7/2004	**Cavan 2-9 Derry 0-25** Celtic Park
		10/7/2004	**Wexford 2-14 Offaly 0-15** Wexford Park
	Qualifiers, Round 3	10/7/2004	**Dublin 1-17 Longford 0-11** Portlaoise
		17/7/2004	**Cork 0-11 Fermanagh 0-18** Croke Park
		17/7/2004	**Derry 2-16 Wexford 2-5** Parnell Park
		17/7/2004	**Galway 0-11 Tyrone 1-16** Croke Park
	Qualifiers, Round 4	24/7/2004	**Derry 0-10 Limerick 0-7** Hyde Park
		24/7/2004	**Fermanagh 1-10 Donegal 0-12** Clones
		1/8/2004	**Roscommon 0-13 Dublin 1-14** Croke Park
		1/8/2004	**Tyrone 3-15 Laois 2-4** Croke Park

All-Ireland

All-Ireland	*Quarter-final*	7/8/2004	**Armagh 0-11 Fermanagh 0-12** Croke Park
		7/8/2004	**Mayo 0-16 Tyrone 1-9** Croke Park
		14/8/2004	**Kerry 1-15 Dublin 1-8** Croke Park
		14/8/2004	**Westmeath 0-13 Derry 2-9** Croke Park
	Semi-final	22/8/2004	**Mayo 0-9 Fermanagh 0-9** Croke Park
		28/8/2004	**Mayo 0-13 Fermanagh 1-8** Croke Park
		29/8/2004	**Derry 1-11 Kerry 1-17** Croke Park
	Final	26/9/2004	**Kerry 1-20 Mayo 2-9** Croke Park

$$\boxed{\textbf{2005}}$$

Kilkenny did not enter the 2005 Championship.

Connacht

First Round	15/5/2005	Galway 3-14 New York 0-6 New York
	22/5/2005	Leitrim 1-11 Sligo 0-9 Carrick-on-Shannon
	29/5/2005	Roscommon 0-12 London 1-8 Ruislip
Semi-final	12/6/2005	Galway 1-11 Leitrim 1-8 Pearse Stadium
	19/6/2005	Mayo 1-16 Roscommon 0-11 Roscommon
Final	10/7/2005	Galway 0-10 Mayo 0-8 Pearse Stadium

Leinster

First Round	7/5/2005	Offaly 1-15 Louth 1-6 Navan
	15/5/2005	Dublin 2-23 Longford 0-10 Croke Park
	15/5/2005	Kildare 1-17 Wicklow 2-12 Croke Park
Quarter-final	29/5/2005	Kildare 0-14 Westmeath 0-11 Croke Park
	29/5/2005	Laois 1-10 Offaly 1-8 Croke Park
	5/6/2005	Dublin 1-12 Meath 1-10 Croke Park
	5/6/2005	Wexford 3-12 Carlow 2-13 Croke Park
Semi-final	19/6/2005	Dublin 1-17 Wexford 2-10 Croke Park
	19/6/2005	Laois 0-21 Kildare 0-9 Croke Park
Final	17/7/2005	Dublin 0-14 Laois 0-13 Croke Park

Munster

First Round	29/5/2005	Kerry 2-22 Tipperary 0-13 Semple Stadium
	29/5/2005	Clare 2-14 Waterford 2-10 Ennis
Semi-final	12/6/2005	Cork 0-18 Clare 0-6 Ennis
	19/6/2005	Kerry 2-10 Limerick 0-10 Limerick
Final	10/7/2005	Cork 0-11 Kerry 1-11 Páirc Uí Chaoimh

Ulster

First Round	15/5/2005	Armagh 2-12 Fermanagh 1-7 Clones
Quarter-finals	22/5/2005	Tyrone 1-13 Down 1-6 Omagh
	29/5/2005	Cavan 0-11 Antrim 0-11 Cavan
	4/6/2005	Cavan 1-15 Antrim 2-6 Casement Park
	5/6/2005	Derry 1-17 Monaghan 2-8 Clones
	12/6/2005	Armagh 0-12 Donegal 0-12 Clones
	19/6/2005	Armagh 3-11 Donegal 1-10 Clones
Semi-final	19/6/2005	Tyrone 0-10 Cavan 1-7 Clones
	25/6/2005	Tyrone 3-19 Cavan 0-7 Clones
	26/6/2005	Derry 0-10 Armagh 1-11 Casement Park
Final	10/7/2005	Armagh 2-8 Tyrone 0-14 Croke Park
	23/7/2005	Armagh 0-13 Tyrone 0-11 Croke Park

Qualifiers			
	Qualifiers, Round 1	25/6/2005	**Antrim 0-13 Meath 5-12** Casement Park
		25/6/2005	**Carlow 0-14 Offaly 1-10** Carlow
		25/6/2005	**Down 1-11 Fermanagh 0-7** Newry
		25/6/2005	**Louth 1-12 Waterford 1-8** Drogheda
		25/6/2005	**Monaghan 2-18 London 1-9** Clones
		25/6/2005	**Sligo 0-18 Longford 0-16** Sligo
		25/6/2005	**Tipperary 1-8 Westmeath 0-12** Semple Stdm
		26/6/2005	**Wicklow 0-12 Donegal 0-16** Aughrim
	Qualifiers, Round 2	2/7/2005	**Cavan 1-11 Donegal 1-10** Cavan
		2/7/2005	**Clare 0-12 Westmeath 0-9** Ennis
		2/7/2005	**Derry 3-8 Down 2-9** Newry
		2/7/2005	**Limerick 2-15 Carlow 0-7** Carlow
		2/7/2005	**Louth 0-11 Roscommon 0-10** Drogheda
		2/7/2005	**Meath 1-12 Leitrim 1-8** Carrick-on-Shannon
		2/7/2005	**Sligo 1-11 Kildare 1-10** Sligo
		9/7/2005	**Monaghan 0-17 Wexford 0-12** Clones
	Qualifiers, Round 3	16/7/2005	**Monaghan 1-12 Louth 0-14** Cavan
		17/7/2005	**Derry 0-13 Limerick 0-9** Castlebar
		17/7/2005	**Meath 1-6 Cavan 1-8** Clones
		17/7/2005	**Sligo 1-13 Clare 0-11** Castlebar
	Qualifiers, Round 4	30/7/2005	**Cork 3-13 Sligo 0-11** Portlaoise
		30/7/2005	**Mayo 0-11 Cavan 0-8** Roscommon
		6/8/2005	**Laois 1-11 Derry 0-11** Croke Park
		6/8/2005	**Tyrone 2-14 Monaghan 1-7** Croke Park
All-Ireland			
	Quarter-final	7/8/2005	**Cork 2-14 Galway 2-11** Croke Park
		7/8/2005	**Kerry 2-15 Mayo 0-18** Croke Park
		13/8/2005	**Dublin 1-14 Tyrone 1-14** Croke Park
		27/8/2005	**Tyrone 2-18 Dublin 1-14** Croke Park
		20/8/2005	**Armagh 2-17 Laois 1-11** Croke Park
	Semi-final	28/8/2005	**Kerry 1-19 Cork 0-9** Croke Park
		4/9/2005	**Tyrone 1-13 Armagh 1-12** Croke Park
	Final	25/9/2005	**Tyrone 1-16 Kerry 2-10** Croke Park

Kilkenny did not enter the 2006 Championship.

Connacht

First Round	14/5/2006	**New York 0-9 Roscommon 1-14** New York
	27/5/2006	**Galway 0-19 Sligo 1-12** Pearse Stadium
	28/5/2006	**London 0-8 Mayo 1-18** Ruislip, London
Semi-final	18/6/2006	**Roscommon 1-8 Galway 3-7** Roscommon
	25/6/2006	**Leitrim 1-9 Mayo 1-10** Carrick-on-Shannon
Final	16/7/2006	**Mayo 0-12 Galway 1-8** Castlebar

Leinster

First Round	14/5/2006	**Meath 1-15 Louth 0-10** Croke Park
	14/5/2006	**Westmeath 0-11 Offaly 0-15** Croke Park
	21/5/2006	**Wicklow 0-12 Carlow 4-9** Wexford
Quarter-final	28/5/2006	**Kildare 0-15 Offaly 3-9** Croke Park
	28/5/2006	**Wexford 1-19 Meath 1-13** Croke Park
	4/6/2006	**Laois 1-17 Carlow 1-9** Portlaoise
	4/6/2006	**Longford 0-13 Dublin 1-12** Longford
Semi-final	25/6/2006	**Dublin 3-17 Laois 0-12** Croke Park
	2/7/2006	**Offaly 2-15 Wexford 1-14** Croke Park
Final	16/7/2006	**Dublin 1-15 Offaly 0-9** Croke Park

Munster

First Round	21/5/2006	**Kerry 0-16 Waterford 0-8** Killarney
	21/5/2006	**Limerick 2-5 Clare 0-8** Limerick
Semi-final	11/6/2006	**Kerry 0-17 Tipperary 1-5** Killarney
	11/6/2006	**Limerick 0-5 Cork 0-9** Limerick
Final	9/7/2006	**Kerry 0-10 Cork 0-10** Killarney
	16/7/2006	**Kerry 0-9 Cork 1-12** Cork

Ulster

First Round	7/5/2006	**Down 1-13 Cavan 0-11** Casement Park
Quarter-finals	14/5/2006	**Armagh 0-10 Monaghan 0-10** Clones
	20/5/2006	**Armagh 1-13 Monaghan 0-10** Clones
	21/5/2006	**Fermanagh 1-9 Antrim 0-9** Enniskillen
	28/5/2006	**Tyrone 0-5 Derry 1-8** Omagh
	4/6/2006	**Donegal 1-12 Down 1-11** Ballybofey
Semi-final	11/6/2006	**Armagh 0-11 Fermanagh 2-5** Clones
	25/6/2006	**Armagh 0-16 Fermanagh 1-8** Clones
	18/6/2006	**Donegal 1-13 Derry 0-11** Clones
Final	9/7/2006	**Armagh 1-9 Donegal 0-9** Croke Park

Qualifiers

Qualifiers, Round 1

17/6/2006	**Antrim 2-9 Clare 1-13** Casement Park
17/6/2006	**Monaghan 2-19 Wicklow 3-6** Clones
17/6/2006	**Sligo 1-7 Down 0-4** Sligo
17/6/2006	**Tyrone 2-16 Louth 2-16** Navan
24/6/2006	**Tyrone 1-12 Louth 1-7** Omagh
17/6/2006	**Waterford 1-9 Longford 1-16** Waterford
18/6/2006	**Carlow 0-12 Meath 1-17** Carlow
18/6/2006	**Westmeath 0-20 London 0-8** Mullingar
24/6/2006	**Kildare 1-18 Cavan 1-13** Newbridge

Qualifiers, Round 2

1 /7/2006	**Derry 1-17 Kildare 0-11** Derry
1 /7/2006	**Longford 1-23 Tipperary 1-10** Longford
1 /7/2006	**Meath 1-19 Roscommon 0-9** Navan
2 /7/2006	**Westmeath 0-13 Limerick 1-9** Mullingar
8 /7/2006	**Clare 0-10 Fermanagh 0-15** Ennis
8 /7/2006	**Laois 0-9 Tyrone 0-6** Portlaoise
9 /7/2006	**Leitrim 0-9 Sligo 1-7** Carrick-on-Shannon
9/7/2006	**Monaghan 0-6 Wexford 0-8** Clones

Qualifiers, Round 3

15/7/2006	**Fermanagh 2-12 Wexford 0-11** Enniskillen
15/7/2006	**Longford 1-16 Derry 2-12** Longford
15/7/2006	**Meath 0-13 Laois 2-13** Navan
15/7/2006	**Sligo 0-14 Westmeath 1-12** Sligo

Qualifiers, Round 4

29/7/2006	**Fermanagh 0-8 Donegal 0-11** Enniskillen
29/7/2006	**Galway 0-10 Westmeath 1-8** Pearse Stadium
29/7/2006	**Kerry 4-11 Longford 1-11** Killarney
30/7/2006	**Laois 1-9 Offaly 0-4** Portlaoise

All-Ireland

Quarter-final

5/8/2006	**Armagh 1-13 Kerry 3-15** Croke Park
5/8/2006	**Cork 1-11 Donegal 1-10** Croke Park
12/8/2006	**Dublin 1-12 Westmeath 0-5** Croke Park
13/8/2006	**Mayo 0-15 Laois 0-15** Croke Park
20/8/2006	**Mayo 0-14 Laois 0-11** Croke Park

Semi-final

20/8/2006	**Kerry 0-16 Cork 0-10** Croke Park
27/8/2006	**Mayo 1-16 Dublin 2-12** Croke Park

Final

17/9/2006	**Kerry 4-15 Mayo 3-5** Croke Park

2007

Kilkenny did not enter the 2007 Championship. On elimination from the provincial championship, counties who played in Division 4 of the National Football League were entered in the Tommy Murphy Cup rather than the All-Ireland Qualifiers.

Connacht

First Round	13/5/2007	**New York 1-3 Sligo 2-18** New York	
	20/5/2007	**Galway 2-10 Mayo 0-9** Pearse Stadium	
	27/5/2007	**London 2-5 Leitrim 1-12** Ruislip, London	
Semi-final	17/6/2007	**Sligo 0-13 Roscommon 2-5** Roscommon	
	24/6/2007	**Leitrim 1-10 Galway 0-17** Carrick-on-Shn	
Final	8/7/2007	**Sligo 1-10 Galway 0-12** Roscommon	

Leinster

First Round	13/5/2007	**Longford 2-13 Westmeath 1-13** Longford
	20/5/2007	**Louth 1-11 Wicklow 0-14** Croke Park
	27/5/2007	**Louth 1-9 Wicklow 0-12** Parnell Park
	3/6/2007	**Louth 2-18 Wicklow 0-11** Croke Park
	20/5/2007	**Meath 2-11 Kildare 1-8** Croke Park
	2/6/2007	**Longford 0-9 Laois 0-14** Tullamore
Quarter-final	3/6/2007	**Dublin 1-11 Meath 0-14** Croke Park
	17/6/2007	**Meath 0-12 Dublin 0-16** Croke Park
	10/6/2007	**Carlow 3-7 Offaly 2-19** Portlaoise
	17/6/2007	**Louth 2-8 Wexford 0-16** Croke Park
Semi-final	24/6/2007	**Dublin 1-12 Offaly 0-10** Croke Park
	1/7/2007	**Laois 1-13 Wexford 0-13** Croke Park
Final	15/7/2007	**Dublin 3-14 Laois 1-14** Croke Park

Munster

First Round	20/5/2007	**Cork 2-14 Limerick 0-7** Páirc Uí Chaoimh
	20/5/2007	**Waterford 1-6 Clare 0-7** Dungarvan
Semi-final	3/6/2007	**Cork 2-18 Tipperary 0-10** Limerick
	3/6/2007	**Waterford 0-4 Kerry 2-15** Dungarvan
Final	20/5/2007	**Kerry 1-15 Cork 1-13** Killarney

Ulster

First Round	13/5/2007	**Cavan 2-11 Down 3-8** Cavan
	20/5/2007	**Down 0-15 Cavan 0-11** Newry
	20/5/2007	**Fermanagh 1-9 Tyrone 0-13** Clones
Quarter-finals	27/5/2007	**Donegal 1-9 Armagh 1-8** Ballybofey
	10/6/2007	**Antrim 0-10 Derry 1-13** Casement Park
	10/6/2007	**Monaghan 2-15 Down 1-15** Newry
Semi-final	17/6/2007	**Tyrone 2-15 Donegal 1-7** Clones
	24/6/2007	**Derry 1-9 Monaghan 0-14** Casement Park
Final	15/7/2007	**Tyrone 1-15 Monaghan 1-13** Clones

Qualifiers	*Qualifiers, Round 1*	7/7/2007	**Armagh 0-9 Derry 0-10** Clones
		7/7/2007	**Down 0-8 Meath 1-10** Newry
		7/7/2007	**Fermanagh 1-12 Wexford 1-8** Clones
		7/7/2007	**Leitrim 1-14 Donegal 1-16** Ck-on-Shannon
		7/7/2007	**Limerick 0-13 Louth 0-14** Limerick
		7/7/2007	**Mayo 1-19 Cavan 3-7** Castlebar
		7/7/2007	**Roscommon 1-13 Kildare 2-13** Roscommon
		7/7/2007	**Westmeath 0-18 Longford 0-9** Mullingar
	Qualifiers, Round 2	14/7/2007	**Derry 2-13 Mayo 1-6** Celtic Park, Derry
		14/7/2007	**Kildare 1-10 Louth 1-16** Newbridge
		14/7/2007	**Meath 0-11 Fermanagh 0-9** Navan
		14/7/2007	**Westmeath 1-8 Donegal 1-13** Mullingar
	Qualifiers, Round 3	14/7/2007	**Galway 1-14 Meath 2-14** Portlaoise
		14/7/2007	**Louth 0-14 Cork 0-16** Portlaoise
		21/7/2007	**Laois 2-11 Derry 1-18** Cavan
		21/7/2007	**Monaghan 2-12 Donegal 1-7** Omagh
All-Ireland	*Quarter-final*	5/8/2007	**Cork 1-11 Sligo 0-8** Croke Park
		5/8/2007	**Meath 1-13 Tyrone 2-8** Croke Park
		11/8/2007	**Dublin 0-18 Derry 0-15** Croke Park
		12/8/2007	**Kerry 1-12 Monaghan 1-11** Croke Park
	Semi-final	19/8/2007	**Cork 1-16 Meath 0-9** Croke Park
		26/8/2007	**Kerry 1-15 Dublin 0-16** Croke Park
	Final	16/9/2007	**Kerry 3-13 Cork 1-9** Croke Park

Kilkenny did not enter the 2008 Championship.

Connacht

First Round	11/5/2008	**New York 0-6 Leitrim 0-17** New York
	18/5/2008	**Galway 2-18 Roscommon 0-6** Pearse Stdm
	25/5/2008	**London 0-7 Sligo 2-17** Ruislip, London
Semi-final	15/6/2008	**Galway 2-14 Leitrim 1-13** Pearse Stadium
	22/6/2008	**Mayo 3-11 Sligo 0-7** Castlebar
Final	13/7/2008	**Galway 2-12 Mayo 1-14** Castlebar

Leinster

First Round	11/5/2008	**Longford 1-10 Westmeath 2-10** Longford
	18/5/2008	**Carlow 0-8 Meath 1-25** Croke Park
	18/5/2008	**Kildare 0-9 Wicklow 0-13** Croke Park
Quarter-final	31/5/2008	**Laois 0-15 Wicklow 0-13** Carlow
	1/6/2008	**Wexford 2-14 Meath 2-13** Carlow
	7/6/2008	**Offaly 1-8 Westmeath 2-11** Tullamore
	8/6/2008	**Dublin 1-22 Louth 0-12** Croke Park
Semi-final	22/6/2008	**Laois 0-12 Wexford 0-18** Croke Park
	29/6/2008	**Westmeath 1-8 Dublin 0-13** Croke Park
Final	20/7/2008	**Wexford 0-9 Dublin 3-23** Croke Park

Munster

First Round	25/5/2008	**Limerick 1-8 Tipperary 1-5** Fermoy
	25/5/2008	**Waterford 0-7 Clare 0-9** Ennis
Semi-final	15/6/2008	**Clare 0-5 Kerry 1-14** Killarney
	15/6/2008	**Cork 2-9 Limerick 0-12** Limerick
Final	6/7/2008	**Cork 1-16 Kerry 1-11** Cork

Ulster

First Round	18/5/2008	**Antrim 1-14 Cavan 1-19** Casement Park
Quarter-finals	25/5/2008	**Fermanagh 2-8 Monaghan 0-10** E-killen
	1/6/2008	**Donegal 1-12 Derry 1-14** Ballybofey
	8/6/2008	**Tyrone 2-8 Down 2-8** Omagh
	14/6/2008	**Tyrone 0-21 Down 1-19** Newry
	15/6/2008	**Cavan 0-13 Armagh 0-17** Cavan
Semi-final	21/6/2008	**Fermanagh 1-11 Derry 1-9** Omagh
	29/6/2008	**Down 0-11 Armagh 1-12** Clones
Final	20/7/2008	**Fermanagh 1-11 Armagh 2-8** Clones
	27/7/2008	**Fermanagh 0-8 Armagh 1-11** Clones

Qualifiers

Qualifiers, Round 1

19/7/2008	**Donegal 3-11 Roscommon 1-9** Ballybofey
19/7/2008	**Kildare 1-16 Cavan 1-15** Newbridge
19/7/2008	**Limerick 4-12 Meath 4-3** Limerick
19/7/2008	**Longford 0-11 Laois 1-10** Longford
19/7/2008	**Louth 1-9 Tyrone 1-17** Drogheda
19/7/2008	**Monaghan 1-13 Derry 1-12** Clones
19/7/2008	**Offaly 2-10 Down 5-19** Tullamore
19/7/2008	**Tipperary 0-6 Westmeath 0-15** Ardinnan

Qualifiers, Round 2

26/7/2008	**Donegal 0-15 Monaghan 0-16** Ballybofey
26/7/2008	**Laois 1-15 Down 2-14** Portlaoise
26/7/2008	**Limerick 0-11 Kildare 1-11** Limerick
26/7/2008	**Tyrone 0-14 Westmeath 1-7** Omagh

Qualifiers, Round 3

2/8/2008	**Mayo 1-9 Tyrone 0-13** Croke Park
2/8/2008	**Wexford 2-13 Down 0-12** Croke Park
3/8/2008	**Fermanagh 0-5 Kildare 0-11** Croke Park
3/8/2008	**Kerry 1-13 Monaghan 0-13** Croke Park

All-Ireland

Quarter-final

9/8/2008	**Armagh 0-12 Wexford 1-14** Croke Park
9/8/2008	**Galway 1-16 Kerry 1-21** Croke Park
10/8/2008	**Cork 2-11 Kildare 1-11** Croke Park
16/8/2008	**Dublin 1-8 Tyrone 3-14** Croke Park

Semi-final

24/8/2008	**Kerry 1-13 Cork 3-7** Croke Park
31/8/2008	**Kerry 3-14 Cork 2-13** Croke Park
31/8/2008	**Tyrone 0-23 Wexford 1-14** Croke Park

Final

21/9/2008	**Tyrone 1-15 Kerry 0-14** Croke Park

2009

Kilkenny did not enter the 2009 Championship.

Connacht

First Round	10/5/2009	**New York 0-10 Mayo 2-19** New York
	24/5/2009	**London 1-7 Galway 1-18** Ruislip, London
	31/5/2009	**Leitrim 2-9 Roscommon 2-13** Ck-on-Shn
Semi-final	20/6/2009	**Mayo 3-18 Roscommon 0-7** Castlebar
	28/6/2009	**Sligo 0-12 Galway 1-13** Sligo
Final	19/7/2009	**Mayo 2-12 Galway 1-14** Pearse Stadium

Leinster

First Round	17/5/2009	**Carlow 1-11 Louth 1-13** Parnell Park
	24/5/2009	**Kildare 1-16 Offaly 1-10** Portlaoise
	24/5/2009	**Longford 1-13 Wicklow 2-12** Portlaoise
Quarter-final	7/6/2009	**Meath 0-12 Dublin 0-14** Croke Park
	13/6/2009	**Kildare 2-12 Wexford 0-11** Carlow
	14/6/2009	**Louth 1-11 Laois 1-15** Parnell Park
	14/6/2009	**Wicklow 1-10 Westmeath 0-16** Tullamore
Semi-final	27/6/2009	**Kildare 2-18 Laois 0-9** Tullamore
	28/6/2009	**Westmeath 0-11 Dublin 4-26** Croke Park
Final	12/7/2009	**Dublin 2-15 Kildare 0-18** Croke Park

Munster

First Round	24/5/2009	**Tipperary 1-9 Limerick 1-11** Semple Stdm
	24/5/2009	**Waterford 1-7 Cork 2-18** Dungarvan
Semi-final	7/6/2009	**Cork 1-10 Kerry 0-13** Killarney
	13/6/2009	**Cork 1-17 Kerry 0-12** Páirc Uí Chaoimh
	7/6/2009	**Limerick 1-13 Clare 1-9** Ennis
Final	5/7/2009	**Limerick 0-11 Cork 2-6** Páirc Uí Chaoimh

Ulster

First Round	17/5/2009	**Fermanagh 0-13 Down 0-10** Enniskillen
Quarter-finals	24/5/2009	**Derry 1-10 Monaghan 0-10** Celtic Park
	31/5/2009	**Tyrone 2-10 Armagh 1-10** Clones
	6/6/2009	**Fermanagh 1-9 Cavan 0-13** Cavan
	14/6/2009	**Donegal 0-12 Antrim 1-10** Ballybofey
Semi final	21/6/2009	**Tyrone 0-15 Derry 0-7** Casement Park
	27/6/2009	**Antrim 0-13 Cavan 1-7** Clones
Final	19/7/2009	**Tyrone 1-18 Antrim 0-15** Clones

Qualifiers	*Qualifiers, Round 1*	4/7/2009	**Donegal 2-13 Carlow 1-6** Ballybofey
		4/7/2009	**Leitrim 0-10 Longford 0-13** Ck-on-Shannon
		4/7/2009	**London 1-7 Down 1-16** Newry
		4/7/2009	**Louth 1-12 Tipperary 2-10** Drogheda
		4/7/2009	**Meath 1-20 Waterford 0-8** Navan
		4/7/2009	**Monaghan 0-13 Armagh 0-12** Clones
		4/7/2009	**Wexford 2-11 Offaly 0-16** Wexford
		4/7/2009	**Wicklow 0-17 Fermanagh 1-11** Aughrim
	Qualifiers, Round 2	11/7/2009	**Derry 3-16 Monaghan 0-20** Clones
		11/7/2009	**Donegal 0-13 Clare 1-7** Ballybofey
		11/7/2009	**Kerry 1-12 Longford 0-11** Longford
		11/7/2009	**Laois 0-7 Down 2-9** Newry
		11/7/2009	**Roscommon 0-11 Wexford 1-8** Wexford
		18/7/2009	**Roscommon 0-11 Wexford 1-8** Roscommon
		11/7/2009	**Sligo 1-13 Tipperary 1-12** Semple Stadium
		11/7/2009	**Westmeath 1-5 Meath 1-15** Mullingar
		11/7/2009	**Wicklow 1-12 Cavan 0-8** Aughrim
	Qualifiers, Round 3	18/7/2009	**Donegal 2-13 Derry 0-18** Ballybofey
		18/7/2009	**Kerry 0-14 Sligo 1-10** Tralee
		18/7/2009	**Wicklow 1-15 Down 0-17** Aughrim
		25/7/2009	**Meath 2-12 Roscommon 0-11** Navan
	Qualifiers, Round 4	25/7/2009	**Galway 0-13 Donegal 0-14** Sligo
		25/7/2009	**Kildare 1-16 Wicklow 2-9** Portlaoise
		26/7/2009	**Antrim 1-10 Kerry 2-12** Tullamore
		1/8/2009	**Limerick 2-9 Meath 1-13** Portlaoise
All-Ireland	*Quarter-final*	1/8/2009	**Cork 1-27 Donegal 2-10** Croke Park
		1/8/2009	**Dublin 1-7 Kerry 1-24** Croke Park
		1/8/2009	**Tyrone 0-16 Kildare 1-11** Croke Park
		8/8/2009	**Mayo 1-15 Meath 2-15** Croke Park
	Semi-final	23/8/2009	**Cork 1-13 Tyrone 0-11** Croke Park
		30/8/2009	**Kerry 2-8 Meath 1-7** Croke Park
	Final	20/9/2009	**Kerry 0-16 Cork 1-9** Croke Park

Kilkenny did not enter the 2010 Championship.

Connacht

First Round	2/5/2010	New York 0-12 Galway 2-13 New York
	30/5/2010	London 0-6 Roscommon 0-14 Ruislip
	5/6/2010	Sligo 0-15 Mayo 1-8 Sligo
	20/6/2010	Roscommon 1-13 Leitrim 0-11 Roscommon
Semi-final	27/6/2010	Sligo 1-10 Galway 1-10 Pearse Stadium
	3/7/2010	Sligo 1-14 Galway 0-16 Sligo
Final	18/7/2010	Roscommon 0-14 Sligo 0-13 Castlebar

Leinster

First Round	16/5/2010	Wicklow 3-13 Carlow 0-12 Portlaoise
	23/5/2010	Louth 1-11 Longford 1-7 Portlaoise
	23/5/2010	Meath 1-20 Offaly 2-7 Portlaoise
Quarter-final	5/6/2010	Louth 1-22 Kildare 1-16 Navan
	6/6/2010	Wicklow 1-11 Westmeath 0-15 Tullamore
	13/6/2010	Dublin 2-16 Wexford 0-15 Croke Park
	13/6/2010	Meath 2-13 Laois 1-16 Croke Park
	19/6/2010	Meath 2-14 Laois 0-10 Tullamore
Semi-final	26/6/2010	Louth 1-15 Westmeath 2-10 Croke Park
	27/6/2010	Meath 5-9 Dublin 0-13 Croke Park
Final	11/7/2010	Meath 1-12 Louth 1-10 Croke Park

Munster

First Round	16/5/2010	Kerry 2-18 Tipperary 2-6 Semple Stadium
	23/5/2010	Clare 0-9 Waterford 1-10 Dungarvan
Semi-final	6/6/2010	Kerry 0-15 Cork 0-15 Killarney
	13/6/2010	Kerry 1-15 Cork 1-14 Páirc Uí Chaoimh
	6/6/2010	Waterford 1-9 Limerick 1-17 Dungarvan
Final	4/7/2010	Kerry 1-17 Limerick 1-14 Killarney

Ulster

First Round	16/5/2010	Derry 1-7 Armagh 1-10 Celtic Park, Derry
Quarter-finals	23/5/2010	Antrim 1-13 Tyrone 2-14 Casement Park
	30/5/2010	Donegal 2-10 Down 1-15 Ballybofey
	6/6/2010	Monaghan 1-18 Armagh 0-9 Casement Park
	12/6/2010	Cavan 0-13 Fermanagh 1-13 Cavan
Semi-final	19/6/2010	Tyrone 0-14 Down 0-10 Casement Park
	27/6/2010	Fermanagh 2-8 Monaghan 0-21 Cavan
Final	18/7/2010	Tyrone 1-14 Monaghan 0-7 Clones

Qualifiers	*Qualifiers, Round 1*	26/6/2010	**Armagh 2-14 Donegal 0-11** Crossmaglen
		26/6/2010	**Carlow 2-9 Derry 1-18** Carlow
		26/6/2010	**Cavan 0-15 Wicklow 2-8** Cavan
		26/6/2010	**Kildare 0-15 Antrim 0-15** Newbridge
		3/7/2010	**Kildare 1-15 Antrim 0-9** Casement Park
		26/6/2010	**Longford 1-12 Mayo 0-14** Longford
		26/6/2010	**Offaly 2-18 Clare 1-18** Tullamore
		27/6/2010	**London 0-9 Wexford 4-22** Ruislip, London
		27/6/2010	**Tipperary 0-13 Laois 0-12** Semple Stadium
	Qualifiers, Round 2	10/7/2010	**Cork 1-19 Cavan 0-4** Páirc Uí Chaoimh
		10/7/2010	**Down 1-14 Longford 1-10** Newry
		10/7/2010	**Dublin 1-21 Tipperary 1-13** Croke Park
		10/7/2010	**Galway 0-13 Wexford 1-11** Pearse Stadium
		10/7/2010	**Leitrim 0-6 Kildare 1-12** Newbridge
		10/7/2010	**Waterford 0-10 Offaly 0-15** Tullamore
		10/7/2010	**Westmeath 1-7 Derry 0-13** Mullingar
		11/7/2010	**Fermanagh 0-7 Armagh 0-11** Enniskillen
	Qualifiers, Round 3	17/7/2010	**Cork 0-12 Wexford 0-5** Wexford
		17/7/2010	**Derry 1-9 Kildare 2-17** Celtic Park, Derry
		17/7/2010	**Down 1-12 Offaly 1-10** Tullamore
		17/7/2010	**Dublin 0-14 Armagh 0-11** Croke Park
	Qualifiers, Round 4	24/7/2010	**Limerick 1-11 Cork 0-16** Limerick
		24/7/2010	**Louth 0-13 Dublin 2-14** Croke Park
		24/7/2010	**Monaghan 1-11 Kildare 1-15** Croke Park
		24/7/2010	**Sligo 0-10 Down 3-20** Cavan
All-Ireland	*Quarter-final*	31/7/2010	**Kerry 1-10 Down 1-16** Croke Park
		1/8/2010	**Meath 1-12 Kildare 2-17** Croke Park
		1/8/2010	**Roscommon 0-10 Cork 1-16** Croke Park
		31/7/2010	**Tyrone 0-13 Dublin 1-15** Croke Park
	Semi-final	22/8/2010	**Kildare 1-14 Down 1-16** Croke Park
		29/8/2010	**Cork 1-15 Dublin 1-14** Croke Park
	Final	19/9/2010	**Cork 0-16 Down 0-15** Croke Park

Kilkenny did not enter the 2011 Championship.

Connacht

First Round	1/5/2011	**New York 1-11 Roscommon 3-21** New York
	22/5/2011	**Sligo 0-10 Leitrim 1-10** Sligo
	29/5/2011	**London 2-10 Mayo 0-19** Ruislip, London
Semi-final	12/6/2011	**Roscommon 2-12 Leitrim 0-6** Ck-on-Shn
	26/6/2011	**Galway 1-6 Mayo 1-12** Castlebar
Final	17/7/2011	**Roscommon 0-11 Mayo 0-13** Roscommon

Leinster

First Round	22/5/2011	**Kildare 0-12 Wicklow 0-5** Portlaoise
	22/5/2011	**Laois 0-10 Longford 0-9** Portlaoise
	28/5/2011	**Wexford 2-16 Offaly 0-8** Tullamore
Quarter-final	5/6/2011	**Kildare 0-16 Meath 0-10** Croke Park
	5/6/2011	**Laois 0-11 Dublin 1-16** Croke Park
	11/6/2011	**Wexford 1-24 Westmeath 0-15** Wexford
	12/6/2011	**Carlow 0-14 Louth 0-13** Portlaoise
Semi-final	26/6/2011	**Kildare 1-11 Dublin 1-12** Croke Park
	26/6/2011	**Wexford 4-12 Carlow 0-10** Croke Park
Final	10/7/2011	**Wexford 1-12 Dublin 2-12** Croke Park

Munster

First Round	22/5/2011	**Clare 0-11 Cork 1-23** Páirc Uí Chaoimh
	22/5/2011	**Tipperary 0-11 Kerry 2-16** Killarney
Semi-final	4/6/2011	**Kerry 1-26 Limerick 3-9** Limerick
	5/6/2011	**Waterford 2-8 Cork 5-17** Páirc Uí Chaoimh
Final	4/7/2011	**Kerry 1-15 Cork 1-12** Killarney

Ulster

First Round	15/5/2011	**Donegal 1-10 Antrim 0-7** Ballybofey
Quarter-finals	22/5/2011	**Derry 1-18 Fermanagh 1-10** Celtic Park
	28/5/2011	**Armagh 1-15 Down 1-10** Armagh
	5/6/2011	**Tyrone 1-13 Monaghan 1-11** Omagh
	12/6/2011	**Cavan 1-8 Donegal 2-14** Cavan
Semi-final	19/6/2011	**Derry 3-14 Armagh 1-11** Clones
	26/6/2011	**Tyrone 0-9 Donegal 2-6** Clones
Final	17/7/2011	**Derry 0-8 Donegal 1-11** Clones

		25/6/2011	**Antrim 0-16 Westmeath 1-7** Casement Park
		25/6/2011	**Cavan 0-11 Longford 2-16** Cavan
		25/6/2011	**Clare 1-12 Down 1-13** Ennis
	Qualifiers, Round 1	25/6/2011	**Laois 2-16 Tipperary 0-11** Portlaoise
		25/6/2011	**London 0-15 Fermanagh 0-9** Ruislip
		25/6/2011	**Louth 2-8 Meath 5-8** Cavan
		25/6/2011	**Offaly 1-18 Monaghan 1-10** Tullamore
		25/6/2011	**Wicklow 1-18 Sligo 0-16** Aughrim
		9/7/2011	**Antrim 1-13 Carlow 2-9** Casement Park
		9/7/2011	**Armagh 0-19 Wicklow 2-13** Armagh
		9/7/2011	**Down 1-16 Leitrim 1-8** Newry
Qualifiers	*Qualifiers, Round 2*	9/7/2011	**Laois 0-10 Kildare 3-16** Portlaoise
		9/7/2011	**Limerick 3-13 Offaly 0-15** Limerick
		9/7/2011	**London 0-13 Waterford 1-17** Ruislip
		9/7/2011	**Longford 0-15 Tyrone 1-17** Longford
		9/7/2011	**Meath 0-11 Galway 0-10** Navan
		16/7/2011	**Wicklow 0-10 Armagh 2-9** Aughrim
	Qualifiers, Round 3	16/7/2011	**Antrim 0-10 Down 3-13** Casement Park
		16/7/2011	**Limerick 0-14 Waterford 0-9** Limerick
		16/7/2011	**Meath 0-14 Kildare 2-11** Navan
		23/7/2011	**Tyrone 2-13 Armagh 0-13** Omagh
	Qualifiers, Round 4	23/7/2011	**Down 0-14 Cork 2-20** Croke Park
		23/7/2011	**Kildare 0-19 Derry 0-13** Croke Park
		23/7/2011	**Limerick 1-18 Wexford 1-17** Portlaoise
		30/7/2011	**Tyrone 3-19 Roscommon 1-14** Croke Park
		30/7/2011	**Donegal 1-12 Kildare 0-14** Croke Park
	Quarter-final	31/7/2011	**Kerry 1-20 Limerick 0-10** Croke Park
		31/7/2011	**Mayo 1-13 Cork 2-6** Croke Park
All-Ireland		6/8/2011	**Dublin 0-22 Tyrone 0-15** Croke Park
	Semi-final	21/8/2011	**Kerry 1-20 Mayo 1-11** Croke Park
		28/8/2011	**Donegal 0-6 Dublin 0-8** Croke Park
	Final	18/9/2011	**Kerry 1-11 Dublin 1-12** Croke Park

Kilkenny did not enter the 2012 Championship.

Connacht

First Round	6/5/2012	**New York 0-6 Sligo 3-21** New York
	20/5/2012	**Roscommon 0-10 Galway 3-15** Roscommon
	3/6/2012	**London 1-8 Leitrim 0-12** Ruislip, London
Semi-final	9/6/2012	**Galway 0-15 Sligo 2-14** Pearse Stadium
	24/6/2012	**Mayo 4-20 Leitrim 0-10** Castlebar
Final	15/7/2012	**Mayo 0-12 Sligo 0-10** Roscommon

Leinster

First Round	20/5/2012	**Longford 1-10 Laois 0-12** Navan
	20/5/2012	**Westmeath 0-14 Louth 2-9** Longford
	27/5/2012	**Meath 0-16 Wicklow 0-11** Carlow
Quarter-final	3/6/2012	**Longford 2-9 Wexford 0-15** Croke Park
	10/6/2012	**Longford 0-15 Wexford 1-13** Tullamore
	3/6/2012	**Louth 0-12 Dublin 2-22** Croke Park
	10/6/2012	**Meath 1-12 Carlow 1-12** Tullamore
	16/6/2012	**Meath 2-21 Carlow 1-9** Tullamore
	16/6/2012	**Offaly 0-6 Kildare 0-19** Portlaoise
Semi-final	1/7/2012	**Dublin 2-11 Wexford 1-10** Croke Park
	1/7/2012	**Meath 1-17 Kildare 1-11** Croke Park
Final	22/7/2012	**Dublin 2-13 Meath 1-13** Croke Park

Munster

First Round	20/5/2012	**Limerick 2-12 Waterford 0-7** Limerick
	27/5/2012	**Tipperary 0-10 Kerry 0-16** Semple Stadium
Semi-final	10/6/2012	**Kerry 0-12 Cork 0-17** Páirc Uí Chaoimh
	9/6/2012	**Limerick 0-15 Clare 1-13** Limerick
Final	8/7/2012	**Cork 3-16 Clare 0-13** Limerick

Ulster

First Round	20/5/2012	**Cavan 1-10 Donegal 1-16** Cavan
Quarter-finals	27/5/2012	**Monaghan 1-12 Antrim 1-9** Clones
	3/6/2012	**Fermanagh 1-8 Down 2-10** Enniskillen
	10/6/2012	**Armagh 1-13 Tyrone 0-19** Armagh
	16/6/2012	**Derry 0-9 Donegal 2-13** Ballybofey
Semi-final	24/6/2012	**Down 1-14 Monaghan 1-13** Armagh
	30/6/2012	**Tyrone 0-10 Donegal 0-12** Clones
Final	22/7/2012	**Donegal 2-18 Down 0-13** Clones

Qualifiers	*Qualifiers, Round 1*	30/6/2012	**Antrim 2-11 London 2-9** Ruislip, London
		30/6/2012	**Laois 1-10 Carlow 0-9** Portlaoise
		30/6/2012	**Longford 0-17 Derry 2-8** Longford
		30/6/2012	**Tipperary 1-12 Offaly 0-10** Semple Stadium
		30/6/2012	**Westmeath 1-15 Louth 0-12** Mullingar
		30/6/2012	**Wicklow 1-17 Waterford 0-15** Aughrim
		1/7/2012	**Cavan 3-13 Fermanagh 0-15** Enniskillen
		1/7/2012	**Roscommon 1-11 Armagh 1-9** Roscommon
	Qualifiers, Round 2	14/7/2012	**Antrim 0-11 Galway 0-10** Casement Park
		14/7/2012	**Leitrim 0-13 Wicklow 0-10** Ck-on-Shannon
		14/7/2012	**Limerick 1-21 Longford 1-15** Longford
		14/7/2012	**Tipperary 1-13 Wexford 0-15** Semple Stadium
		14/7/2012	**Tyrone 1-16 Roscommon 0-8** Roscommon
		15/7/2012	**Kerry 2-10 Westmeath 1-12** Mullingar
		15/7/2012	**Kildare 3-20 Cavan 1-9** Cavan
		15/7/2012	**Laois 2-12 Monaghan 0-12** Portlaoise
	Qualifiers, Round 3	21/7/2012	**Kerry 1-16 Tyrone 1-6** Killarney
		21/7/2012	**Kildare 0-19 Limerick 0-12** Portlaoise
		21/7/2012	**Laois 1-13 Leitrim 1-11** Carrick-on-Shannon
		21/7/2012	**Tipperary 0-10 Antrim 0-8** Semple Stadium
	Qualifiers, Round 4	28/7/2012	**Down 1-13 Tipperary 0-11** Mullingar
		28/7/2012	**Kerry 2-22 Clare 1-6** Limerick
		28/7/2012	**Kildare 0-13 Sligo 0-4** Roscommon
		28/7/2012	**Laois 1-15 Meath 1-12** Tullamore
All-Ireland	*Quarter-final*	5/8/2012	**Cork 2-19 Kildare 0-12** Croke Park
		5/8/2012	**Donegal 1-12 Kerry 1-10** Croke Park
		4/8/2012	**Dublin 1-12 Laois 0-12** Croke Park
		4/8/2012	**Mayo 3-18 Down 2-9** Croke Park
	Semi-final	26/8/2012	**Cork 1-11 Donegal 0-16** Croke Park
		2/9/2012	**Dublin 0-16 Mayo 0-19** Croke Park
	Final	23/9/2012	**Donegal 2-11 Mayo 0-13** Croke Park

2013

Kilkenny did not enter the 2013 Championship.

Connacht

First Round	5/5/2013	New York 0-7 Leitrim 4-19 New York
	19/5/2013	Galway 0-11 Mayo 4-16 Pearse Stadium
	26/5/2013	London 1-12 Sligo 0-14 Ruislip, London
Semi-final	16/6/2013	Roscommon 0-9 Mayo 0-21 Castlebar
	23/6/2013	Leitrim 0-13 London 2-7 Carrick-on-Shn
	30/6/2013	London 2-11 Leitrim 1-13 Roscommon
Final	21/7/2013	London 0-10 Mayo 5-11 Castlebar

Leinster

First Round	19/5/2013	Westmeath 3-15 Carlow 1-10 Mullingar
	26/5/2013	Laois 1-6 Louth 1-16 Portlaoise
	26/5/2013	Wicklow 1-15 Longford 0-16 Aughrim
Quarter-final	1/6/2013	Dublin 1-22 Westmeath 0-9 Croke Park
	1/6/2013	Offaly 1-12 Kildare 0-19 Croke Park
	9/6/2013	Wexford 2-13 Louth 1-15 Drogheda
	15/6/2013	Meath 1-17 Wicklow 1-12 Aughrim
Semi-final	30/6/2013	Dublin 4-16 Kildare 1-9 Croke Park
	30/6/2013	Wexford 0-13 Meath 0-18 Croke Park
Final	14/7/2013	Meath 0-14 Dublin 2-15 Croke Park

Munster

First Round	25/5/2013	Limerick 0-8 Cork 3-17 Limerick
	26/5/2013	Kerry 4-21 Tipperary 0-8 Killarney
Semi-final	1/6/2013	Waterford 1-4 Kerry 2-19 Killarney
	16/6/2013	Clare 1-11 Cork 1-20 Ennis
Final	7/7/2013	Cork 0-17 Kerry 1-16 Killarney

Ulster

First Round	19/5/2013	Cavan 1-15 Armagh 1-11 Cavan
Quarter-finals	26/5/2013	Tyrone 0-10 Donegal 2-10 Ballybofey
	2/6/2013	Derry 1-15 Down 2-17 Celtic Park, Derry
	9/6/2013	Antrim 0-6 Monaghan 0-11 Casement Park
	16/6/2013	Cavan 0-13 Fermanagh 0-11 Enniskillen
Semi-final	23/6/2013	Donegal 0-12 Down 0-9 Cavan
	29/6/2013	Cavan 0-12 Monaghan 1-10 Clones
Final	21/7/2013	Monaghan 0-13 Donegal 0-7 Clones

Qualifiers	*Qualifiers, Round 1*	28/6/2013	**Carlow 0-12 Laois 3-13** Carlow
		29/6/2013	**Galway 1-12 Tipperary 0-11** Pearse Stadium
		29/6/2013	**Longford 2-14 Limerick 0-8** Longford
		29/6/2013	**Louth 1-17 Antrim 1-11** Drogheda
		29/6/2013	**Offaly 0-8 Tyrone 1-27** Tullamore
		29/6/2013	**Westmeath 1-15 Fermanagh 3-10** Enniskillen
		30/6/2013	**Armagh 2-21 Wicklow 0-2** Armagh
		30/6/2013	**Derry 0-15 Sligo 0-8** Owenbeg
	Qualifiers, Round 2	6/7/2013	**Clare 0-10 Laois 3-17** Ennis
		6/7/2013	**Derry 0-13 Down 1-5** Celtic Park. Derry
		6/7/2013	**Galway 1-12 Waterford 0-14** Pearse Stadium
		6/7/2013	**Roscommon 1-7 Tyrone 0-12** Roscommon
		13/7/2013	**Cavan 1-14 Fermanagh 0-10** Cavan
		13/7/2013	**Kildare 1-19 Louth 0-15** Newbridge
		13/7/2013	**Leitrim 0-10 Armagh 8-13** Ck-on-Shannon
		13/7/2013	**Longford 0-16 Wexford 2-15** Longford
	Qualifiers, Round 3	20/7/2013	**Derry 0-20 Cavan 1-22** Celtic Park, Derry
		20/7/2013	**Galway 1-11 Armagh 0-9** Galway
		20/7/2013	**Kildare 0-12 Tyrone 1-11** Newbridge
		20/7/2013	**Wexford 2-8 Laois 0-16** Wexford
	Qualifiers, Round 4	27/7/2013	**Cavan 1-17 London 1-8** Croke Park
		27/7/2013	**Galway 1-16 Cork 1-17** Croke Park
		27/7/2013	**Laois 0-8 Donegal 0-14** Carrick-on-Shannon
		27/7/2013	**Meath 2-9 Tyrone 0-17** Croke Park
All-Ireland	*Quarter-final*	3/8/2013	**Monaghan 0-12 Tyrone 0-14** Croke Park
		4/8/2013	**Dublin 1-16 Cork 0-14** Croke Park
		4/8/2013	**Kerry 0-15 Cavan 0-9** Croke Park
		4/8/2013	**Mayo 4-17 Donegal 1-10** Croke Park
	Semi-final	25/8/2013	**Mayo 1-16 Tyrone 0-13** Croke Park
		1/9/2013	**Kerry 3-11 Dublin 3-18** Croke Park
		2/9/2012	**Dublin 0-16 Mayo 0-19** Croke Park
	Final	3/8/2013	**Dublin 2-12 Mayo 1-14** Croke Park

2014

Kilkenny did not enter the 2014 Championship.

Connacht

First Round	4/5/2014	**New York 0-8 Mayo 4-18** New York
	18/5/2014	**Roscommon 1-9 Leitrim 0-13** Roscommon
	25/5/2014	**London 0-7 Galway 3-17** Ruislip, London
Semi-final	8/6/2014	**Mayo 0-13 Roscommon 1-18** Roscommon
	21/6/2014	**Sligo 0-11 Galway 0-16** Sligo
Final	13/7/2014	**Mayo 3-14 Galway 0-16** Castlebar

Leinster

First Round	17/5/2014	**Westmeath 1-9 Louth 1-14** Mullingar
	18/5/2014	**Longford 0-19 Offaly 0-15** Longford
	18/5/2014	**Wicklow 1-11 Laois 0-21** Aughrim
Quarter-final	7/6/2014	**Longford 1-13 Wexford 1-15** Longford
	8/6/2014	**Laois 0-16 Dublin 2-21** Croke Park
	8/6/2014	**Louth 1-7 Kildare 1-22** Croke Park
	15/6/2014	**Carlow 0-6 Meath 7-13** Carlow
Semi-final	29/6/2014	**Dublin 2-25 Wexford 1-12** Croke Park
	29/6/2014	**Kildare 0-17 Meath 2-16** Croke Park
Final	20/7/2014	**Dublin 3-20 Meath 1-10** Croke Park

Munster

First Round	31/5/2014	**Limerick 1-11 Tipperary 2-14** Limeick
	7/6/2014	**Clare 2-8 Waterford 2-8** Ennis
	14/6/2014	**Clare 3-11 Waterford 0-12** Dungarvan
Semi-final	21/6/2014	**Tipperary 2-11 Cork 0-16** Páirc Uí Chaoimh
	22/6/2014	**Kerry 1-17 Clare 1-13** Ennis
Final	6/7/2014	**Cork 0-12 Kerry 0-24** Páirc Uí Chaoimh

Ulster

First Round	18/5/2014	**Tyrone 2-11 Down 3-8** Omagh
	24/5/2014	**Tyrone 3-11 Down 0-12** Newry
Quarter-finals	25/5/2014	**Derry 0-11 Donegal 1-10** Celtic Park, Derry
	1/6/2014	**Fermanagh 3-13 Antrim 2-18** Enniskillen
	8/6/2014	**Armagh 1-12 Cavan 0-9** Armagh
	15/6/2014	**Tyrone 0-14 Monaghan 1-12** Clones
	22/6/2014	**Antrim 0-12 Donegal 3-16** Clones
Semi-final	28/6/2014	**Monaghan 0-14 Armagh 0-14** Clones
	6/7/2014	**Monaghan 1-18 Armagh 1-13** Clones
Final	20/7/2014	**Monaghan 1-9 Donegal 0-15** Clones

Qualifiers	*Qualifiers, Round 1A*	21/6/2014	**Derry 2-14 Longford 2-16** Celtic Park, Derry
		21/6/2014	**Laois 1-19 Fermanagh 2-15** Portlaoise
		21/6/2014	**Limerick 1-16 London 1-13** Limerick
		21/6/2014	**Wicklow 3-12 Offaly 0-17** Aughrim
	Qualifiers, Round 1B	28/6/2014	**Carlow 0-17 Waterford 1-13** Carlow
		28/6/2014	**Cavan 1-15 Westmeath 1-14** Cavan
		28/6/2014	**Down 4-18 Leitrim 0-9** Newry
		28/6/2014	**Louth 0-10 Tyrone 2-21** Omagh
	Qualifiers, Round 2A	5/7/2014	**Limerick 3-11 Antrim 0-15** Limerick
		5/7/2014	**Tipperary 2-17 Longford 0-6** Thurles
		5/7/2014	**Wicklow 0-10 Sligo 0-12** Aughrin
		6/7/2014	**Wexford 0-17 Laois 0-18** Wexford
	Qualifiers, Round 2B	12/7/2014	**Cavan 0-5 Roscommon 0-16** Cavan
		13/7/2014	**Carlow 2-13 Clare 4-26** Carlow
		13/7/2014	**Down 0-11 Kildare 1-18** Newry
		13/7/2014	**Tyrone 0-10 Armagh 0-13** Omagh
	Qualifiers, Round 3	12/7/2014	**Laois 4-9 Tipperary 3-17** Portlaoise
		12/7/2014	**Sligo 0-12 Limerick 0-10** Sligo
		19/7/2014	**Clare 0-12 Kildare 0-13** Ennis
		19/7/2014	**Roscommon 1-12 Armagh 1-17** Roscommon
	Qualifiers, Round 4	26/7/2014	**Cork 0-21 Sligo 1-11** Tullamore
		26/7/2014	**Galway 4-17 Tipperary 4-12** Tullamore
		2/8/2014	**Meath 0-13 Armagh 0-18** Croke Park
		2/8/2014	**Monaghan 2-16 Kildare 2-14** Croke Park
All-Ireland	*Quarter-final*	3/8/2014	**Kerry 1-20 Galway 2-10** Croke Park
		3/8/2014	**Mayo 1-10 Cork 2-15** Croke Park
		9/8/2014	**Donegal 1-12 Armagh 1-11** Croke Park
		9/8/2014	**Dublin 2-22 Monaghan 0-11** Croke Park
	Semi-final	24/8/2014	**Donegal 3-14 Dublin 0-17** Croke Park
		30/8/2014	**Kerry 3-16 Mayo 3-13** Croke Park
	Final	21/9/2014	**Kerry 2-9 Donegal 0-12** Croke Park

2015

Kilkenny did not enter the 2015 Championship.

Connacht

First Round	3/5/2015	**New York 0-8 Galway 2-18** New York
Quarter-final	17/5/2015	**Leitrim 0-8 Galway 1-13** Carrick-on-Shn.
	24/5/2015	**London 0-10 Roscommon 1-14** Ruislip
Semi-final	14/6/2015	**Galway 2-8 Mayo 1-15** Pearse Stadium
	20/6/2015	**Sligo 1-14 Roscommon 0-13** Sligo
Final	19/7/2015	**Mayo 6-25 Sligo 2-11** Dr Hyde Park

Leinster

First Round	16/5/2015	**Carlow 0-8 Laois 3-16** Carlow
	16/5/2015	**Offaly 0-13 Longford 0-16** Tullamore
	17/5/2015	**Louth 0-16 Westmeath 3-14** Drogheda
Quarter-final	31/5/2015	**Dublin 4-25 Longford 0-10** Croke Park
	6/6/2015	**Kildare 0-16 Laois 0-16** Tullamore
	15/6/2015	**Kildare 3-18 Laois 1-11** Tullamore
	14/6/2015	**Meath 2-19 Wicklow 3-12** Navan
	15/6/2015	**Westmeath 1-21 Wexford 0-15** Mullingar
Semi-final	28/6/2015	**Dublin 5-18 Kildare 0-14** Croke Park
	28/6/2015	**Westmeath 3-19 Meath 2-18** Croke Park
Final	12/7/2015	**Dublin 2-13 Westmeath 0-6** Croke Park

Munster

First Round	23/5/2015	**Clare 0-15 Limerick 0-13** Ennis
	31/5/2015	**Waterford 0-5 Tipperary 1-24** Semple Stdm
Semi-final	14/6/2015	**Cork 1-20 Clare 1-8** Páirc Uí Rinn
	14/6/2015	**Tipperary 2-8 Kerry 2-14** Semple Stadium
Final	5/7/2015	**Kerry 2-15 Cork 3-12** Killarney
	18/7/2015	**Kerry 1-11 Cork 1-6** Killarney

Ulster

First Round	17/5/2015	**Donegal 1-13 Tyrone 1-10** Ballybofey
Quarter-finals	24/5/2015	**Cavan 0-15 Monaghan 0-16** Cavan
	31/5/2015	**Fermanagh 1-13 Antrim 0-8** Enniskillen
	7/6/2015	**Derry 0-12 Down 0-11** Celtic Park, Derry
	14/6/2015	**Armagh 0-8 Donegal 2-11** Armagh
Semi-final	21/6/2015	**Monaghan 1-20 Fermanagh 0-13** Cavan
	27/6/2015	**Derry 0-10 Donegal 1-9** Clones
Final	19/7/2015	**Monaghan 0-11 Donegal 0-10** Clones

		20/6/2015	**Laois 1-16 Antrim 2-15** Portlaoise
	Qualifiers, Round 1A	20/6/2015	**London 0-11 Cavan 2-22** Ruislip
		20/6/2015	**Longford 2-15 Carlow 1-8** Pearse Park
		20/6/2015	**Waterford 1-7 Offaly 0-20** Dungarvan
	Qualifiers, Round 1B	27/6/2015	**Armagh 2-17 Wicklow 2-7** Athletic Grounds
		27/6/2015	**Louth 1-16 Leitrim 0-11** Drogheda
		27/6/2015	**Wexford 2-16 Down 2-11** Wexford Park
		28/6/2015	**Tyrone 1-14 Limerick 0-8** Omagh
	Qualifiers, Round 2A	4/7/2015	**Cavan 1-16 Roscommon 3-17** Breffni Park
		4/7/2015	**Clare 1-12 Longford 2-12** Cusack Park
		4/7/2015	**Offaly 1-13 Kildare 1-15** Tullamore
Qualifiers		5/7/2015	**Fermanagh 1-21 Antrim 0-11** Brewster Park
	Qualifiers, Round 2B	11/7/2015	**Derry 1-16 Wexford 0-10** Owenbeg
		11/7/2015	**Tipperary 3-21 Louth 0-7** Semple Stadium
		11/7/2015	**Tyrone 1-10 Meath 0-11** Healy Park, Omagh
		12/7/2015	**Armagh 0-12 Galway 1-12** Athletic Grounds
	Qualifiers, Round 3A	11/7/2015	**Longford 0-11 Kildare 2-24** Mullingar
		12/7/2015	**Fermanagh 1-14 Roscommon 0-16** E-killen
	Qualifiers, Round 3B	18/7/2015	**Galway 1-11 Derry 0-8** Pearse Stadium
		18/7/2015	**Tipperary 0-7 Tyrone 0-19** Semple Stadium
	Qualifiers, Round 4A	25/7/2015	**Cork 1-13 Kildare 1-21** Semple Stadium
		25/7/2015	**Westmeath 0-7 Fermanagh 1-13** Breffni Park
	Qualifiers, Round 4B	1/8/2015	**Donegal 3-12 Galway 0-11** Croke Park
		1/8/2015	**Sligo 0-14 Tyrone 0-21** Croke Park
	Quarter-final	2/8/2015	**Dublin 2-23 Fermanagh 2-15** Croke Park
		2/8/2015	**Kerry 7-16 Kildare 0-10** Croke Park
		8/8/2015	**Mayo 2-13 Donegal 0-11** Croke Park
All-Ireland		8/8/2015	**Monaghan 0-14 Tyrone 0-18** Croke Park
	Semi-final	23/8/2015	**Kerry 0-18 Tyrone 1-11** Croke Park
		30/8/2015	**Dublin 2-12 Mayo 1-15** Croke Park
		5/9/2015	**Dublin 3-15 Mayo 1-14** Croke Park
	Final	20/9/2015	**Dublin 0-12 Kerry 0-9** Croke Park

Kilkenny did not enter the 2016 Championship. The Laois v Armagh qualifier was replayed as Laois used too many subs in the first game.

Connacht	*First Round*	1/5/2016	**New York 0-17 Roscommon 1-15** N. York
	Quarter-final	22/5/2016	**Leitrim 0-11 Roscommon 1-21** Ck-on-Shn.
		29/5/2016	**London 0-9 Mayo 2-16** Ruislip
	Semi-final	12/6/2016	**Roscommon 4-16 Sligo 2-13** Roscommon
		18/6/2016	**Mayo 0-12 Galway 1-12** Castlebar
	Final	10/7/2016	**Roscommon 1-10 Galway 0-13** Pearse Stdm
		17/7/2016	**Galway 3-16 Roscommon 0-14** Castlebar

Leinster	*First Round*	14/5/2016	**Laois 3-16 Wicklow 0-18** Portlaoise
		14/5/2016	**Louth 2-24 Carlow 3-11** Portlaoise
		14/5/2016	**Offaly 2-21 Longford 2-13** Tullamore
	Quarter-final	21/5/2016	**Wexford 0-8 Kildare 0-9** Croke Park
		4/6/2016	**Laois 2-10 Dublin 2-21** Kilkenny
		12/6/2016	**Louth 1-13 Meath 0-20** Parnell Park
		12/6/2016	**Westmeath 0-13 Offaly 0-12** Mullingar
	Semi-final	26/6/2016	**Dublin 0-21 Meath 0-11** Croke Park
		26/6/2016	**Westmeath 1-12 Kildare 1-11** Croke Park
	Final	17/7/2016	**Dublin 2-19 Westmeath 0-10** Croke Park

Munster	*First Round*	29/5/2016	**Limerick 0-13 Clare 0-16** Limerick
		29/5/2016	**Waterford 1-7 Tipperary 1-15** Dungarvan
	Semi-final	12/6/2016	**Kerry 2-23 Clare 0-17** Killarney
		12/6/2016	**Tipperary 3-15 Cork 2-16** Semple Stadium
	Final	3/7/2016	**Kerry 3-17 Tipperary 2-10** Killarney

Ulster	*First Round*	15/5/2016	**Fermanagh 1-12 Antrim 0-9** Enniskillen
	Quarter-finals	22/5/2016	**Derry 0-12 Tyrone 3-14** Celtic Park, Derry
		29/5/2016	**Cavan 2-16 Armagh 0-14** Cavan
		5/6/2016	**Monaghan 2-22 Down 0-9** Clones
		12/6/2016	**Donegal 2-12 Fermanagh 0-11** Ballbofey
	Semi-final	19/6/2016	**Tyrone 0-16 Cavan 3-7** Clones
		3/7/2016	**Tyrone 5-18 Cavan 2-17** Clones
		25/6/2016	**Donegal 1-11 Monaghan 0-14** Cavan
		2/7/2016	**Donegal 0-17 Monaghan 2-10** Cavan
	Final	17/7/2016	**Donegal 0-11 Tyrone 0-13** Clones

Qualifiers	*Qualifiers, Round 1A*	18/6/2016	**Carlow 1-17 Wicklow 1-12** Carlow
		18/6/2016	**Derry 1-18 Louth 2-10** Owenbeg
		18/6/2016	**Laois 1-11 Armagh 1-10** Portlaoise
		2/7/2016	**Laois 1-10 Armagh 0-10** Portlaoise
		19/6/2016	**Leitrim 0-12 Waterford 0-8** Ck-on-Shannon
	Qualifiers, Round 1B	25/6/2016	**Antrim 0-9 Limerick 2-6** Corrigan Park
		25/6/2016	**Down 3-17 Longford 2-24** Newry
		25/6/2016	**Offaly 0-17 London 1-7** Tullamore
		25/6/2016	**Wexford 1-11 Fermanagh 0-19** Wexford Park
	Qualifiers, Round 2A	2/7/2016	**Sligo 2-15 Leitrim 0-10** Sligo
		9/7/2016	**Cavan 2-13 Carlow 0-12** Breffni Park
		9/7/2016	**Derry 1-14 Meath 1-11** Owenbeg
		10/7/2016	**Clare 0-14 Laois 1-10** Ennis
	Qualifiers, Round 2B	9/7/2016	**Kildare 1-22 Offaly 2-14** Newbridge
		9/7/2016	**Limerick 0-10 Cork 2-12** Semple Stadium
		9/7/2016	**Mayo 2-14 Fermanagh 1-12** Castlebar
		9/7/2016	**Monaghan 1-13 Longford 2-13** Clones
	Qualifiers, Round 3A	16/7/2016	**Cavan 0-18 Derry 1-17** Breffni Park
		16/7/2016	**Sligo 1-13 Clare 2-17** Sligo
	Qualifiers, Round 3B	16/7/2016	**Longford 1-6 Cork 2-9** Pearse Park
		16/7/2016	**Mayo 2-17 Kildare 0-14** Castlebar
	Qualifiers, Round 4A	23/7/2016	**Roscommon 1-9 Clare 2-12** Pearse Stadium
		23/7/2016	**Tipperary 1-21 Derry 2-17** Breffni Park
	Qualifiers, Round 4B	30/7/2016	**Donegal 0-21 Cork 1-15** Croke Park
		30/7/2016	**Westmeath 1-14 Mayo 3-15** Croke Park
All-Ireland	*Quarter-final*	31/7/2016	**Kerry 2-16 Clare 0-11** Croke Park
		31/7/2016	**Tipperary 3-13 Galway 1-10** Croke Park
		6/8/2016	**Dublin 1-15 Donegal 1-10** Croke Park
		6/8/2016	**Mayo 0-13 Tyrone 0-12** Croke Park
	Semi-final	21/8/2016	**Mayo 2-13 Tipperary 0-14** Croke Park
		28/8/2016	**Dublin 0-22 Kerry 2-14** Croke Park
	Final	18/9/2016	**Dublin 2-9 Mayo 0-15** Croke Park
		1/10/2016	**Dublin 1-15 Mayo 1-14** Croke Park

Kilkenny did not enter the 2017 Championship.

Connacht

First Round	7/5/2017	**New York 1-13 Sligo 1-21** New York	
Quarter-final	21/5/2017	**Mayo 2-14 Sligo 1-11** Castlebar	
	28/5/2017	**London 0-16 Leitrim 3-10** Ruislip	
Semi-final	11/6/2017	**Galway 0-15 Mayo 1-11** Pearse Stadium	
	18/6/2017	**Roscommon 2-23 Leitrim 1-9** Dr Hyde Pk	
Final	16/7/2017	**Roscommon 2-15 Galway 0-12** Pearse Stdm	

Leinster

First Round	21/5/2017	**Carlow 2-17 Wexford 2-13** Carlow
	21/5/2017	**Laois 4-15 Longford 0-16** Portlaoise
	21/5/2017	**Louth 1-19 Wicklow 1-14** Parnell Park
	3/6/2017	**Dublin 0-19 Carlow 0-7** Portlaoise
Quarter final	4/6/2017	**Kildare 1-21 Laois 1-7** Tullamore
	4/6/2017	**Meath 0-27 Louth 3-9** Parnell Park
	4/6/2017	**Offaly 0-10 Westmeath 0-10** Tullamore
	11/6/2017	**Westmeath 3-17 Offaly 0-15** Cusack Park
Semi-final	17/6/2017	**Meath 0-13 Kildare 2-16** Tullamore
	25/6/2017	**Dublin 4-29 Westmeath 0-10** Croke Park
Final	16/7/2017	**Dublin 2-23 Kildare 1-17** Croke Park

Munster

First Round	27/5/2017	**Waterford 1-11 Cork 1-12** Dungarvan
	28/5/2017	**Clare 1-13 Limerick 1-12** Ennis
Semi-final	10/6/2017	**Kerry 1-18 Clare 1-12** Ennis
	11/6/2017	**Tipperary 1-9 Cork 1-10** Páirc Uí Rinn
Final	2/7/2017	**Kerry 1-23 Cork 0-15** Killarney

Ulster

First Round	20/5/2017	**Monaghan 1-20 Fermanagh 1-11** Clones
Quarter-finals	21/5/2017	**Donegal 3-19 Antrim 1-9** Ballbofey
	28/5/2017	**Derry 0-11 Tyrone 0-22** Celtic Park
	4/6/2017	**Down 0-15 Armagh 2-7** Newry
	11/6/2017	**Cavan 0-15 Monaghan 1-15** Breffni Park
Semi-final	18/6/2017	**Tyrone 1-21 Donegal 1-12** Clones
	24/6/2017	**Down 1-14 Monaghan 0-15** Athletic Gds
Final	16/7/2017	**Tyrone 2-17 Down 0-15** Clones

Qualifiers	*Qualifiers, Round 1A*	17/6/2017	**Louth 1-10 Longford 2-15** Drogheda
		17/6/2017	**Sligo 0-22 Antrim 3-7** Sligo
		17/6/2017	**Waterford 0-13 Derry 1-17** Dungarvan
		17/6/2017	**Wicklow 3-10 Laois 2-16** Aughrim
	Qualifiers, Round 1B	24/6/2017	**Limerick 0-11 Wexford 0-12** Gaelic Grounds
		25/6/2017	**Armagh 0-20 Fermanagh 0-11** Armagh
		25/6/2017	**London 0-12 Carlow 0-13** Ruislip
		25/6/2017	**Offaly 0-16 Cavan 0-17** Tullamore
	Qualifiers, Round 2A	1/7/2017	**Donegal 0-12 Longford 0-7** Ballybofey
		1/7/2017	**Laois 0-14 Clare 2-18** Portlaoise
		1/7/2017	**Mayo 2-21 Derry 1-13** Castlebar
		1/7/2017	**Meath 0-14 Sligo 1-9** Navan
	Qualifiers, Round 2B	8/7/2017	**Carlow 2-14 Leitrim 0-13** Carlow
		8/7/2017	**Cavan 0-18 Tipperary 2-15** Breffni Park
		8/7/2017	**Westmeath 1-7 Armagh 1-12** Mullingar
		8/7/2017	**Wexford 1-11 Monaghan 3-23** Wexford Park
	Qualifiers, Round 3A	8/7/2017	**Clare 0-13 Mayo 2-14** Ennis
		8/7/2017	**Meath 1-14 Donegal 1-15** Navan
	Qualifiers, Round 3B	15/7/2017	**Carlow 1-7 Monaghan 1-12** Carlow
		15/7/2017	**Tipperary 1-15 Armagh 1-17** Thurles
	Qualifiers, Round 4A	22/7/2017	**Cork 2-20 Mayo 0-27** Limerick
		22/7/2017	**Galway 4-17 Donegal 0-14** Sligo
	Qualifiers, Round 4B	29/7/2017	**Down 1-16 Monaghan 1-24** Croke Park
		29/7/2017	**Kildare 0-17 Armagh 1-17** Croke Park
All-Ireland	*Quarter-final*	30/7/2017	**Kerry 1-18 Galway 0-13** Croke Park
		30/7/2017	**Roscommon 2-9 Mayo 1-12** Croke Park
		7/8/2017	**Mayo 4-19 Roscommon 0-9** Croke Park
		5/8/2017	**Dublin 1-19 Monaghan 0-12** Croke Park
		5/8/2017	**Tyrone 3-17 Armagh 0-8** Croke Park
	Semi-final	20/8/2017	**Mayo 2-14 Kerry 2-14** Croke Park
		26/8/2017	**Mayo 2-16 Kerry 0-17** Croke Park
		27/8/2017	**Dublin 2-17 Tyrone 0-11** Croke Park
	Final	17/9/2017	**Dublin 1-17 Mayo 1-16** Croke Park

Kilkenny did not enter the 2018 Championship. In 2018 the All-Ireland quarter-finals knock-out games were replaced by a group stage with the top two teams in each of two groups progressing to the All-Ireland semi-finals.

Connacht

First Round	6/5/2018	**London 1-11 Sligo 1-21** Ruislip
	6/5/2018	**New York 1-15 Leitrim 0-19** New York
	13/5/2018	**Mayo 0-12 Galway 1-12** Castlebar
Semi-final	26/5/2018	**Roscommon 0-24 Leitrim 0-10** Ck-on-Shan.
	3/6/2018	**Galway 4-24 Sligo 1-12** Pearse Stadium
Final	17/7/2018	**Roscommon 2-6 Galway 0-16** Roscommon

Leinster

First Round	12/5/2018	**Laois 2-21 Wexford 1-18** Wexford
	13/5/2018	**Louth 0-12 Carlow 2-17** Portlaoise
	13/5/2018	**Offaly 1-15 Wicklow 1-20** Portlaoise
Quarter-final	26/5/2018	**Westmeath 1-12 Laois 4-13** Tullamore
	27/5/2018	**Kildare 1-10 Carlow 2-14** Tullamore
	27/5/2018	**Longford 0-16 Meath 0-14** Longford
	27/5/2018	**Dublin 4-25 Wicklow 1-11** Portlaoise
Semi-final	10/6/2018	**Dublin 2-25 Longford 0-12** Croke Park
	10/6/2018	**Laois 0-12 Carlow 0-8** Croke Park
Final	24/6/2018	**Dublin 1-25 Laois 0-10** Croke Park

Munster

First Round	19/5/2018	**Clare 1-23 Limerick 0-14** Limerick
	19/5/2018	**Waterford 0-9 Tipperary 0-20** Dungarvan
Semi-final	26/5/2018	**Tipperary 0-9 Cork 1-17** Semple Stadium
	3/6/2018	**Kerry 0-32 Clare 0-10** Killarney
Final	23/6/2018	**Kerry 3-18 Cork 2-4** Páirc Uí Chaoimh

Ulster

First Round	13/5/2018	**Donegal 2-20 Cavan 1-15** Ballybofey
Quarter-finals	19/5/2018	**Fermanagh 0-12 Armagh 0-7** Enniskillen
	20/5/2018	**Tyrone 1-16 Monaghan 1-18** Omagh
	26/5/2018	**Down 1-18 Antrim 0-14** Newry
	27/5/2018	**Cavan 0-15 Monaghan 1-15** Breffni Park
Semi-final	3/6/2018	**Fermanagh 1-8 Monaghan 0-10** Clones
	10/6/2018	**Down 1-12 Donegal 2-22** Clones
Final	24/6/2018	**Fermanagh 0-12 Donegal 2-18** Clones

Qualifiers	*Qualifiers, Round 1*	9/6/2018	**Derry 2-14 Kildare 2-22** Owenbeg
		9/6/2018	**Limerick 3-7 Mayo 5-19** Limerick
		9/6/2018	**Louth 2-26 London 1-19** Ruislip
		9/6/2018	**Meath 0-19 Tyrone 2-14** Navan
		9/6/2018	**Offaly 2-30 Antrim 1-15** Tullamore
		9/6/2018	**Westmeath 1-11 Armagh 3-16** Mullingar
		9/6/2018	**Wexford 1-18 Waterford 3-14** Wexford
		9/6/2018	**Wicklow 1-5 Cavan 2-16** Aughrim
	Qualifiers, Round 2	23/6/2018	**Carlow 1-10 Tyrone 3-14** Carlow
		23/6/2018	**Cavan 1-14 Down 0-15** Enniskillen
		23/6/2018	**Leitrim 0-25 Louth 1-12** Carrick-on-Shannon
		23/6/2018	**Longford 1-13 Kildare 1-16** Longford
		23/6/2018	**Sligo 1-13 Armagh 1-19** Sligo
		23/6/2018	**Tipperary 1-11 Mayo 1-19** Thurles
		23/6/2018	**Waterford 0-9 Monaghan 5-21** Dungarvan
		24/6/2018	**Offaly 2-14 Clare 1-19** Tullamore
	Qualifiers, Round 3	30/6/2018	**Armagh 2-16 Claire 1-15** Armagh
		30/6/2018	**Cavan 1-12 Tyrone 0-18** Enniskillen
		30/6/2018	**Kildare 0-21 Mayo 0-19** Newbridge
		30/6/2018	**Leitrim 0-9 Monaghan 1-19** Ck-on-Shannon
	Qualifiers, Round 4	7/7/2018	**Cork 0-13 Tyrone 3-20** Portlaoise
		7/7/2018	**Fermanagh 0-18 Kildare 3-20** Navan
		7/7/2018	**Roscommon 2-22 Armagh 1-19** Portlaoise
		8/7/2018	**Laois 1-11 Monaghan 0-19** Navan

All-Ireland

Quarter-final, Group 1

Date	Match	Venue
15/7/2018	**Kerry 1-10 Galway 1-13**	Croke Park
15/7/2018	**Kildare 1-10 Monaghan 0-15**	Croke Park
22/7/2018	**Kildare 0-16 Galway 0-19**	Newbridge
22/7/2018	**Monaghan 1-17 Kerry 1-17**	Clones
4/8/2018	**Kerry 3-25 Kildare 2-16**	Killarney
4/8/2018	**Galway 0-8 Monaghan 0-16**	Pearse Stadium

Quarter-final, Group 1 final table

	Won	Drawn	Lost	Points
Monaghan	2	1	0	5
Galway	2	0	1	4
Kerry	1	1	1	3
Kildare	0	0	3	0

Quarter-final, Group 2

Date	Match	Venue
14/7/2018	**Tyrone 4-24 Roscommon 2-12**	Croke Park
14/7/2018	**Dublin 2-15 Donegal 0-16**	Croke Park
21/7/2018	**Tyrone 0-14 Dublin 1-14**	Omagh
21/7/2018	**Roscommon 0-13 Donegal 0-20**	Roscomn
5/8/2018	**Dublin 4-24 Roscommon 2-16**	Croke Park
5/8/2018	**Donegal 1-13 Tyone 2-17**	Ballybofey

Quarter-final, Group 2 final table

	Won	Drawn	Lost	Points
Dublin	3	0	0	6
Tyrone	2	0	1	4
Donegal	1	0	2	2
Roscommon	0	0	3	0

Semi-final

Date	Match	Venue
11/8/2018	**Dublin 1-24 Galway 2-12**	Croke Park
12/8/2018	**Monaghan 0-15 Tyrone 1-13**	Croke Park

Final

Date	Match	Venue
2/9/2018	**Dublin 2-17 Tyrone 1-14**	Croke Park

Kilkenny did not enter the 2019 Championship.

Connacht

First Round	5/5/2019	**New York 0-4 Mayo 1-22** Ruislip
	5/5/2019	**Roscommon 3-17 Leitrim 0-19** New York
	12/5/2019	**London 1-9 Galway 1-12** Castlebar
Semi-final	19/5/2019	**Roscommon 2-12 Mayo 0-17** Ck-on-Shannon
	25/5/2019	**Galway 3-11 Sligo 0-7** Pearse Stadium
Final	16/6/2019	**Roscommon 1-13 Galway 0-12** Roscommon

Leinster

First Round	12/5/2019	**Louth 0-22 Wexford 1-14** Wexford
	13/5/2019	**Meath 1-13 Offaly 0-14** Portlaoise
	13/5/2019	**Kildare 0-15 Wicklow 1-10** Portlaoise
Quarter-final	26/5/2019	**Dublin 5-21 Louth 0-10** Tullamore
	27/5/2019	**Longford 3-15 Kildare 1-21** Tullamore
	27/5/2019	**Longford 0-10 Kildare 1-18** Tullamore
	27/5/2019	**Carlow 0-9 Meath 2-18** Longford
	27/5/2019	**Laois 0-12 Westmeath 0-10** Portlaoise
Semi-final	10/6/2019	**Dublin 0-26 Kildare 0-11** Croke Park
	10/6/2019	**Laois 0-11 Meath 3-13** Croke Park
Final	24/6/2019	**Dublin 1-17 Meath 0-4** Croke Park

Munster

First Round	11/5/2019	**Clare 0-9 Waterford 0-8** Dungarvan
	11/5/2019	**Tipperary 1-10 Limerick 3-11** Limerick
Semi-final	1/6/2019	**Cork 3-18 Limerick 0-6** Semple Stadium
	1/6/2019	**Kerry 1-15 Clare 0-12** Killarney
Final	22/6/2019	**Kerry 1-19 Cork 3-10** Páirc Uí Chaoimh

Ulster

First Round	12/5/2019	**Tyrone 1-19 Derry 1-13** Ballybofey
Quarter-finals	18/5/2019	**Cavan 1-13 Monaghan 0-12** Enniskillen
	19/5/2019	**Down 3-13 Armagh 2-17** Omagh
	25/5/2019	**Fermanagh 0-9 Donegal 0-15** Newry
	26/5/2019	**Antrim 2-9 Tyrone 2-23** Breffni Park
Semi-final	2/6/2019	**Cavan 0-17 Armagh 1-14** Clones
	8/6/2019	**Cavan 0-23 Armagh 0-17** Clones
	8/6/2019	**Donegal 1-16 Tyrone 0-15** Clones
Final	23/6/2019	**Cavan 2-16 Donegal 1-24** Clones

		8/6/2019	**Offaly 1-21 London 1-11** Tullamore
		8/6/2019	**Leitrim 0-15 Wicklow 0-13** Ck-on-Shannon
		8/6/2019	**Wexford 0-10 Derry 4-16** Wexford
	Qualifiers,	8/6/2019	**Louth 1-11 Antrim 2-16** Drogheda
	Round 1	9/6/2019	**Monaghan 1-10 Fermanagh 1-6** Clones
		9/6/2019	**Down 1-13 Tipperary 1-10** Newry
		9/6/2019	**Carlow 0-7 Longford 2-11** Carlow
		9/6/2019	**Westmeath 1-22 Waterford 0-7** Mullingar
		22/6/2019	**Antrim 0-14 Kildare 1-25** Corrigan Park
		22/6/2019	**Derry 0-12 Laois 1-13** Owenbeg
		22/6/2019	**Down 1-11 Mayo 1-16** Newry
	Qualifiers,	22/6/2019	**Leitrim 0-17 Clare 3-17** Carrick-on-Shannon
Qualifiers	*Round 2*	22/6/2019	**Longford 1-14 Tyrone 2-15** Longford
		22/6/2019	**Monaghan 1-12 Armagh 2-17** Clones
		22/6/2019	**Westmeath 2-13 Limerick 1-10** Mullingar
		23/6/2019	**Offaly 3-17 Sligo 0-15** Tullamore
		29/6/2019	**Kildare 1-15 Tyrone 2-22** Newbridge
	Qualifiers,	29/6/2019	**Westmeath 0-15 Clare 1-13** Mullingar
	Round 3	29/6/2019	**Mayo 2-13 Armagh 1-15** Castlebar
		29/6/2019	**Laois 0-20 Offaly 0-15** Portlaoise
		6/7/2019	**Cavan 0-7 Tyrone 1-20** Clones
	Qualifiers,	6/7/2019	**Cork 4-20 Laois 1-15** Thurles
	Round 4	6/7/2019	**Galway 1-13 Mayo 2-13** Limerick
		7/7/2019	**Meath 2-16 Clare 1-18** Portlaoise

All-Ireland

<table>
<tr><td rowspan="1">Quarter-final, Group 1</td><td>14/7/2019</td><td>Donegal 2-19 Meath 1-13 Ballybofey</td></tr>
</table>

Quarter-final, Group 1	14/7/2019	**Donegal 2-19 Meath 1-13** Ballybofey
	14/7/2019	**Kerry 1-22 Mayo 0-15** Killarney
	21/7/2019	**Mayo 2-17 Meath 0-14** Croke Park
	21/7/2019	**Kerry 1-20 Donegal 1-20** Croke Park
	3/8/2019	**Mayo 1-14 Donegal 1-10** Castlebar
	3/8/2019	**Meath 1-13 Kerry 2-18** Navan

Quarter-final, Group 1 final table		*Won*	*Drawn*	*Lost*	*Points*
	Kerry	2	1	0	5
	Mayo	2	0	1	4
	Donegal	1	1	1	3
	Meath	0	0	3	0

Quarter-final, Group 2		
	14/7/2019	**Roscommon 0-13 Tyrone 0-17** Roscommon
	14/7/2019	**Dublin 5-18 Cork 1-17** Croke Park
	21/7/2019	**Cork 2-12 Tyrone 2-15** Omagh
	21/7/2019	**Dublin 2-26 Roscommon 0-14** Croke Park
	5/8/2019	**Cork 3-9 Roscommon 4-9** Páirc Uí Chaoimh
	5/8/2019	**Tyrone 0-13 Dublin 1-16** Omagh

Quarter-final, Group 2 final table		*Won*	*Drawn*	*Lost*	*Points*
	Dublin	3	0	0	6
	Tyrone	2	0	1	4
	Roscommon	1	0	2	2
	Cork	0	0	3	0

Semi-final	10/8/2019	**Mayo 1-10 Dublin 3-14** Croke Park
	11/8/2019	**Tyrone 0-18 Kerry 1-18** Croke Park
Final	1/9/2019	**Dublin 1-16 Kerry 1-16** Croke Park
	14/9/2019	**Dublin 1-18 Kerry 0-15** Croke Park

ACKNOWLEDGEMENTS

For assistance in various ways in the preparation of this book, thanks are due to Claire Breen, Emma Byrne, Ita Finnegan, Bernie Greer, Peter Greer, Roddy Hegarty, Máire Hegarty, Ruth Moloney, John O'Keefe, Mags O'Keefe, Geraldine O'Neill, Michael O'Neill, Rose O'Neill, Sportsfile and Jonathan Wade.

Printed in Poland
by Amazon Fulfillment
Poland Sp. z o.o., Wrocław